PRACTICAL SQL QUERIES for

Microsoft® SQL Server® 2008 R2

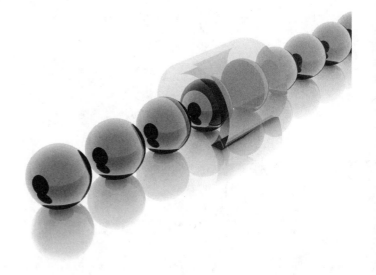

About the Author

Art Tennick (Brighton, U.K.) has worked in relational database design and SQL queries for over 20 years. He has been involved in multidimensional database design, cubes, data mining, and DMX and MDX queries for 10 years. Based in the United Kingdom, he has been a software consultant, trainer, and writer for some 25 years. Recently, he has worked with several major retail and banking corporations to implement BI solutions using Microsoft SQL Server, SSAS, SSIS, SSRS, and Excel 2007/2010. This is his nineteenth book and he has also written over 300 articles for computer magazines in the United States, the United Kingdom, and Ireland. His web site is www.MrCube.net.

About the Technical Editor

Dejan Sarka focuses on development of database and Business Intelligence applications. Besides projects, he spends about half of his time on training and mentoring. He is the founder of the Slovenian SQL Server and .NET Users Group. Dejan Sarka is the main author or coauthor of eight books about databases and SQL Server. Dejan Sarka also developed two courses for Solid Quality Mentors: Data Modeling Essentials and Data Mining with SQL Server 2008.

PRACTICAL SQL QUERIES for

Microsoft® SQL Server® 2008 R2

Art Tennick

New York Chicago San Francisco Lisbon
London Madrid Mexico City Milan
New Delhi San Juan Seoul Singapore
Sydney Toronto

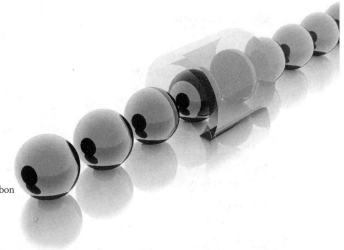

The McGraw·Hill Companies

Cataloging-in-Publication Data is on file with the Library of Congress

McGraw-Hill books are available at special quantity discounts to use as premiums and sales promotions, or for use in corporate training programs. To contact a representative, please e-mail us at bulksales@mcgraw-hill.com.

Practical SQL Queries for Microsoft® SQL Server® 2008 R2

1234567890   DOC DOC   109876543210

ISBN   978-0-07-174687-8
MHID   0-07-174687-0

Sponsoring Editor Wendy Rinaldi	**Indexer** Ted Laux
Editorial Supervisor Patty Mon	**Production Supervisor** George Anderson
Project Manager Deepti Narwat Agarwal, Glyph International	**Composition** Glyph International
Acquisitions Coordinator Joya Anthony	**Illustration** Glyph International
Technical Editor Dejan Sarka	**Art Director, Cover** Jeff Weeks
Copy Editor Margaret Berson	**Cover Designer** Jeff Weeks
Proofreader Laura Bowman	

For my family, including Viv and Buster and Joey.

Contents at a Glance

Contents

Acknowledgments

Thank you to my editor, Wendy Rinaldi—again. In particular, she demonstrated remarkable vision and enthusiasm, and patience. Also thanks again to Joya Anthony of McGraw-Hill and Melinda Lytle. I am also indebted to Dejan Sarka for being such a perceptive technical reviewer.

Introduction

SQL

Structured Query Language (SQL) is a standard language for interrogating and working with relational databases. SQL is supported by many database vendors. The SQL in this book was written against Microsoft SQL Server 2008. However, about 99 percent of the queries will work against earlier versions of SQL Server. In addition, about 95 percent of the queries will work against databases such as Oracle, DB2, MySQL, Access, and others. The Microsoft implementation of the SQL language in SQL Server is called Transact-SQL (T-SQL). All SQL dialects have some small differences, but most of the queries in this book can be adapted to your own database software if it's not SQL Server.

The SQL language is often divided into three sections, data manipulation language (DML), data definition language (DDL), and data control language (DCL). All three sections are covered in this book. DML consists of Select, Insert, Update, and Delete. DDL consists of Create, Alter, and Drop. DCL consists of Grant, Revoke, and Deny. DDL and DCL have their own chapter, but they are discussed briefly in other chapters too. Most of the chapters deal with DML—in particular, we concentrate largely (but not exclusively) on the Select statement of DML.

Generally, when people talk about SQL queries, they are referring to Select statements. You are going to get lots and lots of practice with Select statements! But other areas of SQL are also covered in reasonable detail too.

Prerequisites

You will need two databases. First, the SQL Server AdventureWorksDW2008 database (called AdventureWorksDW in SQL Server 2005), which is the AdventureWorks star/snowflake/OLAP schema—most of the SQL queries are written against that database. Second, the SQL Server AdventureWorks2008 database (called AdventureWorks in SQL Server 2005), which is an OLTP schema. Only one or two queries are written against this database.

Installing Adventure Works

You can download the required SQL Server databases from www.codeplex.com (both 2008 and 2005 versions). As of this writing, the URL was http://www.codeplex.com/MSFTDBProdSamples/Release/ProjectReleases.aspx?ReleaseID=16040. Choose SQL Server 2008 or SQL Server 2005 from the Releases box. URLs can change—if you have difficulty, then search www.codeplex.com on Adventure Works Samples, or try http://msftdbprodsamples.codeplex.com.

SQL Server 2008

Before you begin the download, you might want to check the two hyperlinks for Database Prerequisites and Installing Databases. Download and run SQL2008. AdventureWorks All Databases.x86.msi (there are also 64-bit versions, x64 and ia64). As the installation proceeds, you will have to choose an instance name for your SQL Server. When the installation finishes, you will have some new SQL Server databases, including AdventureWorksDW2008 and AdventureWorks2008.

SQL Server 2005

The download files are called AdventureWorksBICI.msi (there are also 64-bit versions, x64 and IA64) and AdventureWorksDBCI.msi (there are also 64-bit versions, x64 and IA64). With 2005 you can also go through Setup or Control Panel to add the samples—this is not possible in 2008. Unlike with 2008, the download and subsequent installation do not result in the new databases appearing under SQL Server in SSMS—it's not possible to write your first query just yet. You have to manually attach the databases. You can do this from SSMS (right-click on the Databases folder and choose Attach) if you have some DBA knowledge. Or you might ask your SQL Server DBA to do this for you. If you click the Release Notes hyperlink on the download page, you will find out how to do this from SQL—using SQL before you even start a book for learning SQL!

Source Code

All of the source code for the queries in this book is available for download. You can simply copy and paste into the query editor to save you typing. You can copy and paste individual queries or copy and paste blocks of code. If you do the latter, make sure that you highlight only the relevant code before you run the query.

You can download the source code from www.mhprofessional.com/computingdownload.

Acronyms

- ▶ **BI**   Business Intelligence
- ▶ **BIDS**   SQL Server Business Intelligence Development Studio
- ▶ **DMX**   Data Mining Extensions
- ▶ **KPI**   Key Performance Indicator
- ▶ **MDX**   Multdimensional Expressions
- ▶ **SQL**   Structured Query Language
- ▶ **SSAS**   SQL Server Analysis Services
- ▶ **SSIS**   SQL Server Integration Services
- ▶ **SSMS**   SQL Server Management Studio
- ▶ **SSRS**   SQL Server Reporting Services
- ▶ **XMLA**   XML for Analysis

SQL Server 2008 or SQL Server 2005?

The SQL queries in this book are for both SQL Server 2008 and SQL Server 2005.

Enterprise/Developer Edition or Standard Edition?

It makes little difference which edition you use. All of the queries work against the Enterprise/Developer Edition and the Standard Edition of SQL Server.

Writing Queries

1. Open SSMS.
2. If prompted to connect, click Cancel.
3. Click File | New | Database Engine Query.
4. Click Connect in the dialog box.
5. From the drop-down on the toolbar, choose the AdventureWorksDW2008 (or AdventureWorks2008) database.

6. Type, or type and drag, or copy and paste to create the query.

7. Click the Execute button on the toolbar.

There are many other ways of opening the query editor. Here's a popular alternative:

1. In Object Explorer, right-click the SQL Server database AdventureWorksDW2008 or AdventureWorks2008 (AdventureWorksDW or AdventureWorks in SQL Server 2005). If your Object Explorer is closed or empty, click File | Connect Object Explorer.

2. Click New Query.

Chapter Content

Chapter 1, "Select: Single Table"

This is an introductory chapter. It concentrates on retrieving columns and rows of data from a *single* table. A wide variety of techniques are covered—doing column calculations, aliasing columns, handling dates and nulls, and more. Many of the techniques discussed are fundamental ones and give you a sound basis on which to develop more complex SQL. You will meet a lot of syntax from this chapter again in later chapters as you learn more complex SQL.

Chapter 2, "Where"

This chapter is devoted to the Where clause. It's a huge subject area and could easily fill a whole book, let alone a single chapter. Here you'll discover how to search records—how to find what you're looking for. You also see how to return subsets of your tables based on the criteria you specify. Many of your own SQL queries are going to require Where clauses—here you'll become familiar with all of the important concepts and techniques for returning just what you want (and being able to ignore what you don't want).

Chapter 3, "Order By"

If you need to sort the output of your SQL queries, you use the Order By clause. That's the topic for this chapter. It shows you how to sort alphabetically and numerically. It also demonstrates how to extract the top (or best) and the bottom (or worst) of the rows in your tables.

Chapter 4, "Select: Multiple Tables"

The previous three chapters concentrate on single-table queries. It's unlikely that you will always find the data you need in a single table. Often, your data is split across two or more tables. This chapter shows the SQL required to put tables together. The technique is one of performing joins on tables. There are quite a few variations on the join technique. All of the variations (inner joins and outer joins and more) are covered here. You will find the SQL useful when you later move on to build views and stored procedures. If you join tables in a normalized database, then the joining is sometimes referred to as *denormalization*. Denormalization is an important part of building SQL Server relational data warehouses (star schemas, for example) and SSAS multidimensional cubes.

Chapter 5, "Aggregates"

Here we look at how to aggregate data. Aggregating data includes counting, totaling, and averaging data. You may also be interested in how to calculate maximum and minimum values. All of these topics are covered in this chapter. We'll be doing the aggregations on all of the records in a table—so, a summation, for example, will result in a grand total. A later chapter, Chapter 8 on Group By, extends this chapter and shows how to perform aggregations against subsets of tables—in other words, how to calculate subtotals as well as grand totals. Being able to produce aggregates makes your reports for end users more informative—they can see the overall picture rather than lots of individual bits of data. Aggregation is also an important concept to understand as you begin to develop your data warehouses.

Chapter 6, "Select: New Tables"

In this chapter we examine table creation. There are many ways of creating tables—here we concentrate on creating tables using a Select statement (Select Into). A later chapter shows how to do so with a Create statement. You'll learn how to create both permanent and temporary tables. Furthermore, you'll meet three different types of temporary tables and have a quick look at the tempdb system database. New permanent and temporary tables have many uses. They can be used to denormalize and join tables for reporting purposes. In addition, they are invaluable for testing new designs and testing your SQL, when you prefer not to work against live production tables. Also, when your SQL becomes very complex, you can break it down into simpler steps and work against a series of temporary staging tables.

Chapter 7, "Except/Intersect/Union"

Here we examine set operations. The three main keywords introduced are Union, Intersect, and Except. These are set operators that treat each table involved in the operation as a set. If you are familiar with set theory and Venn diagrams from high school math, you already have a good idea how they work. Union puts two or more tables together. Intersect looks at what the tables have in common. Except returns the differences between tables.

Chapter 8, "Group By"

Business users often ask for reports that show totals and subtotals. These totals are often based on particular categories or groups of data. This chapter introduces the SQL required to group your data and produce meaningful totals. The main emphasis is on the Group By clause used with various aggregation functions, for example, Sum(). We also take a quick look at the more specialized Compute and Compute By clauses. Hopefully, you'll learn enough SQL in just this single chapter to begin producing sophisticated reports for your business users.

Chapter 9, "System Functions"

SQL Server has a couple hundred built-in system functions. You can browse them all in Object Explorer, where they are arranged by category. You can always write your own functions in SQL, but it makes sense to use the prewritten ones if they serve your purpose. It's going to save you a lot of work and time if what you want is already there. In this chapter, we investigate some of these system functions. In particular, we concentrate on some of the most popular and useful string functions, mathematical functions, and date functions. Knowledge of these functions will help you to easily manipulate and transform your data, in exactly the way you want to.

Chapter 10, "Subqueries"

A chapter looking at queries within queries—that's Select statements within Select statements. These are often called *subqueries* or *nested queries*. Subqueries have lots of uses, some of them quite advanced, like derived tables. As this is an introductory book, we'll concentrate on one of the more popular and simpler uses for subqueries. We examine how to use a subquery in a Where clause. There are many ways of doing the same thing in SQL, as is often the case. You can arrive at the same results as you do with subqueries by possibly using joins or temporary tables or some procedural programming with variables. Those other topics are covered in other chapters in this book.

Chapter 11, "Delete/Insert/Update"

Many of the other chapters deal with getting data out of your tables and databases—lots and lots of Select statements. This assumes, of course, that the data is already there and is in the form you require. By contrast, this chapter is dedicated to entering and maintaining the data in the first place. Without data, your Select statements will return nothing. Without good data, your Select statements will return erroneous or obsolete data. Here, we look at data entry using the Insert statement and maintaining data accuracy with the Update statement. In addition, you learn how to remove obsolete or unwanted data with the Delete statement. There are also example queries showing how to work with identity (auto-numbering) columns.

Chapter 12, "Views/User-Defined Functions"

As business user demands for more and more sophisticated reports increase, your SQL is going to become more and more complex. Rather than having to code the same syntax over and over again, you can save your SQL. There are three main ways of doing this. You can create views for complex Select statements—a view is really a stored query. You (and others) can reuse it at any time, without having to be aware of all the complex SQL you originally put into it. This is called *encapsulation*. A second way of saving SQL is to create your own user-defined functions. These are normally used for storing calculations (we are not going to cover table functions that can store Selects). A third way is to create stored procedures. Stored procedures can be used to store both calculations and Selects. Views and functions are covered in this chapter. The next chapter discusses stored procedures. Functions and stored procedures allow you to do sophisticated procedural programming, which views do not.

Chapter 13, "Stored Procedures/Programming"

This is the chapter for procedural programmers. It introduces lots of syntax that you may not think of as SQL. Indeed, strictly speaking, some of it is not SQL. We should rather call it T-SQL (Transact-SQL), which is the SQL Server version of SQL that contains lots of keywords and concepts that extend standard SQL. These extensions are very powerful and help you make your SQL queries truly dynamic and versatile. For example, you can dynamically change a Where clause at run time. The main emphasis of the chapter (after exploring some basic programming constructs) is on stored procedures. These allow you to change your SQL dynamically based on conditional factors—and a whole lot more. In addition, stored procedures provide encapsulation of your code. If you get it right, a Select in a stored procedure can also run much faster than it normally would as a stand-alone query. This is SQL on steroids!

Chapter 14, "Data Definition Language (DDL) and Data Control Language (DCL)"

Data definition language (DDL) is that part of SQL concerned with creating and maintaining the database objects you will need. Data control language (DCL) is the part of SQL dedicated to setting up security on the objects you've created. This chapter is dedicated to DDL and DCL. You will see how to create a database, tables, keys, indexes, and other objects. Once those objects have been created, you'll also learn how to create a login and a user and control and test access to the objects.

Chapter 15, "After You Finish"

Throughout this book, you'll be using SSMS to write your SQL queries and display the results. It's unlikely that your users will have SSMS—indeed, it's not recommended for end users as it's simply too powerful and potentially dangerous. This chapter presents some alternative software and methods for getting SQL query results to the end user.

Chapter 1

Select: Single Table

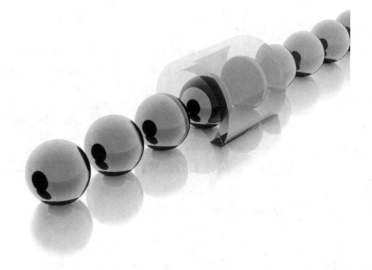

This is an introductory chapter. It concentrates on retrieving columns and rows of data from a *single* table. A wide variety of techniques are covered—doing column calculations, aliasing columns, handling dates and nulls, and more. Many of the techniques discussed are fundamental ones and give you a sound basis on which to develop more complex SQL. You will meet a lot of syntax from this chapter again in later chapters as you learn more complex SQL.

- ▶ **Key concepts**   Selecting columns from a single table, schema names, database names, case sensitivity, aliases, concatenation, data types, date and numeric calculations, XML, nulls, Case functions

- ▶ **Keywords**   Select, From, Use, As, Cast(), Convert(), GetDate(), Datediff(), Distinct, Top, For Xml, IsNull(), Is Null, Coalesce(), Case

Hello World

Your first Select query!

Syntax

```
-- hello world
-- this is a comment as is the line above
select 'Hello World'
```

Result

	(No column name)
1	Hello World

Analysis

I guess this is not the most exciting SQL query ever. However, it does prove a point—a Select statement does *not* have to return data from a table. Select can be used to return literals (strings and numbers), values of variables, function return values, and more. We'll investigate all of these in the course of this book—the rest of this chapter is devoted to returning data from a single relational table.

Select All Columns from a Table

This is different from the previous query—it has a From clause. It returns all the columns or fields (and all the rows or records) from a table called DimCustomer.

Syntax

```
-- basic select
-- make sure you are connected to
-- AdventureWorksDW2008 (SQL Server 2008)
-- or AdventureWorksDW (SQL Server 2005)
select * from DimCustomer
```

Result

	CustomerKey	GeographyKey	CustomerAlternateKey	Title	FirstName	MiddleName	LastName	NameStyle	BirthDate	MaritalStatus	Suffix	Gender
1	11000	26	AW00011000	NULL	Jon	V	Yang	0	1966-04-08	M	NULL	M
2	11001	37	AW00011001	NULL	Eugene	L	Huang	0	1965-05-14	S	NULL	M
3	11002	31	AW00011002	NULL	Ruben	NULL	Torres	0	1965-08-12	M	NULL	M
4	11003	11	AW00011003	NULL	Christy	NULL	Zhu	0	1968-02-15	S	NULL	F
5	11004	19	AW00011004	NULL	Elizabeth	NULL	Johnson	0	1968-08-08	S	NULL	F
6	11005	22	AW00011005	NULL	Julio	NULL	Ruiz	0	1965-08-05	S	NULL	M
7	11006	8	AW00011006	NULL	Janet	G	Alvarez	0	1965-12-06	S	NULL	F
8	11007	40	AW00011007	NULL	Marco	NULL	Mehta	0	1964-05-09	M	NULL	M
9	11008	32	AW00011008	NULL	Rob	NULL	Verhoff	0	1964-07-07	S	NULL	F
10	11009	25	AW00011009	NULL	Shannon	C	Carlson	0	1964-04-01	S	NULL	M
11	11010	22	AW00011010	NULL	Jacquelyn	C	Suarez	0	1964-02-06	S	NULL	F
12	11011	22	AW00011011	NULL	Curtis	NULL	Lu	0	1963-11-04	M	NULL	M
13	11012	611	AW00011012	NULL	Lauren	M	Walker	0	1968-01-18	M	NULL	F
14	11013	543	AW00011013	NULL	Ian	M	Jenkins	0	1968-08-06	M	NULL	M
15	11014	634	AW00011014	NULL	Sydney	NULL	Bennett	0	1968-05-09	S	NULL	F
16	11015	301	AW00011015	NULL	Chloe	NULL	Young	0	1979-02-27	S	NULL	F
17	11016	329	AW00011016	NULL	Wyatt	L	Hill	0	1979-04-28	M	NULL	M
18	11017	39	AW00011017	NULL	Shannon	NULL	Wang	0	1944-06-26	S	NULL	F

Analysis

To return all the columns of a table, you use an asterisk symbol (*). It's normally called *star*—select star from table. Instead of using the star, you can type a list of all the column names separated by commas. *It is good practice to always explicitly have a column list rather than use a star; then there is never any ambiguity about what is returned.* You might be wondering about the strange name of the table, DimCustomer! Tables with a Dim prefix are often so-called "dimension tables." This is a book about SQL queries, not a book about database design, so you don't need to worry about the table name and what a dimension is. The result shows the details for over 18,000 customers. The row or record count is shown in the bottom-right corner of the query editor window.

If your query fails with an invalid object name error, make sure you are connected to the right database—the database is in the drop-down on the toolbar. If you have the correct database and still get the same error, make sure you have capitalized the table name (DimCustomer) as shown in the preceding syntax example (it may just be possible that you have the case-sensitive variety of the database).

Schema Name

Here, there's a dbo. prefix before the table name. The prefix is called the schema. Most of the time, you may be able to ignore the schema name and simply use the table name without the schema prefix. *However, this is generally considered bad practice.* It is possible to have the same table name more than once in a database, if they belong to different schemas. You should always explicitly use the schema name. Instances in which the schema name is not used in this book are for learning purposes only.

Syntax

```
-- schema name
select * from dbo.DimCustomer
```

Result

	CustomerKey	GeographyKey	CustomerAlternateKey	Title	FirstName	MiddleName	LastName	NameStyle	BirthDate	MaritalStatus	Suffix	Gender
1	11000	26	AW00011000	NULL	Jon	V	Yang	0	1966-04-08	M	NULL	M
2	11001	37	AW00011001	NULL	Eugene	L	Huang	0	1965-05-14	S	NULL	M
3	11002	31	AW00011002	NULL	Ruben	NULL	Torres	0	1965-08-12	M	NULL	M
4	11003	11	AW00011003	NULL	Christy	NULL	Zhu	0	1968-02-15	S	NULL	F
5	11004	19	AW00011004	NULL	Elizabeth	NULL	Johnson	0	1968-08-08	S	NULL	F
6	11005	22	AW00011005	NULL	Julio	NULL	Ruiz	0	1965-08-05	S	NULL	M
7	11006	8	AW00011006	NULL	Janet	G	Alvarez	0	1965-12-06	S	NULL	F
8	11007	40	AW00011007	NULL	Marco	NULL	Mehta	0	1964-05-09	M	NULL	M
9	11008	32	AW00011008	NULL	Rob	NULL	Verhoff	0	1964-07-07	S	NULL	F
10	11009	25	AW00011009	NULL	Shannon	C	Carlson	0	1964-04-01	S	NULL	M
11	11010	22	AW00011010	NULL	Jacquelyn	C	Suarez	0	1964-02-06	S	NULL	F
12	11011	22	AW00011011	NULL	Curtis	NULL	Lu	0	1963-11-04	M	NULL	M
13	11012	611	AW00011012	NULL	Lauren	M	Walker	0	1968-01-18	M	NULL	F
14	11013	543	AW00011013	NULL	Ian	M	Jenkins	0	1968-08-06	M	NULL	M
15	11014	634	AW00011014	NULL	Sydney	NULL	Bennett	0	1968-05-09	S	NULL	F
16	11015	301	AW00011015	NULL	Chloe	NULL	Young	0	1979-02-27	S	NULL	F
17	11016	329	AW00011016	NULL	Wyatt	L	Hill	0	1979-04-28	M	NULL	M
18	11017	39	AW00011017	NULL	Shannon	NULL	Wang	0	1944-06-26	S	NULL	F

Analysis

If you expand a database, then expand the Tables folder in the Object Explorer window in SQL Server Management Studio (SSMS), you will notice that the table names have a prefix followed by a dot. This is the schema to which the table belongs. By default, the schema will be dbo. Also, dbo is the default schema for all users—unless your SQL Server database administrator has changed it. If dbo is the default schema, then it's optional in the query—you can simply use the table name without the schema prefix. If the designer of the database has assigned a table to another schema, then you may have to include the schema name. It is recommended that you *always* adopt the two-part names.

Database Name

In the previous query, we qualified the table name with the schema name. This time, the query is further qualified by the database name.

Syntax

```
-- database name
-- the database is AdventureWorksDW2008 in SQL Server 2008
-- the database is AdventureWorksDW in SQL Server 2005
select * from AdventureWorksDW2008.dbo.DimCustomer
select * from AdventureWorksDW2008..DimCustomer
```

Result

	CustomerKey	GeographyKey	CustomerAlternateKey	Title	FirstName	MiddleName	LastName	NameStyle	BirthDate	MaritalStatus	Suffix	Gender
1	11000	26	AW00011000	NULL	Jon	V	Yang	0	1966-04-08	M	NULL	M
2	11001	37	AW00011001	NULL	Eugene	L	Huang	0	1965-05-14	S	NULL	M
3	11002	31	AW00011002	NULL	Ruben	NULL	Torres	0	1965-08-12	M	NULL	M
4	11003	11	AW00011003	NULL	Christy	NULL	Zhu	0	1968-02-15	S	NULL	F
5	11004	19	AW00011004	NULL	Elizabeth	NULL	Johnson	0	1968-08-08	S	NULL	F
6	11005	22	AW00011005	NULL	Julio	NULL	Ruiz	0	1965-08-05	S	NULL	M
7	11006	8	AW00011006	NULL	Janet	G	Alvarez	0	1965-12-06	S	NULL	F
8	11007	40	AW00011007	NULL	Marco	NULL	Mehta	0	1964-05-09	M	NULL	M
9	11008	32	AW00011008	NULL	Rob	NULL	Verhoff	0	1964-07-07	S	NULL	F
10	11009	25	AW00011009	NULL	Shannon	C	Carlson	0	1964-04-01	S	NULL	M
11	11010	22	AW00011010	NULL	Jacquelyn	C	Suarez	0	1964-02-06	S	NULL	F
12	11011	22	AW00011011	NULL	Curtis	NULL	Lu	0	1963-11-04	M	NULL	M
13	11012	611	AW00011012	NULL	Lauren	M	Walker	0	1968-01-18	M	NULL	F
14	11013	543	AW00011013	NULL	Ian	M	Jenkins	0	1968-08-06	M	NULL	M
15	11014	634	AW00011014	NULL	Sydney	NULL	Bennett	0	1968-05-09	S	NULL	F
16	11015	301	AW00011015	NULL	Chloe	NULL	Young	0	1979-02-27	S	NULL	F
17	11016	329	AW00011016	NULL	Wyatt	L	Hill	0	1979-04-28	M	NULL	M
18	11017	39	AW00011017	NULL	Shannon	NULL	Wang	0	1944-06-26	S	NULL	F

Analysis

The result shows the first few columns and records returned. If you are connected to the AdventureWorksDW2008 (or AdventureWorksDW, if you are working on SQL Server 2005) database, then the database name qualifier is not necessary. The current database connection can be seen in the drop-down on the toolbar. If you are currently connected to another database (and don't change the connection in the drop-down), then the database name is necessary. When you do include the database name, you *must* also include the schema name (here the schema is dbo). The second of the two example queries shows a shorthand technique that works only if the schema is dbo. This shorthand is bad practice—you should always *explicitly* mention the dbo schema. It's included here so you can identify what's happening if you inherit code in this format.

Switching Databases

The Use statement here is an alternative to the syntax in the previous query. It's only necessary if the current database context is not AdventureWorksDW2008 (try AdventureWorksDW if you have SQL Server 2005).

Syntax

```
-- alternative
use AdventureWorksDW2008
select * from dimcustomer
```

Result

	CustomerKey	GeographyKey	CustomerAlternateKey	Title	FirstName	MiddleName	LastName	NameStyle	BirthDate	MaritalStatus	Suffix	Gender
1	11000	26	AW00011000	NULL	Jon	V	Yang	0	1966-04-08	M	NULL	M
2	11001	37	AW00011001	NULL	Eugene	L	Huang	0	1965-05-14	S	NULL	M
3	11002	31	AW00011002	NULL	Ruben	NULL	Torres	0	1965-08-12	M	NULL	M
4	11003	11	AW00011003	NULL	Christy	NULL	Zhu	0	1968-02-15	S	NULL	F
5	11004	19	AW00011004	NULL	Elizabeth	NULL	Johnson	0	1968-08-08	S	NULL	F
6	11005	22	AW00011005	NULL	Julio	NULL	Ruiz	0	1965-08-05	S	NULL	M
7	11006	8	AW00011006	NULL	Janet	G	Alvarez	0	1965-12-06	S	NULL	F
8	11007	40	AW00011007	NULL	Marco	NULL	Mehta	0	1964-05-09	M	NULL	M
9	11008	32	AW00011008	NULL	Rob	NULL	Verhoff	0	1964-07-07	S	NULL	F
10	11009	25	AW00011009	NULL	Shannon	C	Carlson	0	1964-04-01	S	NULL	M
11	11010	22	AW00011010	NULL	Jacquelyn	C	Suarez	0	1964-02-06	S	NULL	F
12	11011	22	AW00011011	NULL	Curtis	NULL	Lu	0	1963-11-04	M	NULL	M
13	11012	611	AW00011012	NULL	Lauren	M	Walker	0	1968-01-18	M	NULL	F
14	11013	543	AW00011013	NULL	Ian	M	Jenkins	0	1968-08-06	M	NULL	M
15	11014	634	AW00011014	NULL	Sydney	NULL	Bennett	0	1968-05-09	S	NULL	F
16	11015	301	AW00011015	NULL	Chloe	NULL	Young	0	1979-02-27	S	NULL	F
17	11016	329	AW00011016	NULL	Wyatt	L	Hill	0	1979-04-28	M	NULL	M
18	11017	39	AW00011017	NULL	Shannon	NULL	Wang	0	1944-06-26	S	NULL	F

Analysis

This query and the last one produce an identical result—all the columns and rows from the DimCustomer table. However, the effects of the two queries are subtly different. The last query does not change the current database. This query does change the current database context—if you had been connected to another database, the database name in the drop-down would have changed. I have not included the schema name, but you should always try to do so. As this is a learning book, it means a little less typing for you.

Server Name

Now we have the server name as well. This is a fully qualified table name.

Syntax

```
-- server name
select * from MyServer.AdventureWorksDW2008.dbo.DimCustomer
```

Result

```
Msg 7202, Level 11, State 2, Line 2
Could not find server 'MyServer' in sys.servers. Verify that the correct server name was specified. If necessary, execute t
```

Analysis

A fully qualified table name consists of server name, followed by database name, followed by schema name, and finally the table name. Such syntax might be necessary if you are writing cross-server queries. Most likely your result will be an error. For this syntax to work, you will need a valid server name (maybe not MyServer!), and that server must be linked to the server you are working on. Setting up linked servers is a database administrator's task—it's beyond the scope of an introductory book about SQL queries. I included the syntax here for completeness.

Variations on a Theme

There are four queries here for you to try. There are subtle differences between all four. All four should work and produce the same result (in certain circumstances, you might find that the third query fails). You can run all four together and produce multiple result sets or, probably better, highlight each one individually and run them in turn.

Syntax

```
-- semicolons are optional in this type of query
select * from DimCustomer;
-- SQL syntax is case-insensitive
Select * FROM DimCustomer
-- but object names might be case-sensitive, intellisense helps in 2008
select * from dimcustomer
-- copes with white space and carriage returns
select          *
from
DimCustomer
```

Result

	CustomerKey	GeographyKey	CustomerAlternateKey	Title	FirstName	MiddleName	LastName	NameStyle	BirthDate	MaritalStatus	Suffix	Gender
1	11000	26	AW00011000	NULL	Jon	V	Yang	0	1966-04-08	M	NULL	M
2	11001	37	AW00011001	NULL	Eugene	L	Huang	0	1965-05-14	S	NULL	M
3	11002	31	AW00011002	NULL	Ruben	NULL	Torres	0	1965-08-12	M	NULL	M
4	11003	11	AW00011003	NULL	Christy	NULL	Zhu	0	1968-02-15	S	NULL	F
5	11004	19	AW00011004	NULL	Elizabeth	NULL	Johnson	0	1968-08-08	S	NULL	F
6	11005	22	AW00011005	NULL	Julio	NULL	Ruiz	0	1965-08-05	S	NULL	M
7	11006	8	AW00011006	NULL	Janet	G	Alvarez	0	1965-12-06	S	NULL	F
8	11007	40	AW00011007	NULL	Marco	NULL	Mehta	0	1964-05-09	M	NULL	M
9	11008	32	AW00011008	NULL	Rob	NULL	Verhoff	0	1964-07-07	S	NULL	F
10	11009	25	AW00011009	NULL	Shannon	C	Carlson	0	1964-04-01	S	NULL	M
11	11010	22	AW00011010	NULL	Jacquelyn	C	Suarez	0	1964-02-06	S	NULL	F
12	11011	22	AW00011011	NULL	Curtis	NULL	Lu	0	1963-11-04	M	NULL	M
13	11012	611	AW00011012	NULL	Lauren	M	Walker	0	1968-01-18	M	NULL	F
14	11013	543	AW00011013	NULL	Ian	M	Jenkins	0	1968-08-06	M	NULL	M
15	11014	634	AW00011014	NULL	Sydney	NULL	Bennett	0	1968-05-09	S	NULL	F
16	11015	301	AW00011015	NULL	Chloe	NULL	Young	0	1979-02-27	S	NULL	F
17	11016	329	AW00011016	NULL	Wyatt	L	Hill	0	1979-04-28	M	NULL	M
18	11017	39	AW00011017	NULL	Shannon	NULL	Wang	0	1944-06-26	S	NULL	F

Analysis

Did all four queries work, or just three? It is just possible that the third one might fail. The first of the four queries is terminated with a semicolon (;)—this is sometimes optional, but many SQL programmers consider it good practice to clearly delineate queries. I would recommend the use of semicolons in *all* your queries. In the second query, the From is in uppercase (FROM)—SQL syntax is case-insensitive. The third query is the one that might possibly fail—note the table name is in lowercase (dimcustomer). If it does fail, then your database might be case-sensitive—there are some varieties of the Microsoft AdventureWorks downloads that are case-sensitive. Object names can be case-sensitive. Most SQL Server databases are, in reality, case-insensitive. If you suspect that yours is case-sensitive, ask your SQL Server DBA to make it case-insensitive. Or make sure you capitalize all object names used in this book correctly. You can check the capitalization of object names by browsing to the object in Object Explorer in SSMS. The fourth and final query uses lots of space characters and hard returns—it's on three lines. SQL queries are forgiving of white space and carriage returns.

Specific Column 1/2

Here the star or asterisk has been replaced by a specific column name.

Syntax

```
-- a specific column
select lastname from DimCustomer
```

Result

	lastname
1	Yang
2	Huang
3	Torres
4	Zhu
5	Johnson
6	Ruiz
7	Alvarez
8	Mehta
9	Verhoff
10	Carlson
11	Suarez
12	Lu
13	Walker
14	Jenkins
15	Bennett
16	Young
17	Hill
18	Wang
19	Rai

Analysis

You should still see rows for over 18,000 customers, but there is only the one column. If you suspect that your database is case-sensitive, then replace lastname with LastName (see the next query). You can expand the Columns folder in Object Explorer to check the capitalization. Please be aware that you can drag and drop object names from Object Explorer into the query editor window. Dragging and dropping avoids typos and also capitalizes correctly if you are working on a case-sensitive database.

Specific Column 2/2

This is the same as the last query—except the column name is capitalized differently.

Syntax

```
select LastName from DimCustomer
```

Result

	LastName
1	Yang
2	Huang
3	Torres
4	Zhu
5	Johnson
6	Ruiz
7	Alvarez
8	Mehta
9	Verhoff
10	Carlson
11	Suarez
12	Lu
13	Walker
14	Jenkins
15	Bennett
16	Young
17	Hill
18	Wang
19	Rai

Analysis

For most readers of this book, this query and the previous one both work and produce an identical result. Well, not quite. You might want to glance at the caption for the column header—the one in this query looks better (LastName, rather than lastname). For a small minority of readers (those with a case-sensitive database), only this query will work. I won't mention case sensitivity again, but please bear it in mind as you work through the queries in this book if your database is case-sensitive—most of you can ignore the problem.

Column Aliases 1/2

Often, a database designer may choose obscure names for columns (I have seen live production databases in blue-chip companies with column names like Column1). Or you might simply want a different name for the column. To rename a column you use an alias. There are three queries here to try, either individually (by highlighting individually, if you pasted in the code from the book's download) or together (by having no highlight or highlighting all three).

Syntax

```
-- column alias 1/2
select lastname as Surname from dimcustomer
select lastname Surname from dimcustomer
select Surname = lastname from dimcustomer
```

Result

	Surname
1	Yang
2	Huang
3	Torres
4	Zhu
5	Johnson
6	Ruiz
7	Alvarez
8	Mehta
9	Verhoff
10	Carlson
11	Suarez
12	Lu
13	Walker
14	Jenkins
15	Bennett
16	Young
17	Hill
18	Wang
19	Rai

Analysis

If you ran all three queries together, you may have to scroll down to see all three result sets. All three queries produce the same desired effect, LastName is now Surname. The choice of syntax is, of course, yours. Many SQL programmers prefer the first alternative with the keyword As—perhaps it's more explicit and easier to read.

Column Aliases 2/2

Here our alias is slightly different—there's a space in the alias. There are two queries—please run them separately. If you run them together, you won't see any data being returned.

Syntax

```
-- column alias 2/2
select lastname as Last Name from dimcustomer
select lastname as [Last Name] from dimcustomer
```

Result

	Last Name
1	Yang
2	Huang
3	Torres
4	Zhu
5	Johnson
6	Ruiz
7	Alvarez
8	Mehta
9	Verhoff
10	Carlson
11	Suarez
12	Lu
13	Walker
14	Jenkins
15	Bennett
16	Young
17	Hill
18	Wang
19	Rai

Analysis

The first query fails. If an alias contains a space, then it must be delineated with square brackets. This is a general rule and applies to other objects, not just to aliases. If you have table or original column names, for example, with embedded spaces, then you must use the square brackets; otherwise, you'll receive a syntax error message. If you run the second query separately, then the caption for the column header will be Last Name.

Two or More Columns

So far, you've returned all the columns in a table by using the star or asterisk (*) symbol or a single column only. This query returns two columns.

Syntax

```
-- two or more specific columns
select firstname, lastname from DimCustomer
select lastname, firstname from DimCustomer
```

Result

	lastname	firstname
1	Yang	Jon
2	Huang	Eugene
3	Torres	Ruben
4	Zhu	Christy
5	Johnson	Elizabeth
6	Ruiz	Julio
7	Alvarez	Janet
8	Mehta	Marco
9	Verhoff	Rob
10	Carlson	Shannon
11	Suarez	Jacquelyn
12	Lu	Curtis
13	Walker	Lauren
14	Jenkins	Ian
15	Bennett	Sydney
16	Young	Chloe
17	Hill	Wyatt
18	Wang	Shannon
19	Rai	Clarence

Analysis

Both queries return the same data—but the columns are in a different order. To retrieve two columns, you separate the column names with a comma (,). If you want even more columns, you write a comma-separated list—please note there is no comma after the last column name. If you want all columns, it's a lot easier to use the star or asterisk—it can be tedious to type every single column name. Try not to be tempted to be lazy and always explicitly use column names. You can generate a full list of columns by right-clicking the table in Object Explorer and choosing Script Table as, SELECT To, New Query Editor Window. This can be incredibly useful when there are lots of columns and you want most of them (simply delete the column[s] not required).

Concatenating Columns

Appending one column to another is called *concatenation*—the concatenation symbol is a plus sign (+). Both queries here use two columns, but the output is a single column.

Syntax

```
-- concatenation
select firstname + lastname from dimcustomer
select firstname + lastname as [Full Name] from dimcustomer
```

Result

	Full Name
1	JonYang
2	EugeneHuang
3	RubenTorres
4	ChristyZhu
5	ElizabethJohnson
6	JulioRuiz
7	JanetAlvarez
8	MarcoMehta
9	RobVerhoff
10	ShannonCarlson
11	JacquelynSuarez
12	CurtisLu
13	LaurenWalker
14	IanJenkins
15	SydneyBennett
16	ChloeYoung
17	WyattHill
18	ShannonWang
19	ClarenceRai

Analysis

The second query has an alias—its column header is much more user-friendly. Be careful, please, when concatenating columns. It works on two strings (for example, char or varchar columns), but not on two numeric columns (for example, with a data type of int). In the latter case, it will add the numbers together. You can view the data type of the column in Object Explorer.

Adding Strings

You can improve concatenation by adding your own text. Here, the columns are separated by a comma and a space.

Syntax

```
-- concatenation with text
select firstname + ', ' + lastname as [Full Name] from dimcustomer
```

Result

	Full Name
1	Jon, Yang
2	Eugene, Huang
3	Ruben, Torres
4	Christy, Zhu
5	Elizabeth, Johnson
6	Julio, Ruiz
7	Janet, Alvarez
8	Marco, Mehta
9	Rob, Verhoff
10	Shannon, Carlson
11	Jacquelyn, Suarez
12	Curtis, Lu
13	Lauren, Walker
14	Ian, Jenkins
15	Sydney, Bennett
16	Chloe, Young
17	Wyatt, Hill
18	Shannon, Wang
19	Clarence, Rai

Analysis

You've added some user-defined text. Strictly speaking, we should call it a string and not text—text has a very specific meaning in SQL Server. Text is a data type—string is not a data type and is a safe, generic term. Strings are enclosed within single quotes. Incidentally, the SQL Server dialect of SQL is often called T-SQL or Transact-SQL. Most of the T-SQL syntax in this book is standard SQL (ANSI SQL) and is valid for other database software such as Oracle or DB2 or MySQL.

Concatenation Failure

All we've done here is to change the second column and use a different alias. Expect this query not to work!

Syntax

```
-- concatenation fails
select lastname + ' ' + customerkey as [Name ID] from dimcustomer
```

Result

```
Msg 245, Level 16, State 1, Line 2
Conversion failed when converting the nvarchar value 'Yang ' to data type int.
```

Analysis

If you concatenate two alphabetic columns, then it appends them. If you concatenate two numeric columns, you don't actually get a concatenation—rather, it will add the two numbers together as a summation. If you concatenate an alphabetic column to a numeric one, you get an error. Here, CustomerKey is a numeric column. SQL Server doesn't know whether you want a true concatenation (append) or an addition (summation). You see how to fix the error in the next query.

Cast and Convert

What if you want to concatenate an alphabetic column and a numeric column? To do so, you can use Cast() or Convert(). The two queries produce the same result.

Syntax

```
-- cast or convert
select lastname + ' ' + cast(customerkey as nvarchar) as [Name ID]
from dimcustomer
select lastname + ' ' + convert(nvarchar,customerkey) as [Name ID]
from dimcustomer
```

Result

	Name ID
1	Yang 11000
2	Huang 11001
3	Torres 11002
4	Zhu 11003
5	Johnson 11004
6	Ruiz 11005
7	Alvarez 11006
8	Mehta 11007
9	Verhoff 11008
10	Carlson 11009
11	Suarez 11010
12	Lu 11011
13	Walker 11012
14	Jenkins 11013
15	Bennett 11014
16	Young 11015
17	Hill 11016
18	Wang 11017
19	Rai 11018

Analysis

LastName is an alphabetic column (data type of nvarchar). CustomerKey is a numeric column (data type of int). The Cast() and Convert() functions change the numeric column into an alphabetic one. Cast() and Convert() are generally interchangeable. Many SQL programmers prefer Cast() as it's a little easier to read. However, Convert() has some additional functionality that is useful when working with dates and times. Cast() is ANSI-standard, Convert() is not—Convert() may not work with non-SQL Server databases.

Date Column

Date columns are infamous for causing problems. Here's a date column query.

Syntax

```
-- date format (default ANSI)
select birthdate from dimcustomer
```

Result

	birthdate
1	1966-04-08
2	1965-05-14
3	1965-08-12
4	1968-02-15
5	1968-08-08
6	1965-08-05
7	1965-12-06
8	1964-05-09
9	1964-07-07
10	1964-04-01
11	1964-02-06
12	1963-11-04
13	1968-01-18
14	1968-08-06
15	1968-05-09
16	1979-02-27
17	1979-04-28
18	1944-06-26
19	1944-10-09

Analysis

It works, but the display is not very user-friendly. This is the default display for a SQL Server date (yyyy-mm-dd). The data type of the BirthDate column is date. If you have SQL Server 2005, the data type is datetime and your result will show the time after the date (in this example, as midnight).

Formatting Dates 1/3

The Convert() function is being used to format the date column.

Syntax

```
-- date format US 4 digit year
select convert(varchar,birthdate,101) as [US Date] from dimcustomer
```

Result

	US Date
1	04/08/1966
2	05/14/1965
3	08/12/1965
4	02/15/1968
5	08/08/1968
6	08/05/1965
7	12/06/1965
8	05/09/1964
9	07/07/1964
10	04/01/1964
11	02/06/1964
12	11/04/1963
13	01/18/1968
14	08/06/1968
15	05/09/1968
16	02/27/1979
17	04/28/1979
18	06/26/1944
19	10/09/1944

Analysis

The date column has been converted into an alphabetic column (data type `varchar`). But here, the Convert() function has a third parameter, 101. The Cast() function does not support this extension. The result is a date in U.S. format with a four-digit year.

Formatting Dates 2/3

The third parameter for the Convert() function has been changed from 101 to 1.

Syntax

```
-- date format US 2 digit year
select convert(varchar,birthdate,1) as [US Date] from dimcustomer
```

Result

	US Date
1	04/08/66
2	05/14/65
3	08/12/65
4	02/15/68
5	08/08/68
6	08/05/65
7	12/06/65
8	05/09/64
9	07/07/64
10	04/01/64
11	02/06/64
12	11/04/63
13	01/18/68
14	08/06/68
15	05/09/68
16	02/27/79
17	04/28/79
18	06/26/44
19	10/09/44

Analysis

This time, you have a date in U.S. format, but with a two-digit year. If you wish to research the codes for the third Convert() parameter, highlight the word Convert and press F1.

Formatting Dates 3/3

This time, the third parameter for Convert() is 103.

Syntax

```
-- date format UK 4 digit year
select convert(varchar,birthdate,103) as [UK Date] from dimcustomer
```

Result

	UK Date
1	08/04/1966
2	14/05/1965
3	12/08/1965
4	15/02/1968
5	08/08/1968
6	05/08/1965
7	06/12/1965
8	09/05/1964
9	07/07/1964
10	01/04/1964
11	06/02/1964
12	04/11/1963
13	18/01/1968
14	06/08/1968
15	09/05/1968
16	27/02/1979
17	28/04/1979
18	26/06/1944
19	09/10/1944

Analysis

The parameter 103 gives you a U.K. date format with a four-digit year (a parameter of 3 would result in a two-digit year).

System Date Function

There is no From clause here—we're not working against a table. GetDate() is a system function—it returns the current date and time.

Syntax

```
-- today's date (no table)
select GETDATE()
```

Result

	(No column name)
1	2009-08-29 17:05:47.280

Analysis

You should be looking at the current date and time. I guess your answer is different from mine! GetDate() is not case-sensitive. Microsoft provides lots of useful system functions. We are going to use this one to do some date calculations, shortly. If you wish to view the system functions, expand your database in Object Explorer, then expand Programmability, Functions, System Functions. GetDate() can be seen under the Date and Time Functions folder.

Date Column Calculation

Here we introduce another system function for working with dates, Datediff(). Hopefully, this is quite a useful query for you.

Syntax

```
-- date calculation
select birthdate, datediff(yy,birthdate,GETDATE()) as Age
from dimcustomer
```

Result

	birthdate	Age
1	1966-04-08	43
2	1965-05-14	44
3	1965-08-12	44
4	1968-02-15	41
5	1968-08-08	41
6	1965-08-05	44
7	1965-12-06	44
8	1964-05-09	45
9	1964-07-07	45
10	1964-04-01	45
11	1964-02-06	45
12	1963-11-04	46
13	1968-01-18	41
14	1968-08-06	41
15	1968-05-09	41
16	1979-02-27	30
17	1979-04-28	30
18	1944-06-26	65
19	1944-10-09	65

Analysis

Often, you'll want to see how much time has elapsed since a start date or start time. For example, if you are in marketing, you might want to see the age of your customers. It doesn't make sense to have a column (unless it's a calculated column) in the table called Age—you'll be updating the column every year for every customer! This is probably a better solution—it makes use of the Datediff() function. The function is working out the number of years between the birth date of the customer and the current date. The first parameter of the Datediff() function is yy. To see a full list of parameter codes, highlight the word Datediff and press F1. My help system takes me to Dateadd(), not Datediff(), for some reason—but the codes are the same. This anomaly may well be fixed in your version of SQL Server.

Numeric Column Calculation 1/2

As well as date column calculations, you can perform calculations using numeric columns. Here, you're attempting to find out how many children of a customer live away from home. Expect this query to fail—at least, partially.

Syntax

```
-- columns calculation
select totalchildren, numberchildrenathome,
totalchildren - numberchildrenathome as AwayFromHome
from DimCustomer
```

Result

```
Msg 8115, Level 16, State 2, Line 2
Arithmetic overflow error converting expression to data type tinyint.
```

Analysis

You might just see a quick flicker of data on the Results tab before you are flipped to the Messages tab, with an error about a tinyint overflow. If you then click the Results tab, you will see some records returned—so you may be tempted to conclude that the query was successful. However, you will see a note at the bottom that the query completed with errors. Also, there are only 82 rows returned (bottom-right corner), and from earlier queries we know there are over 18,000 customers. The problem is addressed in the next query.

Numeric Column Calculation 2/2

The Cast() function is used here to change the two columns (TotalChildren and NumberChildrenAtHome) involved in the calculation into a data type of smallint.

Syntax

```
-- columns calculation working
select totalchildren, numberchildrenathome,
cast(totalchildren as smallint) - cast(numberchildrenathome as smallint)
as AwayFromHome from DimCustomer
```

Result

	totalchildren	numberchildrenathome	AwayFromHome
1	2	0	2
2	3	3	0
3	3	3	0
4	0	0	0
5	5	5	0
6	0	0	0
7	0	0	0
8	3	3	0
9	4	4	0
10	0	0	0
11	0	0	0
12	4	4	0
13	2	0	2
14	2	0	2
15	3	0	3
16	0	0	0
17	0	0	0
18	4	0	4

Analysis

If you examine the two columns in the Object Explorer, you will notice they both have a data type of tinyint. A tinyint only supports positive integers. A tinyint column subtracted from a tinyint column will attempt to give the answer (aliased as AwayFromHome) as a tinyint as well. However, the customer on row 83 has a negative number as AwayFromHome—the previous query failed exactly at this record. The Cast() function is used to change both tinyint columns into smallint ones, and the result will be a smallint. A smallint supports negative (as well as positive) integers. Now, the query completes successfully. I am not sure how you can have a negative number of children away from home (but that's the data we have to work with)!

Arithmetic Calculation

What if we are coming out of a recession? Maybe all of our customers are due a ten percent raise in yearly income.

Syntax

```
-- numeric calculation
select YearlyIncome, YearlyIncome * 1.1 as [After Increase] from
dimcustomer
```

Result

	YearlyIncome	After Increase
1	90000.00	99000.00000
2	60000.00	66000.00000
3	60000.00	66000.00000
4	70000.00	77000.00000
5	80000.00	88000.00000
6	70000.00	77000.00000
7	70000.00	77000.00000
8	60000.00	66000.00000
9	60000.00	66000.00000
10	70000.00	77000.00000
11	70000.00	77000.00000
12	60000.00	66000.00000
13	100000.00	110000.00000
14	100000.00	110000.00000
15	100000.00	110000.00000
16	30000.00	33000.00000
17	30000.00	33000.00000
18	20000.00	22000.00000

Analysis

This is a simple arithmetic calculation. All basic arithmetic operators are supported for add (+), subtract (-), multiply (*), and divide (/). There are also an integer division (\) and a modulo (%). System functions provide a wide range of mathematical and aggregate functions (you can browse these in Object Explorer).

Distinct Values

Definitely no recession—all of our customers have an occupation (EnglishOccupation column). But many have the same occupation—maybe we simply want to see an enumeration of the possible occupations.

Syntax

```
-- distinct on one column
select englishoccupation from DimCustomer
select distinct englishoccupation from DimCustomer
```

Result

	englishoccupation
1	Professional
2	Manual
3	Clerical
4	Management
5	Skilled Manual

Analysis

The second query includes the Distinct operator. Distinct suppresses duplicate values for the column(s) in the columns list. Distinct followed by a star (*) suppresses duplicate records. The first query returns duplicated records.

Distinct on Multiple Columns

In the second query here, the Distinct operator is applied to two columns. Please try both queries and compare the number of records returned.

Syntax

```
-- distinct on more than one column
select englishoccupation, englisheducation from DimCustomer
select distinct englishoccupation, englisheducation from DimCustomer
```

Result

	englishoccupation	englisheducation
1	Clerical	Bachelors
2	Skilled Manual	Partial College
3	Professional	Partial High School
4	Manual	Bachelors
5	Manual	Graduate Degree
6	Management	Graduate Degree
7	Professional	High School
8	Management	Bachelors
9	Management	Partial College
10	Clerical	Graduate Degree
11	Skilled Manual	Graduate Degree
12	Skilled Manual	Bachelors
13	Professional	Bachelors
14	Professional	Partial College
15	Professional	Graduate Degree
16	Manual	High School
17	Clerical	High School
18	Clerical	Partial High School

Analysis

As you examine the records you'll notice Clerical more than once. You will also see Bachelors more than once. However, you won't see Clerical together with Bachelors more than once. The Distinct operator is working on both columns together.

Top

When you are developing your queries against large tables, it can take a while for results to be returned. Here's a simple technique to reduce the number of rows while you perfect your SQL.

Syntax

```
-- just a few records
select * from DimCustomer
select top 7 * from DimCustomer
```

Result

	CustomerKey	GeographyKey	CustomerAlternateKey	Title	FirstName	MiddleName	LastName	NameStyle	BirthDate	MaritalStatus	Suffix	Gender
1	11000	26	AW00011000	NULL	Jon	V	Yang	0	1966-04-08	M	NULL	M
2	11001	37	AW00011001	NULL	Eugene	L	Huang	0	1965-05-14	S	NULL	M
3	11002	31	AW00011002	NULL	Ruben	NULL	Torres	0	1965-08-12	M	NULL	M
4	11003	11	AW00011003	NULL	Christy	NULL	Zhu	0	1968-02-15	S	NULL	F
5	11004	19	AW00011004	NULL	Elizabeth	NULL	Johnson	0	1968-08-08	S	NULL	F
6	11005	22	AW00011005	NULL	Julio	NULL	Ruiz	0	1965-08-05	S	NULL	M
7	11006	8	AW00011006	NULL	Janet	G	Alvarez	0	1965-12-06	S	NULL	F

Analysis

The first query returns 18,484 rows. The second query returns just 7 rows—it uses the Top keyword. Top has many more uses than this—we'll return to Top when we examine sorting records later in the book. If you don't sort the rows, you can't be sure which 7 rows are going to be returned.

XML

Normally, your SQL queries return a set of records or rows—this is often called a *result set* or *record set*. You can handle this in a wide variety of ways in front-end applications; a popular way is to use a data grid. Sometimes, though, your client software may want the data in XML format. The second and third queries here show two ways of retrieving XML data.

Syntax

```
-- xml
select * from DimCustomer
select * from DimCustomer for xml auto
select * from DimCustomer for xml auto, elements
```

Result

XML_F52E2B61-18A1-11d1-B105-00805F49916B
1 <DimCustomer><CustomerKey>11000</CustomerKey><Ge...

Analysis

The first query returns a simple result set. The second and third queries return the data in XML format—they both use the For Xml clause. You can view the XML by clicking its blue hyperlink. The second query shows attribute-centric XML, while the third query returns element-centric XML. The result shown is from the third query.

Nulls 1/3

Null values can present interesting challenges. The MiddleName column in the DimCustomer table has a number of null values. Please run the two queries and compare the results. Null values represent missing values—they are *not* the same as empty strings or zeroes.

Syntax

```
-- handling nulls 1/3
select firstname, middlename, lastname from DimCustomer
select firstname + ' ' + middlename + ' ' + lastname as [Full Name]
from dimcustomer
```

Result

	Full Name
1	Jon V Yang
2	Eugene L Huang
3	NULL
4	NULL
5	NULL
6	NULL
7	Janet G Alvarez
8	NULL
9	NULL
10	Shannon C Carlson
11	Jacquelyn C Suarez
12	NULL
13	Lauren M Walker
14	Ian M Jenkins
15	NULL
16	NULL
17	Wyatt L Hill
18	NULL

Analysis

The first query shows that Ruben Torres has a null value for the MiddleName column. The second query demonstrates what happens when you try to concatenate a null value to the other two columns. By default, any operation involving a null value will result in Null. The result is from the second query. Unless otherwise mentioned, most results shown in this book are from the last query (when more than one query is shown for the syntax to try).

Nulls 2/3

There are two queries here showing how to handle nulls. Both queries produce an identical result—but they use different syntax.

Syntax

```
-- handling nulls 2/3
select firstname + ' ' + isnull(middlename,'') + ' ' + lastname
as [Full Name] from dimcustomer
select firstname + ' ' +
case
when middlename is null    then ''
else middlename + ' '
end
+ lastname as [Full Name] from dimcustomer
```

Result

	Full Name
1	Jon V Yang
2	Eugene L Huang
3	Ruben Torres
4	Christy Zhu
5	Elizabeth Johnson
6	Julio Ruiz
7	Janet G Alvarez
8	Marco Mehta
9	Rob Verhoff
10	Shannon C Carlson
11	Jacquelyn C Suarez
12	Curtis Lu
13	Lauren M Walker
14	Ian M Jenkins
15	Sydney Bennett
16	Chloe Young
17	Wyatt L Hill
18	Shannon Wang

Analysis

Now you can see the row for Ruben Torres. The first query uses the IsNull() function to replace null values with an empty string. The second query uses the Is Null clause to do the same. Please note that the IsNull() function is one word while the Is Null clause is two words. The second query also introduces the Case function.

Nulls 3/3

You can also achieve the same effect with the Coalesce() function.

Syntax

```
-- handling nulls 3/3 coalesce
select coalesce(firstname + ' ' + middlename + ' ' +lastname,
firstname + ' ' +lastname) as [Full Name] from dimcustomer
```

Result

	Full Name
1	Jon V Yang
2	Eugene L Huang
3	Ruben Torres
4	Christy Zhu
5	Elizabeth Johnson
6	Julio Ruiz
7	Janet G Alvarez
8	Marco Mehta
9	Rob Verhoff
10	Shannon C Carlson
11	Jacquelyn C Suarez
12	Curtis Lu
13	Lauren M Walker
14	Ian M Jenkins
15	Sydney Bennett
16	Chloe Young
17	Wyatt L Hill
18	Shannon Wang

Analysis

The syntax for Coalesce() is not quite as easy as that for the IsNull() function or the Is Null clause. It accepts a list of expressions as parameters, separated by commas. It then returns the first expression in the list that's a non-null value. For Jon V Yang, it returns FirstName and MiddleName and LastName. For Ruben Torres, it returns FirstName and LastName (without the MiddleName).

Case 1/2

The Case function has many, many uses. It's commonly used to change values or to assign continuous values to buckets (if you are involved in SQL Server Analysis Services [SSAS] data mining, you will recognize the latter as a technique called *discretization*). Here, the Case function is being used for discretization.

Syntax

```
-- case 1/2
select yearlyincome from dimcustomer
select
case
when yearlyincome <= 30000 then 'Low'
when yearlyincome <= 70000 then 'Medium'
else 'High'
end
as [Income Group]
from dimcustomer
```

Result

	Income Group
1	High
2	Medium
3	Medium
4	Medium
5	High
6	Medium
7	Medium
8	Medium
9	Medium
10	Medium
11	Medium
12	Medium
13	High
14	High
15	High
16	Low
17	Low
18	Low

Analysis

The result of the first query shows a wide range of income values. The second query shows only three values for the YearlyIncome column aliased as Income Group. Please note that the original column name, YearlyIncome, is repeated after each When.

Case 2/2

This time, the Case function is used to change values.

Syntax

```
-- case 2/2
select maritalstatus from DimCustomer
select
case maritalstatus
when 'M' then 'Married'
when 'S' then 'Single'
else 'Unknown'
end
as 'Married?'
from dimcustomer
```

Result

	Married?
1	Married
2	Single
3	Married
4	Single
5	Single
6	Single
7	Single
8	Married
9	Single
10	Single
11	Single
12	Married
13	Married
14	Married
15	Single
16	Single
17	Married
18	Single

Analysis

The contents of the MaritalStatus column have been changed and aliased as 'Married?'. This is a subtly different syntax from the previous query. Here, the column name, MaritalStatus, appears only once after Case—it does not appear after each When. These are known respectively as simple and searched Case statements.

Chapter 2

Where

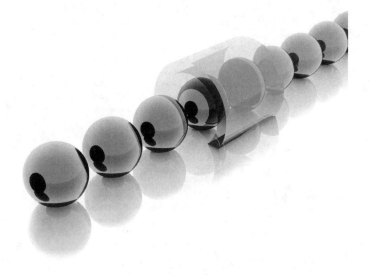

Tis chapter is devoted to the Where clause. It's a huge subject area and could easily fill a whole book, let alone a single chapter. Here you'll discover how to search records (relational database experts prefer to call them *rows*)—how to find what you're looking for. You'll also see how to return subsets of your tables based on the criteria you specify. Many of your own SQL queries are going to require Where clauses—here you'll become familiar with all of the important concepts and techniques for returning just what you want (and being able to ignore what you don't want).

▶   **Key concepts**   Searching for records, filtering, search criteria, date searching, equalities and inequalities, null values, Unicode and ASCII, wildcards, full-text searches

▶   **Keywords**   Where, And, Or, In(), Not, Between, Is Null, Is Not Null, Like, Left(), N, Charindex(), Contains

All Rows in a Table

A query such as this will return all of the rows or records in the table. We are still using the AdventureWorksDW2008 database.

Syntax

```
-- returns all rows
select FirstName, LastName, EnglishEducation, EnglishOccupation
from DimCustomer
```

Result

	FirstName	LastName	EnglishEducation	EnglishOccupation
1	Jon	Yang	Bachelors	Professional
2	Eugene	Huang	Bachelors	Professional
3	Ruben	Torres	Bachelors	Professional
4	Christy	Zhu	Bachelors	Professional
5	Elizabeth	Johnson	Bachelors	Professional
6	Julio	Ruiz	Bachelors	Professional
7	Janet	Alvarez	Bachelors	Professional
8	Marco	Mehta	Bachelors	Professional
9	Rob	Verhoff	Bachelors	Professional
10	Shannon	Carlson	Bachelors	Professional
11	Jacquelyn	Suarez	Bachelors	Professional
12	Curtis	Lu	Bachelors	Professional
13	Lauren	Walker	Bachelors	Management
14	Ian	Jenkins	Bachelors	Management
15	Sydney	Bennett	Bachelors	Management
16	Chloe	Young	Partial College	Skilled Manual
17	Wyatt	Hill	Partial College	Skilled Manual
18	Shannon	Wang	High School	Skilled Manual

Analysis

The query returns four columns only—I've not used a star for all the columns. When you have a subset of all possible columns in a table, it's sometimes referred to as a *vertical partition* of the table. If you examine the row count in the bottom-right corner, you'll notice that 18,484 records are returned. You can also click the Messages tab to examine the row count.

Top

This query incorporates a Top clause to limit the number of rows returned.

Syntax

```
-- select just a few
select top 3 FirstName, LastName, EnglishEducation, EnglishOccupation
from DimCustomer
```

Result

	FirstName	LastName	EnglishEducation	EnglishOccupation
1	Jon	Yang	Bachelors	Professional
2	Eugene	Huang	Bachelors	Professional
3	Ruben	Torres	Bachelors	Professional

Analysis

Here there are only 3 rows, not the 18,484 we had in the previous query. When you have a subset of the rows in a table, it's often referred to as a *horizontal partition*. Without any sorting of the data, you can't predict exactly which 3 rows are going to be returned. Also, please remember to include the schema name as you adapt this and other queries for your own databases. As a reminder, it's also good practice to terminate the query with a semicolon.

Where =

Where clauses are used in many, many SQL queries. They are used to limit the number of rows returned according to certain criteria.

Syntax

```
-- where one column =
select FirstName, LastName, EnglishEducation, EnglishOccupation
from DimCustomer
where englisheducation = 'Partial College'
```

Result

	FirstName	LastName	EnglishEducation	EnglishOccupation
1	Chloe	Young	Partial College	Skilled Manual
2	Wyatt	Hill	Partial College	Skilled Manual
3	Clarence	Rai	Partial College	Clerical
4	Destiny	Wilson	Partial College	Skilled Manual
5	Ethan	Zhang	Partial College	Skilled Manual
6	Seth	Edwards	Partial College	Skilled Manual
7	Russell	Xie	Partial College	Skilled Manual
8	Harold	Sai	Partial College	Clerical
9	Jessie	Zhao	Partial College	Clerical
10	Jill	Jimenez	Partial College	Clerical
11	Jimmy	Moreno	Partial College	Clerical
12	Jennifer	Russell	Partial College	Skilled Manual
13	Marc	Martin	Partial College	Clerical
14	Jesse	Murphy	Partial College	Skilled Manual
15	Amanda	Carter	Partial College	Skilled Manual
16	Megan	Sanchez	Partial College	Skilled Manual
17	Nathan	Simmons	Partial College	Skilled Manual
18	Heidi	Lopez	Partial College	Clerical

Analysis

You should have 5,064 rows, not 18,484 rows. When you include a Where clause, you are asking for a horizontal partition of the table. Many SQL developers refer to this as a *filter*. Here the criterion for the filter is on the EnglishEducation column. Its data type is nvarchar, so you need the criterion to be a string—strings are delineated by single quotes. The column(s) used in the Where clause do not necessarily have to also be in the Select list of columns.

Where <>

Instead of an equality in the Where clause, we have an inequality.

Syntax

```
-- where one column <>
select FirstName, LastName, EnglishEducation, EnglishOccupation
from DimCustomer
where englisheducation <> 'Partial College'
```

Result

	FirstName	LastName	EnglishEducation	EnglishOccupation
1	Jon	Yang	Bachelors	Professional
2	Eugene	Huang	Bachelors	Professional
3	Ruben	Torres	Bachelors	Professional
4	Christy	Zhu	Bachelors	Professional
5	Elizabeth	Johnson	Bachelors	Professional
6	Julio	Ruiz	Bachelors	Professional
7	Janet	Alvarez	Bachelors	Professional
8	Marco	Mehta	Bachelors	Professional
9	Rob	Verhoff	Bachelors	Professional
10	Shannon	Carlson	Bachelors	Professional
11	Jacquelyn	Suarez	Bachelors	Professional
12	Curtis	Lu	Bachelors	Professional
13	Lauren	Walker	Bachelors	Management
14	Ian	Jenkins	Bachelors	Management
15	Sydney	Bennett	Bachelors	Management
16	Shannon	Wang	High School	Skilled Manual
17	Luke	Lal	High School	Skilled Manual
18	Jordan	King	High School	Skilled Manual

Analysis

These are all of the customers who do not have an EnglishEducation of Partial College. There are 13,420 rows (18,484 less 5,064).

Where And

Here we've introduced the And operator into the Where clause.

Syntax

```
-- where one column = with and
select FirstName, LastName, EnglishEducation, EnglishOccupation
from DimCustomer
where englisheducation = 'Partial College'
and englisheducation = 'High School'
```

Result

FirstName	LastName	EnglishEducation	EnglishOccupation

Analysis

You should discover that no rows at all are returned. The And operator is working on the same column, EnglishEducation, twice. An individual customer, in this table design, can only have one education level—it's impossible for any customer to have two or more education levels. That's why no rows qualify for the criteria defined in the query.

Where <> And

This variation on the last query makes a little more sense.

Syntax

```
-- where one column <> with and
select FirstName, LastName, EnglishEducation, EnglishOccupation
from DimCustomer
where englisheducation <> 'Partial College'
and englisheducation <> 'High School'
```

Result

	FirstName	LastName	EnglishEducation	EnglishOccupation
1	Jon	Yang	Bachelors	Professional
2	Eugene	Huang	Bachelors	Professional
3	Ruben	Torres	Bachelors	Professional
4	Christy	Zhu	Bachelors	Professional
5	Elizabeth	Johnson	Bachelors	Professional
6	Julio	Ruiz	Bachelors	Professional
7	Janet	Alvarez	Bachelors	Professional
8	Marco	Mehta	Bachelors	Professional
9	Rob	Verhoff	Bachelors	Professional
10	Shannon	Carlson	Bachelors	Professional
11	Jacquelyn	Suarez	Bachelors	Professional
12	Curtis	Lu	Bachelors	Professional
13	Lauren	Walker	Bachelors	Management
14	Ian	Jenkins	Bachelors	Management
15	Sydney	Bennett	Bachelors	Management
16	Alejandro	Beck	Partial High School	Clerical
17	Bethany	Yuan	Partial High School	Clerical
18	Wendy	Dominguez	Partial High School	Clerical

Analysis

You should see 10,126 rows. These are for all those customers who do not have Partial College and who do not have High School—thus, for example, a customer with an education level of Bachelors qualifies.

Where Or 1/2

We are now trying out the Or operator, rather than the And operator.

Syntax

```
-- where one column = with or 1/2
select FirstName, LastName, EnglishEducation, EnglishOccupation
from DimCustomer
where englisheducation = 'Partial College'
or englisheducation = 'High School'
```

Result

	FirstName	LastName	EnglishEducation	EnglishOccupation
1	Chloe	Young	Partial College	Skilled Manual
2	Wyatt	Hill	Partial College	Skilled Manual
3	Shannon	Wang	High School	Skilled Manual
4	Clarence	Rai	Partial College	Clerical
5	Luke	Lal	High School	Skilled Manual
6	Jordan	King	High School	Skilled Manual
7	Destiny	Wilson	Partial College	Skilled Manual
8	Ethan	Zhang	Partial College	Skilled Manual
9	Seth	Edwards	Partial College	Skilled Manual
10	Russell	Xie	Partial College	Skilled Manual
11	Harold	Sai	Partial College	Clerical
12	Jessie	Zhao	Partial College	Clerical
13	Jill	Jimenez	Partial College	Clerical
14	Jimmy	Moreno	Partial College	Clerical
15	Theresa	Ramos	High School	Skilled Manual
16	Denise	Stone	High School	Skilled Manual
17	Jaime	Nath	High School	Skilled Manual
18	Ebony	Gonzalez	High School	Skilled Manual

Analysis

There should be 8,358 records. If you scroll down, you'll see only those customers with an EnglishEducation of either Partial College or High School. When we used the And operator earlier, a similar query returned zero rows. And and Or operators use different logic.

Where Or 2/2

Another Or operator has been added to extend the criteria for the Where clause.

Syntax

```
-- where one column = with or 2/2
select FirstName, LastName, EnglishEducation, EnglishOccupation
from DimCustomer
where englisheducation = 'Partial College'
or englisheducation = 'High School' or englisheducation = 'Graduate Degree'
```

Result

	FirstName	LastName	EnglishEducation	EnglishOccupation
55	Blake	Anderson	High School	Professional
56	Leah	Ye	High School	Professional
57	Gina	Martin	High School	Professional
58	Donald	Gonzalez	Graduate Degree	Management
59	Damien	Chander	Graduate Degree	Management
60	Angela	Butler	Graduate Degree	Management
61	Alyssa	Cox	Graduate Degree	Management
62	Emily	Johnson	High School	Professional
63	Ryan	Brown	Partial College	Professional
64	Tamara	Liang	Partial College	Professional
65	Trevor	Bryant	Partial College	Professional
66	Dalton	Perez	Partial College	Professional
67	Aimee	He	Graduate Degree	Management
68	Cedric	Ma	Partial College	Skilled Manual
69	Chad	Kumar	Partial College	Skilled Manual
70	Edwin	Nara	Partial College	Skilled Manual
71	Mallory	Rubio	Partial College	Skilled Manual
72	Latasha	Navarro	Partial College	Skilled Manual

Analysis

This time, there are 11,547 records. You can see only those customers with an education level of Partial College or High School or Graduate Degree. You may have to scroll down a little to see examples of all three. If you have programmed in various languages, you might recognize this as an inclusive Or.

Case Sensitivity

This is an identical query to the last, except the criteria are all in lowercase.

Syntax

```
-- case sensitive?
select FirstName, LastName, EnglishEducation, EnglishOccupation
from DimCustomer
where englisheducation = 'partial college'
or englisheducation = 'high school' or englisheducation = 'graduate degree'
```

Result

	FirstName	LastName	EnglishEducation	EnglishOccupation
55	Blake	Anderson	High School	Professional
56	Leah	Ye	High School	Professional
57	Gina	Martin	High School	Professional
58	Donald	Gonzalez	Graduate Degree	Management
59	Damien	Chander	Graduate Degree	Management
60	Angela	Butler	Graduate Degree	Management
61	Alyssa	Cox	Graduate Degree	Management
62	Emily	Johnson	High School	Professional
63	Ryan	Brown	Partial College	Professional
64	Tamara	Liang	Partial College	Professional
65	Trevor	Bryant	Partial College	Professional
66	Dalton	Perez	Partial College	Professional
67	Aimee	He	Graduate Degree	Management
68	Cedric	Ma	Partial College	Skilled Manual
69	Chad	Kumar	Partial College	Skilled Manual
70	Edwin	Nara	Partial College	Skilled Manual
71	Mallory	Rubio	Partial College	Skilled Manual
72	Latasha	Navarro	Partial College	Skilled Manual

Analysis

Again you have 11,547 rows. If you see no records in your result, then your database is case-sensitive—in which case, you'll have to use the last query. If this query works for you, your database is case-insensitive and you can use either this query or the previous one to achieve the same outcome.

Where In

Typing out a long list of Or operators can get a little tedious. Our query here uses a shorthand—the In keyword.

Syntax

```
-- in
select FirstName, LastName, EnglishEducation, EnglishOccupation
from DimCustomer
where englisheducation in ('partial college','high school','graduate
degree')
```

Result

	FirstName	LastName	EnglishEducation	EnglishOccupation
55	Blake	Anderson	High School	Professional
56	Leah	Ye	High School	Professional
57	Gina	Martin	High School	Professional
58	Donald	Gonzalez	Graduate Degree	Management
59	Damien	Chander	Graduate Degree	Management
60	Angela	Butler	Graduate Degree	Management
61	Alyssa	Cox	Graduate Degree	Management
62	Emily	Johnson	High School	Professional
63	Ryan	Brown	Partial College	Professional
64	Tamara	Liang	Partial College	Professional
65	Trevor	Bryant	Partial College	Professional
66	Dalton	Perez	Partial College	Professional
67	Aimee	He	Graduate Degree	Management
68	Cedric	Ma	Partial College	Skilled Manual
69	Chad	Kumar	Partial College	Skilled Manual
70	Edwin	Nara	Partial College	Skilled Manual
71	Mallory	Rubio	Partial College	Skilled Manual
72	Latasha	Navarro	Partial College	Skilled Manual

Analysis

The In keyword requires a comma-separated list of values enclosed within parentheses. You will still get 11,547 rows.

Where Not In

Our query this time shows how to use the Not operator.

Syntax

```
-- not in
select FirstName, LastName, EnglishEducation, EnglishOccupation
from DimCustomer
where englisheducation not in ('partial college','high school',
'graduate degree')
```

Result

	FirstName	LastName	EnglishEducation	EnglishOccupation
1	Jon	Yang	Bachelors	Professional
2	Eugene	Huang	Bachelors	Professional
3	Ruben	Torres	Bachelors	Professional
4	Christy	Zhu	Bachelors	Professional
5	Elizabeth	Johnson	Bachelors	Professional
6	Julio	Ruiz	Bachelors	Professional
7	Janet	Alvarez	Bachelors	Professional
8	Marco	Mehta	Bachelors	Professional
9	Rob	Verhoff	Bachelors	Professional
10	Shannon	Carlson	Bachelors	Professional
11	Jacquelyn	Suarez	Bachelors	Professional
12	Curtis	Lu	Bachelors	Professional
13	Lauren	Walker	Bachelors	Management
14	Ian	Jenkins	Bachelors	Management
15	Sydney	Bennett	Bachelors	Management
16	Alejandro	Beck	Partial High School	Clerical
17	Bethany	Yuan	Partial High School	Clerical
18	Wendy	Dominguez	Partial High School	Clerical

Analysis

The Not operator, as you might expect, negates the criteria in a Where clause. No matter how far down you scroll, you won't see Partial College or High School or Graduate Degree.

Where and Or 1/3

Where clauses can quickly become quite complex with various combinations of And, Or, and Not operators. This query uses both And and Or.

Syntax

```
-- and with or 1/3
select FirstName, LastName, EnglishEducation, EnglishOccupation
from dimcustomer
where englisheducation = 'Partial College'
and englishoccupation = 'Clerical' or englishoccupation = 'Manual'
```

Result

	FirstName	LastName	EnglishEducation	EnglishOccupation
1	Clarence	Rai	Partial College	Clerical
2	Harold	Sai	Partial College	Clerical
3	Jessie	Zhao	Partial College	Clerical
4	Jill	Jimenez	Partial College	Clerical
5	Jimmy	Moreno	Partial College	Clerical
6	Marc	Martin	Partial College	Clerical
7	Heidi	Lopez	Partial College	Clerical
8	Evan	James	Partial College	Clerical
9	Tanya	Moreno	Partial College	Clerical
10	Deanna	Ramos	Graduate Degree	Manual
11	Nicole	Brown	Bachelors	Manual
12	Carla	Raman	Bachelors	Manual
13	Jerome	Romero	Bachelors	Manual
14	Arthur	Carlson	Bachelors	Manual
15	Jessie	Jimenez	Partial College	Manual
16	Robin	Ramos	Partial College	Manual
17	Deanna	Gutierrez	Partial College	Manual
18	Roy	Navarro	Partial College	Manual

Analysis

The result shows Partial College with Clerical—there is no Clerical *without* Partial College. The occupation Manual appears with any education level including Partial College. To fully understand the logic of this, you need to realize that the And operator takes precedence over the Or operator. If you are totally new to SQL, this is not at all obvious—hopefully, the next query makes it a little clearer. If you reverse the And and Or sections of the Where clause, you receive the same result. And takes logical precedence over Or. It is good practice to always explicitly specify the precedence as in the next query, then there is no ambiguity.

Where and Or 2/3

In this query, the And operator has been enclosed within parentheses.

Syntax

```
-- and with or 2/3
select FirstName, LastName, EnglishEducation, EnglishOccupation
from dimcustomer
where (englisheducation = 'Partial College'
and englishoccupation = 'Clerical') or englishoccupation = 'Manual'
```

Result

	FirstName	LastName	EnglishEducation	EnglishOccupation
1	Clarence	Rai	Partial College	Clerical
2	Harold	Sai	Partial College	Clerical
3	Jessie	Zhao	Partial College	Clerical
4	Jill	Jimenez	Partial College	Clerical
5	Jimmy	Moreno	Partial College	Clerical
6	Marc	Martin	Partial College	Clerical
7	Heidi	Lopez	Partial College	Clerical
8	Evan	James	Partial College	Clerical
9	Tanya	Moreno	Partial College	Clerical
10	Deanna	Ramos	Graduate Degree	Manual
11	Nicole	Brown	Bachelors	Manual
12	Carla	Raman	Bachelors	Manual
13	Jerome	Romero	Bachelors	Manual
14	Arthur	Carlson	Bachelors	Manual
15	Jessie	Jimenez	Partial College	Manual
16	Robin	Ramos	Partial College	Manual
17	Deanna	Gutierrez	Partial College	Manual
18	Roy	Navarro	Partial College	Manual

Analysis

The result is the same as the last query. This version uses parentheses to explicitly show the precedence of the And operator over the Or operator (in the previous query this was implicit). Quite possibly, this version is easier to both read and understand.

Where and Or 3/3

Please note that the parentheses are in a different position.

Syntax

```
-- and with or 3/3
select FirstName, LastName, EnglishEducation, EnglishOccupation
from dimcustomer
where englisheducation = 'Partial College'
and (englishoccupation = 'Clerical' or englishoccupation = 'Manual')
```

Result

	FirstName	LastName	EnglishEducation	EnglishOccupation
1	Clarence	Rai	Partial College	Clerical
2	Harold	Sai	Partial College	Clerical
3	Jessie	Zhao	Partial College	Clerical
4	Jill	Jimenez	Partial College	Clerical
5	Jimmy	Moreno	Partial College	Clerical
6	Marc	Martin	Partial College	Clerical
7	Heidi	Lopez	Partial College	Clerical
8	Evan	James	Partial College	Clerical
9	Tanya	Moreno	Partial College	Clerical
10	Jessie	Jimenez	Partial College	Manual
11	Robin	Ramos	Partial College	Manual
12	Deanna	Gutierrez	Partial College	Manual
13	Roy	Navarro	Partial College	Manual
14	Shawn	Rai	Partial College	Manual
15	Mindy	Luo	Partial College	Manual
16	Raymond	Rodriguez	Partial College	Manual
17	Deanna	Suarez	Partial College	Manual
18	Terrence	Carson	Partial College	Manual

Analysis

You get a totally different result this time (2003 rather than 3639 rows)! All customers have Partial College together with either Clerical or Manual. The parentheses now explicitly give Or precedence over And. In complex Where clauses, it's recommended that you use parentheses wherever possible.

Where Comparing Columns

So far, you've been comparing columns to hard-coded, literal values. It's also possible to compare a column to another column in a Where clause.

Syntax

```
-- comparing two columns
select FirstName, LastName, TotalChildren, NumberChildrenAtHome
from dimcustomer
where TotalChildren < NumberChildrenAtHome
```

Result

	FirstName	LastName	TotalChildren	NumberChildrenAtHome
1	Angela	Butler	0	1
2	Alyssa	Cox	0	1
3	Nicholas	Robinson	0	1
4	Jose	Flores	2	4
5	Nathan	Johnson	2	3
6	Molly	Rodriguez	2	4
7	April	Anand	1	3
8	Devin	Martin	2	3
9	Clarence	Anand	2	3
10	Mayra	Prasad	2	3
11	Latoya	Goel	2	4
12	Anne	Hernandez	2	3
13	Lisa	Cai	2	3
14	Larry	Munoz	2	4
15	Robin	Alvarez	2	3
16	Alexis	Coleman	2	3
17	Ricky	Vazquez	3	4
18	Latasha	Rubio	3	4

Analysis

An interesting result? I'm still not sure how TotalChildren can possibly be less than NumberChildrenAtHome. Maybe the latter includes nephews and nieces and friends of the customer's own children?

Where with Numeric Column =

You can also have numeric criteria in a Where clause—after all, many of your columns are likely to be numeric. There are four queries here for you to try—expect one of them to fail.

Syntax

```
-- numeric column =
select FirstName, LastName, YearlyIncome from dimcustomer
where YearlyIncome = 90000.00
select FirstName, LastName, YearlyIncome from dimcustomer
where YearlyIncome = 90000
select FirstName, LastName, YearlyIncome from dimcustomer
where YearlyIncome = 90,000
select FirstName, LastName, YearlyIncome from dimcustomer
where YearlyIncome = '90,000'
```

Result

	FirstName	LastName	YearlyIncome
1	Jon	Yang	90000.00
2	Trevor	Bryant	90000.00
3	Dalton	Perez	90000.00
4	Cheryl	Diaz	90000.00
5	Bianca	Lin	90000.00
6	Bryce	Richardson	90000.00
7	Carol	Howard	90000.00
8	Mason	Roberts	90000.00
9	Nicholas	Thompson	90000.00
10	Trinity	Richardson	90000.00
11	Eduardo	Martin	90000.00
12	Elizabeth	Jones	90000.00
13	Taylor	Howard	90000.00
14	Nathan	Lal	90000.00
15	Jonathan	Phillips	90000.00
16	Amanda	Cook	90000.00
17	Robert	Collins	90000.00
18	Christian	Thomas	90000.00

Analysis

In SQL, string values are enclosed in single quotes—numeric values are not. The first two queries show the correct syntax for using a numeric criterion—YearlyIncome has a data type of money. The third query may generate a syntax error—it's confused by the thousands separator for some collation settings. Strangely, the fourth query works. The single quotes denote a string (which overcomes the thousands separator problem) and then SQL Server kindly and implicitly converts the string into a number for you. The syntax of the fourth query is not recommended.

Where with Numeric Column <>

This is a simple inequality criterion on a numeric column.

Syntax

```
-- numeric column <>
select FirstName, LastName, YearlyIncome from dimcustomer
where YearlyIncome <> 90000
```

Result

	FirstName	LastName	YearlyIncome
1	Eugene	Huang	60000.00
2	Ruben	Torres	60000.00
3	Christy	Zhu	70000.00
4	Elizabeth	Johnson	80000.00
5	Julio	Ruiz	70000.00
6	Janet	Alvarez	70000.00
7	Marco	Mehta	60000.00
8	Rob	Verhoff	60000.00
9	Shannon	Carlson	70000.00
10	Jacquelyn	Suarez	70000.00
11	Curtis	Lu	60000.00
12	Lauren	Walker	100000.00
13	Ian	Jenkins	100000.00
14	Sydney	Bennett	100000.00
15	Chloe	Young	30000.00
16	Wyatt	Hill	30000.00
17	Shannon	Wang	20000.00
18	Clarence	Rai	30000.00

Analysis

The main thing to consider with numeric columns is the presence or absence of decimal places. This query filters out YearlyIncome of 90000; it would not filter out a YearlyIncome of 90000.01 (if it existed). You can check the exact data type of a column by browsing in Object Explorer.

Where with Numeric Column >

Maybe you wish to see those customers with a YearlyIncome of more than 90000.

Syntax

```
-- numeric column >
select FirstName, LastName, YearlyIncome from dimcustomer
where YearlyIncome > 90000
```

Result

	FirstName	LastName	YearlyIncome
1	Lauren	Walker	100000.00
2	Ian	Jenkins	100000.00
3	Sydney	Bennett	100000.00
4	Donald	Gonzalez	160000.00
5	Damien	Chander	170000.00
6	Savannah	Baker	120000.00
7	Angela	Butler	130000.00
8	Alyssa	Cox	130000.00
9	Aimee	He	100000.00
10	Jonathan	Hill	100000.00
11	Gabrielle	Adams	100000.00
12	Sarah	Thomas	110000.00
13	Nicholas	Robinson	110000.00
14	Jose	Flores	110000.00
15	Nathan	Johnson	100000.00
16	Molly	Rodriguez	120000.00
17	April	Anand	160000.00
18	Devin	Martin	170000.00

Analysis

A fairly straightforward query—it returns 2198 rows.

Where with Numeric Column >=

Now, this query is for those customers with a YearlyIncome equal to or greater than 90000.

Syntax

```
-- numeric column >=
select FirstName, LastName, YearlyIncome from dimcustomer
where YearlyIncome >= 90000
```

Result

	FirstName	LastName	YearlyIncome
1	Jon	Yang	90000.00
2	Lauren	Walker	100000.00
3	Ian	Jenkins	100000.00
4	Sydney	Bennett	100000.00
5	Donald	Gonzalez	160000.00
6	Damien	Chander	170000.00
7	Savannah	Baker	120000.00
8	Angela	Butler	130000.00
9	Alyssa	Cox	130000.00
10	Trevor	Bryant	90000.00
11	Dalton	Perez	90000.00
12	Cheryl	Diaz	90000.00
13	Aimee	He	100000.00
14	Bianca	Lin	90000.00
15	Bryce	Richardson	90000.00
16	Carol	Howard	90000.00
17	Jonathan	Hill	100000.00
18	Gabrielle	Adams	100000.00

Analysis

This query returns 3040 rows.

Where with Non-numeric Column >=

This is similar to the last query except the Where clause contains a non-numeric column.

Syntax

```
-- non numeric column >=
select FirstName, LastName, EnglishEducation from dimcustomer
where EnglishEducation >= 'High School'
```

Result

	FirstName	LastName	EnglishEducation
1	Chloe	Young	Partial College
2	Wyatt	Hill	Partial College
3	Shannon	Wang	High School
4	Clarence	Rai	Partial College
5	Luke	Lal	High School
6	Jordan	King	High School
7	Destiny	Wilson	Partial College
8	Ethan	Zhang	Partial College
9	Seth	Edwards	Partial College
10	Russell	Xie	Partial College
11	Alejandro	Beck	Partial High School
12	Harold	Sai	Partial College
13	Jessie	Zhao	Partial College
14	Jill	Jimenez	Partial College
15	Jimmy	Moreno	Partial College
16	Bethany	Yuan	Partial High School
17	Theresa	Ramos	High School
18	Denise	Stone	High School

Analysis

The EnglishEducation column is a string (nvarchar). Relational operators on strings take into account alphabetic order. The result includes High School and Partial College; it does not include Bachelors.

Where with Numeric Column <

Here, we have a simple variation on our continuing theme.

Syntax

```
-- numeric column <
select FirstName, LastName, YearlyIncome from dimcustomer
where YearlyIncome < 90000
```

Result

	FirstName	LastName	YearlyIncome
1	Eugene	Huang	60000.00
2	Ruben	Torres	60000.00
3	Christy	Zhu	70000.00
4	Elizabeth	Johnson	80000.00
5	Julio	Ruiz	70000.00
6	Janet	Alvarez	70000.00
7	Marco	Mehta	60000.00
8	Rob	Verhoff	60000.00
9	Shannon	Carlson	70000.00
10	Jacquelyn	Suarez	70000.00
11	Curtis	Lu	60000.00
12	Chloe	Young	30000.00
13	Wyatt	Hill	30000.00
14	Shannon	Wang	20000.00
15	Clarence	Rai	30000.00
16	Luke	Lal	40000.00
17	Jordan	King	40000.00
18	Destiny	Wilson	40000.00

Analysis

This query returns 15444 rows.

Where with Numeric Column <=

There's nothing new here—just some practice for you.

Syntax

```
-- numeric column <=
select FirstName, LastName, YearlyIncome from dimcustomer
where YearlyIncome <= 90000
```

Result

	FirstName	LastName	YearlyIncome
1	Jon	Yang	90000.00
2	Eugene	Huang	60000.00
3	Ruben	Torres	60000.00
4	Christy	Zhu	70000.00
5	Elizabeth	Johnson	80000.00
6	Julio	Ruiz	70000.00
7	Janet	Alvarez	70000.00
8	Marco	Mehta	60000.00
9	Rob	Verhoff	60000.00
10	Shannon	Carlson	70000.00
11	Jacquelyn	Suarez	70000.00
12	Curtis	Lu	60000.00
13	Chloe	Young	30000.00
14	Wyatt	Hill	30000.00
15	Shannon	Wang	20000.00
16	Clarence	Rai	30000.00
17	Luke	Lal	40000.00
18	Jordan	King	40000.00

Analysis

This query returns 16286 rows.

Where with Numeric Column Range 1/3

It's fairly easy to return customers with a range of incomes.

Syntax

```
-- numeric column > and <
select FirstName, LastName, YearlyIncome from dimcustomer
where YearlyIncome > 90000 and YearlyIncome < 120000
```

Result

	FirstName	LastName	YearlyIncome
1	Lauren	Walker	100000.00
2	Ian	Jenkins	100000.00
3	Sydney	Bennett	100000.00
4	Aimee	He	100000.00
5	Jonathan	Hill	100000.00
6	Gabrielle	Adams	100000.00
7	Sarah	Thomas	110000.00
8	Nicholas	Robinson	110000.00
9	Jose	Flores	110000.00
10	Nathan	Johnson	100000.00
11	Lisa	Cai	100000.00
12	Larry	Munoz	110000.00
13	Tristan	Alexander	110000.00
14	Victoria	Stewart	100000.00
15	Katelyn	Kelly	110000.00
16	Megan	Barnes	110000.00
17	Arturo	Lal	110000.00
18	Theresa	Serrano	110000.00

Analysis

This query returns 1045 rows.

Where with Numeric Column Range 2/3

This time you have an inclusive range—it returns customers with incomes of 90000 and 120000 and all values between those two limits.

Syntax

```
-- numeric column >= and <=
select FirstName, LastName, YearlyIncome from dimcustomer
where YearlyIncome >= 90000 and YearlyIncome <= 120000
```

Result

	FirstName	LastName	YearlyIncome
1	Jon	Yang	90000.00
2	Lauren	Walker	100000.00
3	Ian	Jenkins	100000.00
4	Sydney	Bennett	100000.00
5	Savannah	Baker	120000.00
6	Trevor	Bryant	90000.00
7	Dalton	Perez	90000.00
8	Cheryl	Diaz	90000.00
9	Aimee	He	100000.00
10	Bianca	Lin	90000.00
11	Bryce	Richardson	90000.00
12	Carol	Howard	90000.00
13	Jonathan	Hill	100000.00
14	Gabrielle	Adams	100000.00
15	Sarah	Thomas	110000.00
16	Nicholas	Robinson	110000.00
17	Mason	Roberts	90000.00
18	Jose	Flores	110000.00

Analysis

This query returns 2219 rows.

Where with Numeric Column Range 3/3

This query introduces the Between operator—it's used in conjunction with the And operator. Are you expecting 1045 or 2219 rows?

Syntax

```
-- numeric column between and
select FirstName, LastName, YearlyIncome from dimcustomer
where YearlyIncome between 90000 and 120000
```

Result

	FirstName	LastName	YearlyIncome
1	Jon	Yang	90000.00
2	Lauren	Walker	100000.00
3	Ian	Jenkins	100000.00
4	Sydney	Bennett	100000.00
5	Savannah	Baker	120000.00
6	Trevor	Bryant	90000.00
7	Dalton	Perez	90000.00
8	Cheryl	Diaz	90000.00
9	Aimee	He	100000.00
10	Bianca	Lin	90000.00
11	Bryce	Richardson	90000.00
12	Carol	Howard	90000.00
13	Jonathan	Hill	100000.00
14	Gabrielle	Adams	100000.00
15	Sarah	Thomas	110000.00
16	Nicholas	Robinson	110000.00
17	Mason	Roberts	90000.00
18	Jose	Flores	110000.00

Analysis

This query returns 2219 rows. Between … And is inclusive.

Numeric with Or

A simple practice query.

Syntax

```
-- numeric column or
select FirstName, LastName, YearlyIncome from dimcustomer
where YearlyIncome = 90000 or YearlyIncome = 120000
```

Result

	FirstName	LastName	YearlyIncome
1	Jon	Yang	90000.00
2	Savannah	Baker	120000.00
3	Trevor	Bryant	90000.00
4	Dalton	Perez	90000.00
5	Cheryl	Diaz	90000.00
6	Bianca	Lin	90000.00
7	Bryce	Richardson	90000.00
8	Carol	Howard	90000.00
9	Mason	Roberts	90000.00
10	Molly	Rodriguez	120000.00
11	Ricky	Vazquez	120000.00
12	Latasha	Rubio	120000.00
13	Nicholas	Thompson	90000.00
14	Jacqueline	Powell	120000.00
15	Xavier	Hill	120000.00
16	Trinity	Richardson	90000.00
17	Eduardo	Martin	90000.00
18	Elizabeth	Jones	90000.00

Analysis

This query returns 1174 rows.

Numeric with In

Another simple practice query.

Syntax

```
-- numeric column in
select FirstName, LastName, YearlyIncome from dimcustomer
where YearlyIncome in (90000,120000)
```

Result

	FirstName	LastName	YearlyIncome
1	Jon	Yang	90000.00
2	Savannah	Baker	120000.00
3	Trevor	Bryant	90000.00
4	Dalton	Perez	90000.00
5	Cheryl	Diaz	90000.00
6	Bianca	Lin	90000.00
7	Bryce	Richardson	90000.00
8	Carol	Howard	90000.00
9	Mason	Roberts	90000.00
10	Molly	Rodriguez	120000.00
11	Ricky	Vazquez	120000.00
12	Latasha	Rubio	120000.00
13	Nicholas	Thompson	90000.00
14	Jacqueline	Powell	120000.00
15	Xavier	Hill	120000.00
16	Trinity	Richardson	90000.00
17	Eduardo	Martin	90000.00
18	Elizabeth	Jones	90000.00

Analysis

This query returns 1174 rows.

Null Values 1/2

You may have null values in your own tables. If so, you need to know how to handle them. There are two queries here.

Syntax

```
-- null values
select FirstName, MiddleName, LastName from DimCustomer
select FirstName, MiddleName, LastName from DimCustomer
where MiddleName is null
```

Result

	FirstName	MiddleName	LastName
1	Ruben	NULL	Torres
2	Christy	NULL	Zhu
3	Elizabeth	NULL	Johnson
4	Julio	NULL	Ruiz
5	Marco	NULL	Mehta
6	Rob	NULL	Verhoff
7	Curtis	NULL	Lu
8	Sydney	NULL	Bennett
9	Chloe	NULL	Young
10	Shannon	NULL	Wang
11	Destiny	NULL	Wilson
12	Russell	NULL	Xie
13	Alejandro	NULL	Beck
14	Harold	NULL	Sai
15	Jill	NULL	Jimenez
16	Denise	NULL	Stone
17	Jaime	NULL	Nath
18	Ebony	NULL	Gonzalez

Analysis

The first query returns all records (18484) and includes the customers Jon Yang and Ruben Torres. The second query returns 7830 records—Ruben Torres is there but Jon Yang is not.

Null Values 2/2

This time we have added the Not logical operator.

Syntax

```
-- not null values
select FirstName, MiddleName, LastName from DimCustomer
where MiddleName is not null
```

Result

	FirstName	MiddleName	LastName
1	Jon	V	Yang
2	Eugene	L	Huang
3	Janet	G	Alvarez
4	Shannon	C	Carlson
5	Jacquelyn	C	Suarez
6	Lauren	M	Walker
7	Ian	M	Jenkins
8	Wyatt	L	Hill
9	Clarence	D	Rai
10	Luke	L	Lal
11	Jordan	C	King
12	Ethan	G	Zhang
13	Seth	M	Edwards
14	Jessie	R	Zhao
15	Jimmy	L	Moreno
16	Bethany	G	Yuan
17	Theresa	G	Ramos
18	Jennifer	C	Russell

Analysis

This query returns 10654 rows. Jon Yang has reappeared but Ruben Torres has gone.

Date Criteria

There are three queries here. The second and third queries show how to handle date criteria.

Syntax

```
-- dates
select FirstName, LastName, BirthDate from DimCustomer
select FirstName, LastName, BirthDate from DimCustomer
where BirthDate = '1944-06-26'
select FirstName, LastName, BirthDate from DimCustomer
where BirthDate <= '1944-06-26'
```

Result

	FirstName	LastName	BirthDate
1	Shannon	Wang	1944-06-26
2	Cameron	Griffin	1944-06-26

Analysis

The result shown is from the second query. Dates as criteria can be problematic. Please note they are enclosed in single quotes like strings. Also, note the format of the date (YYYY-MM-DD, 1944-06-26)—this is just one of the formats you can use. Other formats such as MM/DD/YYYY (06/26/1944) and DD/MM/YYYY (26/06/1944) may cause difficulties for non-U.S. and U.S. users, respectively. You might want to experiment further, maybe trying MMM DD, YYYY (Jun 26, 1944) or MMMM DD, YYYY (June 26, 1944) formats. A reasonably safe format is YYYYMMDD (19440626).

There are further complications. BirthDate has a date data type. You may well meet other columns with a datetime data type. Such columns will also record the hours and minutes and seconds and milliseconds. When developing your criteria, you will have to pay attention to the time as well as the date—for example, 1944-06-26 00:00:00.000.

Wildcards

There may be occasions when you need to perform a wildcard search. The wildcard operator is Like. One of the possible wildcard characters is %.

Syntax

```
-- like %
select FirstName, LastName from DimCustomer
select FirstName, LastName from DimCustomer
where LastName like 'L%'
```

Result

	FirstName	LastName
1	Curtis	Lu
2	Luke	Lal
3	Jaclyn	Lu
4	Heidi	Lopez
5	Tiffany	Liang
6	Casey	Luo
7	Tamara	Liang
8	Jessie	Liu
9	Bianca	Lin
10	Samantha	Long
11	Hannah	Long
12	Jasmine	Lee
13	Tiffany	Li
14	Madison	Lee
15	Todd	Li
16	Shannon	Liu
17	Xavier	Long
18	Colin	Lin

Analysis

The wildcard character, %, finds zero, one, or more than one characters. The second query here finds all customers whose LastName begins with the letter 'L'—no matter how many characters they have in their LastName.

Left()

Often, in SQL, you may find more than one way of doing the same thing. This query returns the same rows as the previous query.

Syntax

```
-- alternative
select FirstName, LastName from DimCustomer
where left(LastName,1) = 'L'
```

Result

	FirstName	LastName
1	Curtis	Lu
2	Luke	Lal
3	Jaclyn	Lu
4	Heidi	Lopez
5	Tiffany	Liang
6	Casey	Luo
7	Tamara	Liang
8	Jessie	Liu
9	Bianca	Lin
10	Samantha	Long
11	Hannah	Long
12	Jasmine	Lee
13	Tiffany	Li
14	Madison	Lee
15	Todd	Li
16	Shannon	Liu
17	Xavier	Long
18	Colin	Lin

Analysis

The syntax uses the Left() system string function. Again, it finds all customers whose LastName begins with the letter 'L'.

Not Like

We've introduced the Not operator before the Like operator.

Syntax

```
-- not like
select FirstName, LastName from DimCustomer
where LastName not like 'L%'
```

Result

	FirstName	LastName
1	Jon	Yang
2	Eugene	Huang
3	Ruben	Torres
4	Christy	Zhu
5	Elizabeth	Johnson
6	Julio	Ruiz
7	Janet	Alvarez
8	Marco	Mehta
9	Rob	Verhoff
10	Shannon	Carlson
11	Jacquelyn	Suarez
12	Lauren	Walker
13	Ian	Jenkins
14	Sydney	Bennett
15	Chloe	Young
16	Wyatt	Hill
17	Shannon	Wang
18	Clarence	Rai

Analysis

This finds all those customers whose LastName does not begin with the letter 'L'.

Unicode Characters

Please note the use of the N prefix.

Syntax

```
-- like N%
select FirstName, LastName from DimCustomer
where LastName like N'L%'
```

Result

	FirstName	LastName
1	Curtis	Lu
2	Luke	Lal
3	Jaclyn	Lu
4	Heidi	Lopez
5	Tiffany	Liang
6	Casey	Luo
7	Tamara	Liang
8	Jessie	Liu
9	Bianca	Lin
10	Samantha	Long
11	Hannah	Long
12	Jasmine	Lee
13	Tiffany	Li
14	Madison	Lee
15	Todd	Li
16	Shannon	Liu
17	Xavier	Long
18	Colin	Lin

Analysis

Some SQL Server string data types (for example, char and varchar) contain ASCII characters only. Other string data types (for example, nchar and nvarchar) contain Unicode characters. In general, the mapping from ASCII to Unicode happens automatically. In certain circumstances, the mapping may not work. A discussion of SQL Server collations and the difference between ASCII and Unicode is outside the scope of this book. However, if you find that searches are not returning the expected results, you may want to try the N prefix as shown in the syntax for this query. This prefix means you are searching with a Unicode rather than an ASCII character. Many graphical query designers automatically add the N prefix before strings for you.

More on Like

Here, the pattern for the wildcard search has changed.

Syntax

```
-- two letters
select FirstName, LastName from DimCustomer
where LastName like 'Li%'
```

Result

	FirstName	LastName
1	Tiffany	Liang
2	Tamara	Liang
3	Jessie	Liu
4	Bianca	Lin
5	Tiffany	Li
6	Todd	Li
7	Shannon	Liu
8	Colin	Lin
9	Shannon	Liang
10	Bianca	Liu
11	Laura	Lin
12	Crystal	Liang
13	Jorge	Liang
14	Ernest	Lin
15	Jose	Li
16	Micah	Liang
17	Jamie	Liang
18	Wesley	Liang

Analysis

This finds all customers whose LastName begins with the letters 'Li'.

Single Character Wildcard

The wildcard character is now an underscore (_) rather than a percent symbol (%).

Syntax

```
-- two letters, three in length
select FirstName, LastName from DimCustomer
where LastName like 'Li_'
```

Result

	FirstName	LastName
1	Jessie	Liu
2	Bianca	Lin
3	Shannon	Liu
4	Colin	Lin
5	Bianca	Liu
6	Laura	Lin
7	Ernest	Lin
8	Omar	Liu
9	Tiffany	Lin
10	Trisha	Lin
11	Alejandro	Lin
12	Cedric	Liu
13	Rosa	Lin
14	Jaclyn	Liu
15	Kelvin	Lin
16	Cedric	Lin
17	Arturo	Liu
18	Arturo	Lin

Analysis

This is very similar to the last query, but it returns a different set of records. It shows only those customers whose LastName begins with the letters 'Li' and whose LastName is exactly three characters in length. The percent symbol (%) means any number of characters, including zero characters. The underscore (_) means exactly one character.

Complex Wildcards 1/3

Sometimes you may need more complex wildcard searches.

Syntax

```
-- two letters, multiple times
select FirstName, LastName from DimCustomer
where LastName like 'L%' or LastName like 'M%' or LastName like 'N%'
```

Result

	FirstName	LastName
1	Marco	Mehta
2	Curtis	Lu
3	Luke	Lal
4	Jimmy	Moreno
5	Jaime	Nath
6	Marc	Martin
7	Jesse	Murphy
8	Leonard	Nara
9	Jaclyn	Lu
10	Heidi	Lopez
11	Deanna	Munoz
12	Michele	Nath
13	Angela	Murphy
14	Tiffany	Liang
15	Carolyn	Navarro
16	Casey	Luo
17	Gina	Martin
18	Tamara	Liang

Analysis

The result is all those customers whose LastName begins with any one of the letters 'L', 'M', and 'N'. Typing in complex searches with repeated use of the Or operator can get tedious.

Complex Wildcards 2/3

This is a much better alternative. Please note the use of square brackets.

Syntax

```
-- better
select FirstName, LastName from DimCustomer
where LastName like '[L-N]%'
```

Result

	FirstName	LastName
1	Marco	Mehta
2	Curtis	Lu
3	Luke	Lal
4	Jimmy	Moreno
5	Jaime	Nath
6	Marc	Martin
7	Jesse	Murphy
8	Leonard	Nara
9	Jaclyn	Lu
10	Heidi	Lopez
11	Deanna	Munoz
12	Michele	Nath
13	Angela	Murphy
14	Tiffany	Liang
15	Carolyn	Navarro
16	Casey	Luo
17	Gina	Martin
18	Tamara	Liang

Analysis

You have the same result as the last query, but the syntax is more elegant. The use of square brackets denotes a range of values.

Complex Wildcards 3/3

This is the opposite of the last query. Note the use of the caret character (^).

Syntax

```
-- and not like a range
select FirstName, LastName from DimCustomer
where LastName like '[^L-N]%'
```

Result

	FirstName	LastName
1	Jon	Yang
2	Eugene	Huang
3	Ruben	Torres
4	Christy	Zhu
5	Elizabeth	Johnson
6	Julio	Ruiz
7	Janet	Alvarez
8	Rob	Verhoff
9	Shannon	Carlson
10	Jacquelyn	Suarez
11	Lauren	Walker
12	Ian	Jenkins
13	Sydney	Bennett
14	Chloe	Young
15	Wyatt	Hill
16	Shannon	Wang
17	Clarence	Rai
18	Jordan	King

Analysis

The use of the caret character (^) denotes not in the range.

Working with Long Strings 1/2

All of the next few queries involve working with long strings. In order to do so, we are going to use another table in another database. The new database is AdventureWorks2008 rather than AdventureWorksDW2008 (if you have SQL Server 2005 and not SQL Server 2008, please use the AdventureWorks database rather than AdventureWorksDW). To switch the database context, use the drop-down on the toolbar—then try the first two queries here. Then switch the context back to AdventureWorksDW2008 and try the third query.

Syntax

```
-- new table, new database
-- change database context to AdventureWorks2008
select * from ProductDescription
select * from Production.ProductDescription
-- or
select * from AdventureWorks2008.Production.ProductDescription
```

Result

	ProductDescriptionID	Description	rowguid	ModifiedDate
1	3	Chromoly steel.	301EED3A-1A82-4855-99CB-2AFE8290D641	2003-06-01 00:00:00.000
2	4	Aluminum alloy cups; large diameter spindle.	DFEBA528-DA11-4650-9D86-CAFDA7294EB0	2003-06-01 00:00:00.000
3	5	Aluminum alloy cups and a hollow axle.	F7178DA7-1A7E-4997-8470-067371181305E	2003-06-01 00:00:00.000
4	8	Suitable for any type of riding, on or off-road. Fits ...	8E6746E5-AD97-46E2-BD24-FCEA075C3B52	2003-06-01 00:00:00.000
5	64	This bike delivers a high-level of performance on...	7B1C4E90-85E2-4792-B47B-E0C424E2EC94	2003-06-01 00:00:00.000
6	88	For true trail addicts. An extremely durable bike t...	4C1AD253-357E-4A98-B02E-02180AA406F6	2003-06-01 00:00:00.000
7	128	Serious back-country riding. Perfect for all levels ...	130709E6-8512-49B9-9F62-1F5C99152056	2004-03-11 10:32:17.973
8	168	Top-of-the-line competition mountain bike. Perfor...	DB979DA6-4CC8-4171-9ECF-65003FF8178A	2003-06-01 00:00:00.000
9	170	Suitable for any type of off-road trip. Fits any bud...	EA772412-6369-4416-9CC9-C1A5D1FF9C52	2003-06-01 00:00:00.000
10	209	Entry level adult bike; offers a comfortable ride cr...	F5FF5FFD-CB7C-4AD6-BBC9-4D250BB6E98D	2003-06-01 00:00:00.000
11	249	Value-priced bike with many features of our top-o...	4291F144-7693-4460-8B0B-1373E0433021	2003-06-01 00:00:00.000
12	320	Same technology as all of our Road series bikes,...	E130DED9-D0EC-4656-BF4D-1A3A46491891	2003-06-01 00:00:00.000
13	321	Same technology as all of our Road series bikes....	C7B429DA-DC51-47DB-A18E-5891E76CCC16	2003-06-01 00:00:00.000
14	337	A true multi-sport bike that offers streamlined ridin...	DB560F0B-E70B-42A7-A1F5-3B7E42D3679D	2003-06-01 00:00:00.000
15	375	Cross-train, race, or just socialize on a sleek, aer...	747B2185-0320-4FE5-8E8F-27B84A40A838	2003-06-01 00:00:00.000
16	376	Cross-train, race, or just socialize on a sleek, aer...	F1D9955B-BC1C-4D34-BE8B-CDEE33E77087	2003-06-01 00:00:00.000
17	409	Alluminum-alloy frame provides a light, stiff ride, w...	3DC76714-7572-4547-9D79-ABB708950B2C	2003-06-01 00:00:00.000
18	457	This bike is ridden by race winners. Developed ...	3DDB8DEA-FC37-4E44-8C1D-0BF7C6A723E3	2003-06-01 00:00:00.000

Analysis

The first query is always going to fail as the ProductDescription table is in the Production schema (I am assuming that your default schema is dbo). The second query will work provided the database context is correct. The third query is always going to work as it's an unambiguous fully qualified object name. Make sure your database context is back to AdventureWorksDW2008 (or AdventureWorksDW in SQL Server 2005) for the rest of the queries in this book.

Working with Long Strings 2/2

A simple Select resulting in two columns.

Syntax

```
-- long string
select ProductDescriptionID, Description
from AdventureWorks2008.Production.ProductDescription
```

Result

	ProductDescriptionID	Description
1	3	Chromoly steel.
2	4	Aluminum alloy cups; large diameter spindle.
3	5	Aluminum alloy cups and a hollow axle.
4	8	Suitable for any type of riding, on or off-road. Fits any budget. Smooth-shifting with a comfortable ride.
5	64	This bike delivers a high-level of performance on a budget. It is responsive and maneuverable, and offers peace-of-mind when you decide to go ...
6	88	For true trail addicts. An extremely durable bike that will go anywhere and keep you in control on challenging terrain - without breaking your budg...
7	128	Serious back-country riding. Perfect for all levels of competition. Uses the same HL Frame as the Mountain-100.
8	168	Top-of-the-line competition mountain bike. Performance-enhancing options include the innovative HL Frame, super-smooth front suspension, and...
9	170	Suitable for any type of off-road trip. Fits any budget.
10	209	Entry level adult bike; offers a comfortable ride cross-country or down the block. Quick-release hubs and rims.
11	249	Value-priced bike with many features of our top-of-the-line models. Has the same light, stiff frame, and the quick acceleration we're famous for.
12	320	Same technology as all of our Road series bikes, but the frame is sized for a woman. Perfect all-around bike for road or racing.
13	321	Same technology as all of our Road series bikes. Perfect all-around bike for road or racing.
14	337	A true multi-sport bike that offers streamlined riding and a revolutionary design. Aerodynamic design lets you ride with the pros, and the gearing wil...
15	375	Cross-train, race, or just socialize on a sleek, aerodynamic bike. Advanced seat technology provides comfort all day.
16	376	Cross-train, race, or just socialize on a sleek, aerodynamic bike designed for a woman. Advanced seat technology provides comfort all day.
17	409	Alluminum-alloy frame provides a light, stiff ride, whether you are racing in the velodrome or on a demanding club ride on country roads.
18	457	This bike is ridden by race winners. Developed with the Adventure Works Cycles professional race team, it has a extremely light heat-treated alu...

Analysis

The Description column is quite large—in fact, it's an `nvarchar(400)`. We're going to use this column for some long string searches.

Like %

Please note the fully qualified table name in the syntax again.

Syntax

```
-- like %
select ProductDescriptionID, Description
from AdventureWorks2008.Production.ProductDescription
where Description like 'Alu%'
```

Result

	ProductDescriptionID	Description
1	4	Aluminum alloy cups; large diameter spindle.
2	5	Aluminum alloy cups and a hollow axle.
3	871	Aluminum alloy rim with stainless steel spokes; bu...
4	1185	Aluminum cage is lighter than our mountain versi...

Analysis

This finds four product descriptions starting with 'aluminum'.

Like %%

This is new—there are two wildcard characters in the query.

Syntax

```
-- like %%
select ProductDescriptionID, Description
from AdventureWorks2008.Production.ProductDescription
where Description like '%Alu%'
```

Result

	ProductDescriptionID	Description
1	4	Aluminum alloy cups; large diameter spindle.
2	5	Aluminum alloy cups and a hollow axle.
3	249	Value-priced bike with many features of our top-of-the-line ...
4	457	This bike is ridden by race winners. Developed with the A...
5	513	All-occasion value bike with our basic comfort and safety f...
6	594	Travel in style and comfort. Designed for maximum comfort...
7	620	Triple crankset; alumunim crank arm; flawless shifting.
8	634	Composite road fork with an aluminum steerer tube.
9	637	Our best value utilizing the same, ground-breaking frame t...
10	642	The ML frame is a heat-treated aluminum frame made with...
11	644	The ML frame is a heat-treated aluminum frame made with...
12	647	Each frame is hand-crafted in our Bothell facility to the opti...
13	661	Made from the same aluminum alloy as our top-of-the line ...
14	698	Tough aluminum alloy bars for downhill.
15	701	Anatomically shaped aluminum tube bar will suit all riders.
16	702	Designed for racers; high-end anatomically shaped bar fro...
17	704	A light yet stiff aluminum bar for long distance riding.
18	850	Clipless pedals - aluminum.

Analysis

This is an interesting query. It still finds the four records where the description starts with 'aluminum', but it also finds those rows where the word 'aluminum' appears in the middle of the description. As well as locating 'aluminum' (U.S. spelling), it also locates 'aluminium' (French and U.K. spelling). Running a double wildcard character query like this one against long string columns can be very inefficient, especially when you have lots of records in the table. This inefficiency is mainly caused by the first wildcard.

Charindex()

Just to give you some practice with another function, here's the Charindex() system string function.

Syntax

```
-- alternative
select ProductDescriptionID, Description
from AdventureWorks2008.Production.ProductDescription
where charindex('alu',Description,1) > 0
```

Result

	ProductDescriptionID	Description
1	4	Aluminum alloy cups; large diameter spindle.
2	5	Aluminum alloy cups and a hollow axle.
3	249	Value-priced bike with many features of our top-of-the-line ...
4	457	This bike is ridden by race winners. Developed with the A...
5	513	All-occasion value bike with our basic comfort and safety f...
6	594	Travel in style and comfort. Designed for maximum comfort...
7	620	Triple crankset; alumunim crank arm; flawless shifting.
8	634	Composite road fork with an aluminum steerer tube.
9	637	Our best value utilizing the same, ground-breaking frame t...
10	642	The ML frame is a heat-treated aluminum frame made with...
11	644	The ML frame is a heat-treated aluminum frame made with...
12	647	Each frame is hand-crafted in our Bothell facility to the opti...
13	661	Made from the same aluminum alloy as our top-of-the line ...
14	698	Tough aluminum alloy bars for downhill.
15	701	Anatomically shaped aluminum tube bar will suit all riders.
16	702	Designed for racers; high-end anatomically shaped bar fro...
17	704	A light yet stiff aluminum bar for long distance riding.
18	850	Clipless pedals - aluminum.

Analysis

This gives you the same result as last time. This too can be very inefficient on long strings when there are thousands of rows. Charindex() is searching from the first letter of the description. If it finds the search text, it returns the start position of that text. If it doesn't find the search text, it returns zero.

Contains 1/3

The syntax here uses the Contains predicate in the Where clause. We are using a new table, JobCandidate, which is in the HumanResources schema.

Syntax

```
-- better, contains - another table
select JobCandidateID, Resume
from AdventureWorks2008.HumanResources.JobCandidate
where contains(Resume,'cycle')
```

Result

	JobCandidateID	Resume
1	4	<ns:Resume xmlns:ns="http://schemas.m...
2	5	<ns:Resume xmlns:ns="http://schemas.m...

Analysis

This query finds the word 'cycle' anywhere within the Resume column of the table. The Contains predicate assumes that full-text searching is enabled on your database and that a Full Text Catalog exists on the table. Enabling full-text search and constructing a Full Text Catalog on a table is beyond the scope of this book (but to point you in the right direction, you right-click on a table and choose Full-Text index). The Resume column has a data type of XML and has an awful lot of data in it. When you have long strings to search (for example, XML, text, ntext, varchar(max), nvarchar(max)) and potentially lots of records, you will find full-text searching much faster than using the Like operator with wildcards.

Contains 2/3

Here's some more practice with using Contains.

Syntax

```
-- contains again
select JobCandidateID, Resume
from AdventureWorks2008.HumanResources.JobCandidate
where contains(Resume,'tricycles')
```

Result

	JobCandidateID	Resume
1	1	<ns:Resume xmlns:ns="http://schemas.microsoft.co...
2	7	<ns:Resume xmlns:ns="http://schemas.microsoft.co...

Analysis

Remember, you can click on the XML data hyperlink to read it.

Contains 3/3

You can even have wildcards with the Contains predicate.

Syntax

```
-- contains with wildcard
select JobCandidateID, Resume
from AdventureWorks2008.HumanResources.JobCandidate
where contains(Resume,'"cycle*"')
```

Result

	JobCandidateID	Resume
1	2	<ns:Resume xmlns:ns="http://schemas.microsoft.co...
2	4	<ns:Resume xmlns:ns="http://schemas.microsoft.co...
3	5	<ns:Resume xmlns:ns="http://schemas.microsoft.co...

Analysis

This is still going to be faster than using the Like operator. The wildcard operators for Contains are different from those for Like. Instead of a percent symbol (%), you use an asterisk (*). Also, note the double quotes embedded within the single quotes.

Chapter 3

Order By

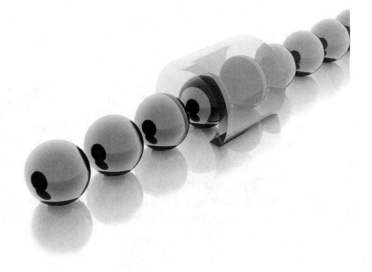

I f you need to sort the output of your SQL queries, you use the Order By clause. That's the topic for this chapter. It shows you how to sort alphabetically and numerically. It also demonstrates how to extract the top (or best) and the bottom (or worst) of the rows in your tables.

▶ **Key concepts**   Sorting records, sorting on alphabetic columns, sorting on numeric columns, showing the top records, showing the bottom records

▶ **Keywords**   Order By, Asc, Desc, Top, Percent, With Ties

No Particular Order

Let's start with a simple Select on two columns from the DimCustomer table.

Syntax

```
-- names in any old order
select LastName, FirstName from DimCustomer
```

Result

	LastName	FirstName
1	Yang	Jon
2	Huang	Eugene
3	Torres	Ruben
4	Zhu	Christy
5	Johnson	Elizabeth
6	Ruiz	Julio
7	Alvarez	Janet
8	Mehta	Marco
9	Verhoff	Rob
10	Carlson	Shannon
11	Suarez	Jacquelyn
12	Lu	Curtis
13	Walker	Lauren
14	Jenkins	Ian
15	Bennett	Sydney
16	Young	Chloe
17	Hill	Wyatt
18	Wang	Shannon

Analysis

Neither the LastName nor the FirstName columns are in any particular (alphabetical) order. If you were to include the CustomerKey column, you might see that it appears to be sorted numerically in ascending order. That column is the primary key of the table and has a special type of index (clustered index) defined for it. Often, SQL Server will return data in the order of a cluster-indexed primary key. However, you can't guarantee that this will happen every time—the only way to be certain of some kind of sort is to use an Order By clause.

Order By

Often, of course, you'll want to sort the rows being returned—either alphabetically (on strings) or numerically (on numeric columns). This query includes an Order By clause.

Syntax

```
-- order on lastname
select LastName, FirstName from DimCustomer
order by LastName
```

Result

	LastName	FirstName
80	Adams	Alexandra
81	Adams	Thomas
82	Adams	Ian
83	Agbonile	Osarumw...
84	Alan	Kelvin
85	Alan	Cheryl
86	Alan	Xavier
87	Alan	Alisha
88	Alan	Meghan
89	Alan	Bob
90	Alan	Kari
91	Alan	Jamie
92	Albrecht	Brian
93	Alexander	Rachel
94	Alexander	Oscar
95	Alexander	Robert
96	Alexander	Gabriel
97	Alexander	Ryan

Analysis

The LastName column is now sorted in ascending alphabetic order. You may have to scroll down a long way to see the effect—there are an awful lot of customers with a surname of Adams! You will also notice that the FirstName column is in no particular order for each LastName.

Asc

The keyword Asc has been added to the Order By clause.

Syntax

```
-- explicit asc
select LastName, FirstName from DimCustomer
order by LastName asc
```

Result

	LastName	FirstName
80	Adams	Alexandra
81	Adams	Thomas
82	Adams	Ian
83	Agbonile	Osarumw...
84	Alan	Kelvin
85	Alan	Cheryl
86	Alan	Xavier
87	Alan	Alisha
88	Alan	Meghan
89	Alan	Bob
90	Alan	Kari
91	Alan	Jamie
92	Albrecht	Brian
93	Alexander	Rachel
94	Alexander	Oscar
95	Alexander	Robert
96	Alexander	Gabriel
97	Alexander	Ryan

Analysis

The customer surnames are still sorted in ascending alphabetic order. As you might have guessed, the keyword Asc means ascending. It's the default setting for an Order By clause, so you don't have to include it. However, it's explicit and it's considered good practice to include it.

Desc

In this query, the keyword Desc has been used instead of Asc.

Syntax

```
-- desc
select LastName, FirstName from DimCustomer
order by LastName desc
```

Result

	LastName	FirstName
1	Zukowski	Jake
2	Zimmerman	Henry
3	Zimmerman	Tiffany
4	Zimmerman	Candice
5	Zimmerman	Bianca
6	Zimmerman	Christy
7	Zimmerman	Jack
8	Zimmerman	Curtis
9	Zimmerman	Krystal
10	Zimmerman	Jenny
11	Zhu	Alisha
12	Zhu	Karen
13	Zhu	Clarence
14	Zhu	Bianca
15	Zhu	Margaret
16	Zhu	Wesley
17	Zhu	Colin
18	Zhu	Colleen

Analysis

Desc means descending. Your customers are now sorted in descending order based on LastName. Desc is not the default for Order By, so you must specifically include it when you require a descending sort. Notice, once again, that the FirstName column is not sorted within each LastName.

Alternative Syntax

The Order By clause includes a number rather than a column name.

Syntax

```
-- alternative
select LastName, FirstName from DimCustomer
order by 1 desc
```

Result

	LastName	FirstName
1	Zukowski	Jake
2	Zimmerman	Henry
3	Zimmerman	Tiffany
4	Zimmerman	Candice
5	Zimmerman	Bianca
6	Zimmerman	Christy
7	Zimmerman	Jack
8	Zimmerman	Curtis
9	Zimmerman	Krystal
10	Zimmerman	Jenny
11	Zhu	Alisha
12	Zhu	Karen
13	Zhu	Clarence
14	Zhu	Bianca
15	Zhu	Margaret
16	Zhu	Wesley
17	Zhu	Colin
18	Zhu	Colleen

Analysis

The syntax means sort the first column (1) in the Select list in descending order. In this example, that column is LastName—so this is the same as the last query. However, this is not good practice—it's quite possible that you might change the Select list at a later date and end up sorting on a completely different column. I've only included this version of the syntax for completeness—and just in case you inherit code from others that adopts this approach.

Sorting on Two Columns 1/3

There is now a comma-separated list of columns in the Order By clause.

Syntax

```
-- on two columns
select LastName, FirstName from DimCustomer
order by LastName asc, FirstName asc
```

Result

	LastName	FirstName
80	Adams	Thomas
81	Adams	Wyatt
82	Adams	Xavier
83	Agbonile	Osarum...
84	Alan	Alisha
85	Alan	Bob
86	Alan	Cheryl
87	Alan	Jamie
88	Alan	Kari
89	Alan	Kelvin
90	Alan	Meghan
91	Alan	Xavier
92	Albrecht	Brian
93	Alexander	Aaron
94	Alexander	Abigail
95	Alexander	Aidan
96	Alexander	Alexandra
97	Alexander	Alexandria

Analysis

You may have to scroll down to see various combinations of LastName and FirstName. The rows are sorted by LastName, and within each LastName the rows are sorted by FirstName.

Sorting on Two Columns 2/3

This query has both the Asc and Desc keywords.

Syntax

```
-- asc and desc
-- on two columns
select LastName, FirstName from DimCustomer
order by LastName asc, FirstName desc
```

Result

	LastName	FirstName
80	Adams	Alex
81	Adams	Adam
82	Adams	Aaron
83	Agbonile	Osarumwense
84	Alan	Xavier
85	Alan	Meghan
86	Alan	Kelvin
87	Alan	Kari
88	Alan	Jamie
89	Alan	Cheryl
90	Alan	Bob
91	Alan	Alisha
92	Albrecht	Brian
93	Alexander	Zachary
94	Alexander	Xavier
95	Alexander	Victoria
96	Alexander	Tristan
97	Alexander	Trevor

Analysis

This is not the same as the previous query. The FirstName column is in descending order within each LastName, which is sorted in ascending order.

Sorting on Two Columns 3/3

Here the two columns in the Order By clause have been reversed.

Syntax

```
-- reversing columns
select LastName, FirstName from DimCustomer
order by FirstName desc, LastName asc
```

Result

	LastName	FirstName
1	Bailey	Zoe
2	Bell	Zoe
3	Brooks	Zoe
4	Cook	Zoe
5	Cooper	Zoe
6	Cox	Zoe
7	Gray	Zoe
8	Howard	Zoe
9	James	Zoe
10	Kelly	Zoe
11	Morgan	Zoe
12	Morris	Zoe
13	Murphy	Zoe
14	Peterson	Zoe
15	Ramirez	Zoe
16	Reed	Zoe
17	Richardson	Zoe
18	Rivera	Zoe

Analysis

The primary sort is on FirstName descending. The secondary sort is on LastName ascending. If you were also to reverse the two column names in the Select list, the output would be easier to decipher.

Order By with Where

As you create your own SQL queries, you are not limited to single clauses or keywords. This query shows how to combine a Where clause with an Order By clause.

Syntax

```
-- order with where
select LastName, FirstName from DimCustomer
where LastName <> 'Adams'
order by LastName asc, FirstName asc
```

Result

	LastName	FirstName
1	Agbonile	Osarumwense
2	Alan	Alisha
3	Alan	Bob
4	Alan	Cheryl
5	Alan	Jamie
6	Alan	Kari
7	Alan	Kelvin
8	Alan	Meghan
9	Alan	Xavier
10	Albrecht	Brian
11	Alexander	Aaron
12	Alexander	Abigail
13	Alexander	Aidan
14	Alexander	Alexandra
15	Alexander	Alexandria
16	Alexander	Alexia
17	Alexander	Alexis
18	Alexander	Alyssa

Analysis

We have lost all of the customers named Adams—and the rest of the customers are sorted by LastName then FirstName. It's important that the Order By clause appears after the Where clause; it doesn't work the other way around.

Numeric Sort

You can sort numerically as well as alphabetically. There are two queries here using the YearlyIncome column.

Syntax

```
-- numeric column
select LastName, FirstName, YearlyIncome from DimCustomer
order by YearlyIncome
select LastName, FirstName, YearlyIncome from DimCustomer
order by YearlyIncome desc
```

Result

	LastName	FirstName	YearlyIncome
1	Chander	Damien	170000.00
2	Martin	Devin	170000.00
3	Coleman	Alexis	170000.00
4	Liu	Shannon	170000.00
5	Griffin	Hunter	170000.00
6	Deng	Dustin	170000.00
7	Lopez	Andre	170000.00
8	Zheng	Arturo	170000.00
9	Liang	Wesley	170000.00
10	Alonso	Hector	170000.00
11	Phillips	Charles	170000.00
12	Gonzales	Justin	170000.00
13	Schmidt	Kristina	170000.00
14	Zhou	Glenn	170000.00
15	Shan	Bonnie	170000.00
16	Washington	Luis	170000.00
17	Ruiz	Audrey	170000.00
18	Anand	Colleen	170000.00

Analysis

The first query is an (implicit) ascending sort; the second is a descending sort. The YearlyIncome column is numeric (data type money). The result is from the second query.

Top

Who is the customer (singular) with the highest income?

Syntax

```
-- top
select top 1 LastName, FirstName, YearlyIncome from DimCustomer
order by YearlyIncome desc
```

Result

	LastName	FirstName	YearlyIncome
1	Chander	Damien	170000.00

Analysis

There's a Top clause in this query—it's asking for the top one (1). But top one at what? The Top clause works with the Order By clause (if you have that clause). Therefore, we are asking for the top paid customer—here it's Damien Chander (your answer may be different). In fact, the result is not predictable, and the next query shows why.

You should be aware of an alternative syntax:

```
select top (1) LastName, FirstName, YearlyIncome from DimCustomer
order by YearlyIncome desc
```

This alternative syntax incorporates parentheses. This is, in fact, the recommended way to do it. I have avoided this best practice, in this book, for reasons of backward compatibility.

Top with Ties

Who are the customers (plural) with the highest income? There are two queries here for you to try.

Syntax

```
-- top with ties
select top 1 with ties LastName, FirstName, YearlyIncome from DimCustomer
order by YearlyIncome desc
select top 113 LastName, FirstName, YearlyIncome from DimCustomer
order by YearlyIncome desc
```

Result

	LastName	FirstName	YearlyIncome
1	Chander	Damien	170000.00
2	Martin	Devin	170000.00
3	Coleman	Alexis	170000.00
4	Liu	Shannon	170000.00
5	Griffin	Hunter	170000.00
6	Deng	Dustin	170000.00
7	Lopez	Andre	170000.00
8	Zheng	Arturo	170000.00
9	Liang	Wesley	170000.00
10	Alonso	Hector	170000.00
11	Phillips	Charles	170000.00
12	Gonzales	Justin	170000.00
13	Schmidt	Kristina	170000.00
14	Zhou	Glenn	170000.00
15	Shan	Bonnie	170000.00
16	Washington	Luis	170000.00
17	Ruiz	Audrey	170000.00
18	Anand	Colleen	170000.00

Analysis

The first query has the With Ties hint after the Top clause. Now you can see why our previous query did not give the full picture. There are, in fact, 112 customers with the same top income (170000). If you also run the second query, you can see that the customer in row 113 has a lower income (160000).

Bottom

Which customers shared the lowest income?

Syntax

```
-- bottom
select top 1 with ties LastName, FirstName, YearlyIncome from DimCustomer
order by YearlyIncome asc
```

Result

	LastName	FirstName	YearlyIncome
1	Beck	Alejandro	10000.00
2	Yuan	Bethany	10000.00
3	Dominguez	Wendy	10000.00
4	Hernandez	Diana	10000.00
5	Carson	Shaun	10000.00
6	Townsend	Larry	10000.00
7	Ramos	Deanna	10000.00
8	Brown	Nicole	10000.00
9	Raman	Carla	10000.00
10	Carlson	Arthur	10000.00
11	Jimenez	Jessie	10000.00
12	Ramos	Robin	10000.00
13	Gutierrez	Deanna	10000.00
14	Navarro	Roy	10000.00
15	Rai	Shawn	10000.00
16	Luo	Mindy	10000.00
17	Romero	Jerome	10000.00
18	Munoz	Melody	10000.00

Analysis

We're still using Top to find the worst incomes. Unlike in the DMX and MDX languages, there is no Bottom in SQL! Instead, you simply reverse the sort order. This time we use Asc rather than Desc. There are 1155 customers who share the lowest YearlyIncome of 10000.

Top Percent 1/2

Sometimes you might be interested in top percentages.

Syntax

```
-- top percent
-- 1849 rows
select top 10 percent LastName, FirstName, YearlyIncome from DimCustomer
order by YearlyIncome desc
-- 2198 rows
select top 10 percent with ties LastName, FirstName, YearlyIncome
from DimCustomer
order by YearlyIncome desc
```

Result

	LastName	FirstName	YearlyIncome
1	Chander	Damien	170000.00
2	Martin	Devin	170000.00
3	Coleman	Alexis	170000.00
4	Liu	Shannon	170000.00
5	Griffin	Hunter	170000.00
6	Deng	Dustin	170000.00
7	Lopez	Andre	170000.00
8	Zheng	Arturo	170000.00
9	Liang	Wesley	170000.00
10	Alonso	Hector	170000.00
11	Phillips	Charles	170000.00
12	Gonzales	Justin	170000.00
13	Schmidt	Kristina	170000.00
14	Zhou	Glenn	170000.00
15	Shan	Bonnie	170000.00
16	Washington	Luis	170000.00
17	Ruiz	Audrey	170000.00
18	Anand	Colleen	170000.00

Analysis

The first query includes the Percent keyword. The second query does too, but it also has the With Ties qualifier. The first should return about 1849 rows and the second 2198 rows. There is a large number of customers with a YearlyIncome of 100000—you may have to scroll down quite a way (or use CTRL-END).

Top Percent 2/2

There is no Bottom Percent—you have to reverse the sort order in the Order By clause.

Syntax

```
-- bottom percent
-- 1849 rows
select top 10 percent LastName, FirstName, YearlyIncome from DimCustomer
order by YearlyIncome asc
-- 2922 rows
select top 10 percent with ties LastName, FirstName, YearlyIncome
from DimCustomer
order by YearlyIncome asc
```

Result

	LastName	FirstName	YearlyIncome
1	Beck	Alejandro	10000.00
2	Yuan	Bethany	10000.00
3	Dominguez	Wendy	10000.00
4	Hernandez	Diana	10000.00
5	Carson	Shaun	10000.00
6	Townsend	Larry	10000.00
7	Ramos	Deanna	10000.00
8	Brown	Nicole	10000.00
9	Raman	Carla	10000.00
10	Carlson	Arthur	10000.00
11	Jimenez	Jessie	10000.00
12	Ramos	Robin	10000.00
13	Gutierrez	Deanna	10000.00
14	Navarro	Roy	10000.00
15	Rai	Shawn	10000.00
16	Luo	Mindy	10000.00
17	Romero	Jerome	10000.00
18	Munoz	Melody	10000.00

Analysis

There are two queries to try. If you run both, you can see that a lot of customers share a salary of 20000.

Column Name

This is our final query in this chapter on sorting records.

Syntax

```
-- don't have to show column
select LastName, FirstName from DimCustomer
order by YearlyIncome asc
```

Result

	LastName	FirstName
1	Beck	Alejandro
2	Yuan	Bethany
3	Dominguez	Wendy
4	Hernandez	Diana
5	Carson	Shaun
6	Townsend	Larry
7	Ramos	Deanna
8	Brown	Nicole
9	Raman	Carla
10	Carlson	Arthur
11	Jimenez	Jessie
12	Ramos	Robin
13	Gutierrez	Deanna
14	Navarro	Roy
15	Rai	Shawn
16	Luo	Mindy
17	Romero	Jerome
18	Munoz	Melody

Analysis

The column you use in the Order By clause does not have to appear in the Select list as well—though, if it doesn't, as in this example, it makes the result a little more difficult to interpret.

Chapter 4

Select: Multiple Tables

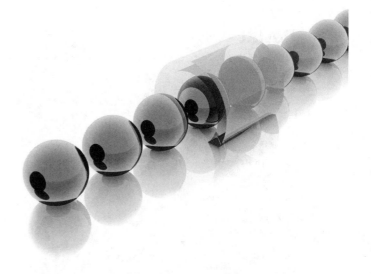

The previous three chapters concentrated on single-table queries. It's unlikely that you will always find the data you need in a single table. Often, your data is split across two or more tables. This chapter shows the SQL required to put tables together. The technique is one of performing joins on tables. There are quite a few variations on the join technique. All of the variations (inner joins and outer joins and more) are covered here. You will find the SQL useful when you later move on to build views and stored procedures. If you join tables in a normalized database, the joining is sometimes referred to as *denormalization*. Denormalization is an important part of building SQL Server relational data warehouses (star schemas, for example) and SSAS multidimensional cubes.

- ▶ **Key concepts**   Querying multiple tables, inner joins, left outer joins, right outer joins, full outer joins, self joins, cross joins, matching records, nonmatching records, table aliases
- ▶ **Keywords**   Inner Join, On, Left Outer Join, Right Outer Join, Full Outer Join

Single Table

If you've worked through the previous chapters, this should be revision. It's a single table Select to serve as a base query for some upcoming queries that are going to involve more than just one table.

Syntax

```
-- single table
select EnglishProductName, ProductSubcategoryKey from DimProduct
where ProductSubcategoryKey is not null
```

Result

	EnglishProductName	ProductSubcategoryKey
1	HL Road Frame - Black, 58	14
2	HL Road Frame - Red, 58	14
3	Sport-100 Helmet, Red	31
4	Sport-100 Helmet, Red	31
5	Sport-100 Helmet, Red	31
6	Sport-100 Helmet, Black	31
7	Sport-100 Helmet, Black	31
8	Sport-100 Helmet, Black	31
9	Mountain Bike Socks, M	23
10	Mountain Bike Socks, L	23
11	Sport-100 Helmet, Blue	31
12	Sport-100 Helmet, Blue	31
13	Sport-100 Helmet, Blue	31
14	AWC Logo Cap	19
15	AWC Logo Cap	19
16	AWC Logo Cap	19
17	Long-Sleeve Logo Jersey, S	21
18	Long-Sleeve Logo Jersey, S	21

Analysis

You will notice that each product belongs to a particular product subcategory, denoted by the ProductSubcategoryKey column. To simplify our introduction to multiple table queries, we are ignoring those products that do not have a product subcategory. The null values have been suppressed for now—we'll see how to deal with them later in the chapter. As the query stands, you should have 397 rows. It would be useful to see the name of the products' subcategories rather than their keys—we need another table in order to do this.

If you know something about relational database design (in particular, normalization), you might be surprised to see duplicate product names in the result. In fact, AdventureWorksDW2008 (or AdventureWorksDW in SQL Server 2005) is not a normalized database. It's deliberately denormalized into a star schema (strictly speaking, it's a snowflaked star). Star and snowflake schemas are used in data warehousing and building SSAS cubes. These topics are beyond the scope of this book. But, if you're interested, the same product name can appear more than once if other columns in the record are different—for example, the same product can have a different price at different times. Such a table is called a *slowly changing dimension table*.

How Not to Join Tables 1/3

In order to show the product subcategory name alongside the product name, this query adds a second table (DimProductSubcategory, which contains the subcategory name). We are trying to join the two tables together.

Syntax

```
-- how not to do it 1/3
select EnglishProductName, EnglishProductSubcategoryName
from DimProduct, DimProductSubcategory
order by EnglishProductName
```

Result

	EnglishProductName	EnglishProductSubcategoryName
1	Adjustable Race	Mountain Bikes
2	Adjustable Race	Road Bikes
3	Adjustable Race	Touring Bikes
4	Adjustable Race	Handlebars
5	Adjustable Race	Bottom Brackets
6	Adjustable Race	Brakes
7	Adjustable Race	Chains
8	Adjustable Race	Cranksets
9	Adjustable Race	Derailleurs
10	Adjustable Race	Forks
11	Adjustable Race	Headsets
12	Adjustable Race	Mountain Frames
13	Adjustable Race	Pedals
14	Adjustable Race	Road Frames
15	Adjustable Race	Saddles
16	Adjustable Race	Touring Frames
17	Adjustable Race	Wheels
18	Adjustable Race	Bib-Shorts

Analysis

This is not what we want! In the last query you saw 397 products—now it seems there are 22422. In this query, the two tables are separated by a comma in the From clause. This syntax is something called a *cross join*. It shows every single combination of product name and product subcategory name—even when the combination is wrong. Please take a look at the Adjustable Race product. Cross joins do have certain very limited uses in SQL queries, but a cross join is not appropriate here. The Order By clause is there purely to sort the records—nothing else.

How Not to Join Tables 2/3

Both the tables, DimProduct and DimProductSubcategory, have a column in common. It's called ProductSubcategoryKey. In this query, we're trying to join the two tables together on this shared column—to see if we can get the right match between products and their subcategories.

Syntax

```
-- how not to do it 2/3
select EnglishProductName, EnglishProductSubcategoryName
from DimProduct, DimProductSubcategory
where ProductSubcategoryKey = ProductSubcategoryKey
```

Result

```
Msg 209, Level 16, State 1, Line 3
Ambiguous column name 'ProductSubcategoryKey'.
Msg 209, Level 16, State 1, Line 3
Ambiguous column name 'ProductSubcategoryKey'.
```

Analysis

Well, it was a good try. Unfortunately, you see an ambiguous column name error. When a column name is shared between tables, it must be qualified with the table name.

How Not to Join Tables 3/3

In the Where clause, the ambiguous column name has been qualified with the table name. Does this look better?

Syntax

```
-- how not to do it 3/3
select EnglishProductName, EnglishProductSubcategoryName
from DimProduct, DimProductSubcategory
where DimProduct.ProductSubcategoryKey =
DimProductSubcategory.ProductSubcategoryKey
```

Result

	EnglishProductName	EnglishProductSubcategoryName
1	HL Road Frame - Black, 58	Road Frames
2	HL Road Frame - Red, 58	Road Frames
3	Sport-100 Helmet, Red	Helmets
4	Sport-100 Helmet, Red	Helmets
5	Sport-100 Helmet, Red	Helmets
6	Sport-100 Helmet, Black	Helmets
7	Sport-100 Helmet, Black	Helmets
8	Sport-100 Helmet, Black	Helmets
9	Mountain Bike Socks, M	Socks
10	Mountain Bike Socks, L	Socks
11	Sport-100 Helmet, Blue	Helmets
12	Sport-100 Helmet, Blue	Helmets
13	Sport-100 Helmet, Blue	Helmets
14	AWC Logo Cap	Caps
15	AWC Logo Cap	Caps
16	AWC Logo Cap	Caps
17	Long-Sleeve Logo Jersey, S	Jerseys
18	Long-Sleeve Logo Jersey, S	Jerseys

Analysis

This is looking good. You are back with 397 products, and the products-to-subcategory matches seem reasonable. I guess an AWC Logo Cap might belong to the Caps subcategory. In an earlier query you saw a product called Adjustable Race—here, it has disappeared. That's because the Adjustable Race product does not have a product subcategory.

If you inherit SQL queries written by others, you might see syntax similar to this. The join between the tables is in the Where clause and it produces the correct result. Yet it's wrong! First, it does not conform to standard ANSI SQL rules. Second, as a result of this nonconformance, it's possible that SQL Server will not support it in future versions. Thirdly, there is a more efficient and elegant and explicit method of joining tables together—please look at the next query.

How to Join Tables 1/2

These are classic inner join queries. The syntax is substantially different from that of our last query.

Syntax

```
-- how to do it 1/2
select EnglishProductName, EnglishProductSubcategoryName
from DimProduct inner join DimProductSubcategory
on DimProduct.ProductSubcategoryKey =
DimProductSubcategory.ProductSubcategoryKey
select EnglishProductName, EnglishProductSubcategoryName
from DimProduct join DimProductSubcategory
on DimProduct.ProductSubcategoryKey =
DimProductSubcategory.ProductSubcategoryKey
```

Result

	EnglishProductName	EnglishProductSubcategoryName
1	HL Road Frame - Black, 58	Road Frames
2	HL Road Frame - Red, 58	Road Frames
3	Sport-100 Helmet, Red	Helmets
4	Sport-100 Helmet, Red	Helmets
5	Sport-100 Helmet, Red	Helmets
6	Sport-100 Helmet, Black	Helmets
7	Sport-100 Helmet, Black	Helmets
8	Sport-100 Helmet, Black	Helmets
9	Mountain Bike Socks, M	Socks
10	Mountain Bike Socks, L	Socks
11	Sport-100 Helmet, Blue	Helmets
12	Sport-100 Helmet, Blue	Helmets
13	Sport-100 Helmet, Blue	Helmets
14	AWC Logo Cap	Caps
15	AWC Logo Cap	Caps
16	AWC Logo Cap	Caps
17	Long-Sleeve Logo Jersey, S	Jerseys
18	Long-Sleeve Logo Jersey, S	Jerseys

Analysis

Yes, we get the same result—397 products and Adjustable Race missing. This time the tables are separated by the Inner Join operator (or simply Join as in the second example), not by a comma. The join is specified in the On clause. We are joining the shared column across the two tables. Here, the column is ProductSubcategoryKey. In the DimProductSubcategory table it's a primary key. In the DimProduct table it's a foreign key. The DimProductSubcategory table is sometimes called the parent or the *one* table. The DimProduct table is sometimes called the child or *many* table. One subcategory can have many products.

If the child table appears first in the From clause, the On clause is from foreign key to primary key. If the parent table appears first, the On clause is from the primary key to the foreign key. Both varieties produce the same result.

How to Join Tables 2/2

This is the same query, but rewritten in a more elegant way.

Syntax

```
-- how to do it 2/2
select EnglishProductName, EnglishProductSubcategoryName
from DimProduct as P inner join DimProductSubcategory as S
on P.ProductSubcategoryKey = S.ProductSubcategoryKey
```

Result

	EnglishProductName	EnglishProductSubcategoryName
1	HL Road Frame - Black, 58	Road Frames
2	HL Road Frame - Red, 58	Road Frames
3	Sport-100 Helmet, Red	Helmets
4	Sport-100 Helmet, Red	Helmets
5	Sport-100 Helmet, Red	Helmets
6	Sport-100 Helmet, Black	Helmets
7	Sport-100 Helmet, Black	Helmets
8	Sport-100 Helmet, Black	Helmets
9	Mountain Bike Socks, M	Socks
10	Mountain Bike Socks, L	Socks
11	Sport-100 Helmet, Blue	Helmets
12	Sport-100 Helmet, Blue	Helmets
13	Sport-100 Helmet, Blue	Helmets
14	AWC Logo Cap	Caps
15	AWC Logo Cap	Caps
16	AWC Logo Cap	Caps
17	Long-Sleeve Logo Jersey, S	Jerseys
18	Long-Sleeve Logo Jersey, S	Jerseys

Analysis

The table names have been aliased as P and S. These aliases then substitute for the full table names in the On clause. It makes the code more succinct and arguably easier to read. However, once you have specified an alias, you must use the alias, not the original table name in the On clause.

Ambiguity Problem

Maybe you do want to see the key value as well as the name of the subcategory for each product. There are two queries. The first will fail. The second fixes the problem.

Syntax

```
-- ambiguity
select EnglishProductName, EnglishProductSubcategoryName,
ProductSubcategoryKey from DimProduct as P inner join
DimProductSubcategory as S
on P.ProductSubcategoryKey = S.ProductSubcategoryKey
select EnglishProductName, EnglishProductSubcategoryName,
S.ProductSubcategoryKey from DimProduct as P inner join
DimProductSubcategory as S
on P.ProductSubcategoryKey = S.ProductSubcategoryKey
```

Result

	EnglishProductName	EnglishProductSubcategoryName	ProductSubcategoryKey
1	HL Road Frame - Black, 58	Road Frames	14
2	HL Road Frame - Red, 58	Road Frames	14
3	Sport-100 Helmet, Red	Helmets	31
4	Sport-100 Helmet, Red	Helmets	31
5	Sport-100 Helmet, Red	Helmets	31
6	Sport-100 Helmet, Black	Helmets	31
7	Sport-100 Helmet, Black	Helmets	31
8	Sport-100 Helmet, Black	Helmets	31
9	Mountain Bike Socks, M	Socks	23
10	Mountain Bike Socks, L	Socks	23
11	Sport-100 Helmet, Blue	Helmets	31
12	Sport-100 Helmet, Blue	Helmets	31
13	Sport-100 Helmet, Blue	Helmets	31
14	AWC Logo Cap	Caps	19
15	AWC Logo Cap	Caps	19
16	AWC Logo Cap	Caps	19
17	Long-Sleeve Logo Jersey, S	Jerseys	21
18	Long-Sleeve Logo Jersey, S	Jerseys	21

Analysis

The ProductSubcategoryKey column is shared between the two tables. It must be fully qualified by the table name (or table alias) whether it's in a Select list or in an On clause.

Joining Three Tables

It's almost as easy to join three tables together as it is two tables. The third table here is DimProductCategory. It's going to let us see not just product and product subcategory, but product category as well.

Syntax

```
-- three tables
select EnglishProductName, EnglishProductSubcategoryName,
EnglishProductCategoryName from DimProduct as P inner join
DimProductSubcategory as S
on P.ProductSubcategoryKey = S.ProductSubcategoryKey
inner join DimProductCategory as C
on S.ProductCategoryKey = C.ProductCategoryKey
```

Result

	EnglishProductName	EnglishProductSubcategoryName	EnglishProductCategoryName
1	HL Road Frame - Black, 58	Road Frames	Components
2	HL Road Frame - Red, 58	Road Frames	Components
3	Sport-100 Helmet, Red	Helmets	Accessories
4	Sport-100 Helmet, Red	Helmets	Accessories
5	Sport-100 Helmet, Red	Helmets	Accessories
6	Sport-100 Helmet, Black	Helmets	Accessories
7	Sport-100 Helmet, Black	Helmets	Accessories
8	Sport-100 Helmet, Black	Helmets	Accessories
9	Mountain Bike Socks, M	Socks	Clothing
10	Mountain Bike Socks, L	Socks	Clothing
11	Sport-100 Helmet, Blue	Helmets	Accessories
12	Sport-100 Helmet, Blue	Helmets	Accessories
13	Sport-100 Helmet, Blue	Helmets	Accessories
14	AWC Logo Cap	Caps	Clothing
15	AWC Logo Cap	Caps	Clothing
16	AWC Logo Cap	Caps	Clothing
17	Long-Sleeve Logo Jersey, S	Jerseys	Clothing
18	Long-Sleeve Logo Jersey, S	Jerseys	Clothing

Analysis

The result seems totally reasonable. An AWC Logo Cap product belongs to the Caps subcategory. The Caps subcategory belongs to the Clothing category.

To join two tables, you need one Inner Join (or Join) operator and one On clause. In order to join three tables, you'll require two Inner Join (or Join) operators and two On clauses—and so on.

Complex Query 1/2

Here's a practice query to help you extend your SQL to ask for more sophisticated results. A Where clause has been added.

Syntax

```
-- with where
select EnglishProductName, EnglishProductSubcategoryName,
EnglishProductCategoryName from DimProduct as P inner join
DimProductSubcategory as S
on P.ProductSubcategoryKey = S.ProductSubcategoryKey
inner join DimProductCategory as C
on S.ProductCategoryKey = C.ProductCategoryKey
where EnglishProductCategoryName = 'Bikes'
or EnglishProductCategoryName = 'Accessories'
```

Result

	EnglishProductName	EnglishProductSubcategoryName	EnglishProductCategoryName
1	Sport-100 Helmet, Red	Helmets	Accessories
2	Sport-100 Helmet, Red	Helmets	Accessories
3	Sport-100 Helmet, Red	Helmets	Accessories
4	Sport-100 Helmet, Black	Helmets	Accessories
5	Sport-100 Helmet, Black	Helmets	Accessories
6	Sport-100 Helmet, Black	Helmets	Accessories
7	Sport-100 Helmet, Blue	Helmets	Accessories
8	Sport-100 Helmet, Blue	Helmets	Accessories
9	Sport-100 Helmet, Blue	Helmets	Accessories
10	Road-150 Red, 62	Road Bikes	Bikes
11	Road-150 Red, 44	Road Bikes	Bikes
12	Road-150 Red, 48	Road Bikes	Bikes
13	Road-150 Red, 52	Road Bikes	Bikes
14	Road-150 Red, 56	Road Bikes	Bikes
15	Road-450 Red, 58	Road Bikes	Bikes
16	Road-450 Red, 60	Road Bikes	Bikes
17	Road-450 Red, 44	Road Bikes	Bikes
18	Road-450 Red, 48	Road Bikes	Bikes

Analysis

The Where clause has to come after any joins.

Complex Query 2/2

Another practice query—with an extra Order By clause.

Syntax

```
-- with where and order
select EnglishProductName, EnglishProductSubcategoryName,
EnglishProductCategoryName from DimProduct as P inner join
DimProductSubcategory as S
on P.ProductSubcategoryKey = S.ProductSubcategoryKey
inner join DimProductCategory as C
on S.ProductCategoryKey = C.ProductCategoryKey
where EnglishProductCategoryName = 'Bikes'
or EnglishProductCategoryName = 'Accessories'
order by EnglishProductName
```

Result

	EnglishProductName	EnglishProductSubcategoryName	EnglishProductCategoryName
1	All-Purpose Bike Stand	Bike Stands	Accessories
2	Bike Wash - Dissolver	Cleaners	Accessories
3	Cable Lock	Locks	Accessories
4	Fender Set - Mountain	Fenders	Accessories
5	Headlights - Dual-Beam	Lights	Accessories
6	Headlights - Weatherproof	Lights	Accessories
7	Hitch Rack - 4-Bike	Bike Racks	Accessories
8	HL Mountain Tire	Tires and Tubes	Accessories
9	HL Road Tire	Tires and Tubes	Accessories
10	Hydration Pack - 70 oz.	Hydration Packs	Accessories
11	LL Mountain Tire	Tires and Tubes	Accessories
12	LL Road Tire	Tires and Tubes	Accessories
13	Minipump	Pumps	Accessories
14	ML Mountain Tire	Tires and Tubes	Accessories
15	ML Road Tire	Tires and Tubes	Accessories
16	Mountain Bottle Cage	Bottles and Cages	Accessories
17	Mountain Pump	Pumps	Accessories
18	Mountain Tire Tube	Tires and Tubes	Accessories

Analysis

The Order By clause must come after the Where clause.

Outer Joins

Often, when you join tables, there may be a mismatch of records. For example, you may have a product that does not belong to any product subcategory. Or you may have a product subcategory that does not have any products belonging to it. Inner joins find matched records across two or more tables. In order to find mismatched records as well, you will need an outer join (not an inner join). The next few queries investigate outer joins. Here's a base query to get us started—for now, it's still an inner join.

Syntax

```
-- two tables again 397 rows
select EnglishProductName, EnglishProductSubcategoryName,
S.ProductSubcategoryKey from DimProduct as P inner join
DimProductSubcategory as S
on P.ProductSubcategoryKey = S.ProductSubcategoryKey
```

Result

	EnglishProductName	EnglishProductSubcategoryName	ProductSubcategoryKey
1	HL Road Frame - Black, 58	Road Frames	14
2	HL Road Frame - Red, 58	Road Frames	14
3	Sport-100 Helmet, Red	Helmets	31
4	Sport-100 Helmet, Red	Helmets	31
5	Sport-100 Helmet, Red	Helmets	31
6	Sport-100 Helmet, Black	Helmets	31
7	Sport-100 Helmet, Black	Helmets	31
8	Sport-100 Helmet, Black	Helmets	31
9	Mountain Bike Socks, M	Socks	23
10	Mountain Bike Socks, L	Socks	23
11	Sport-100 Helmet, Blue	Helmets	31
12	Sport-100 Helmet, Blue	Helmets	31
13	Sport-100 Helmet, Blue	Helmets	31
14	AWC Logo Cap	Caps	19
15	AWC Logo Cap	Caps	19
16	AWC Logo Cap	Caps	19
17	Long-Sleeve Logo Jersey, S	Jerseys	21
18	Long-Sleeve Logo Jersey, S	Jerseys	21

Analysis

There are 397 rows. If you scroll down through the records, you will notice that every product (EnglishProductName) has an associated product subcategory (EnglishProductSubcategoryName). Conversely, every product subcategory listed has a product name next to it. This is an inner join—it includes an Inner Join (or Join) operator.

There is no product called Adjustable Race—that's a product with no matching product subcategory.

Left Outer Join 1/2

There are two outer join queries here. To be specific, they are left outer joins. The queries produce identical results—there is only a minor difference in the syntax. The first one uses a Left Outer Join operator—the second one, a Left Join operator. They both mean the same thing, but maybe it's better to be more explicit and use the full Left Outer Join version.

Syntax

```
-- now 606 records
select EnglishProductName, EnglishProductSubcategoryName
from DimProduct as P left outer join DimProductSubcategory as S
```

```
on P.ProductSubcategoryKey = S.ProductSubcategoryKey
select EnglishProductName, EnglishProductSubcategoryName
from DimProduct as P left join DimProductSubcategory as S
on P.ProductSubcategoryKey = S.ProductSubcategoryKey
```

Result

	EnglishProductName	EnglishProductSubcategoryName
1	Adjustable Race	NULL
2	Bearing Ball	NULL
3	BB Ball Bearing	NULL
4	Headset Ball Bearings	NULL
5	Blade	NULL
6	LL Crankarm	NULL
7	ML Crankarm	NULL
8	HL Crankarm	NULL
9	Chainring Bolts	NULL
10	Chainring Nut	NULL
11	Chainring	NULL
12	Crown Race	NULL
13	Chain Stays	NULL
14	Decal 1	NULL
15	Decal 2	NULL
16	Down Tube	NULL
17	Mountain End Caps	NULL
18	Road End Caps	NULL

Analysis

This time there are more records, 606 in total. Now a product called Adjustable Race is there—and it does not have a product subcategory. In fact, the query returns all products, whether they have a matching subcategory or not. If you scroll all the way down, you'll see some products with subcategories and some without. Inner joins return matching records; outer joins return matching *and* nonmatching records.

Our examples here are *left* outer joins. A left outer join returns all the records from the left table. The left table is the table before (to the left of) the join operator. This is sometimes called the *preserved* table.

Left Outer Join 2/2

It might be informative to see only those products that do not have a product subcategory. This query has an additional Where with an Is Null clause.

Syntax

```
-- with is null 209 which is 606 minus 397
select EnglishProductName, EnglishProductSubcategoryName
from DimProduct as P left outer join DimProductSubcategory as S
on P.ProductSubcategoryKey = S.ProductSubcategoryKey
where EnglishProductSubcategoryName is null
```

Result

	EnglishProductName	EnglishProductSubcategoryName
1	Adjustable Race	NULL
2	Bearing Ball	NULL
3	BB Ball Bearing	NULL
4	Headset Ball Bearings	NULL
5	Blade	NULL
6	LL Crankarm	NULL
7	ML Crankarm	NULL
8	HL Crankarm	NULL
9	Chainring Bolts	NULL
10	Chainring Nut	NULL
11	Chainring	NULL
12	Crown Race	NULL
13	Chain Stays	NULL
14	Decal 1	NULL
15	Decal 2	NULL
16	Down Tube	NULL
17	Mountain End Caps	NULL
18	Road End Caps	NULL

Analysis

You should see the Adjustable Race product again, with no matching product subcategory. If you examine all the rows, none of them have a product subcategory. There should be 209 rows. A couple of queries ago we had an inner join that returned 397 rows—that included just the products with subcategories. In the previous query (left outer join), you saw 606 records—that included products both with and without subcategories. Here we have 209 records (606—397); this includes a left outer join with an Is Null clause and shows only those products that don't have a subcategory.

Right Outer Join 1/2

This time, the join clause is Right Outer Join (or Right Join).

Syntax

```
-- right outer 397 no mismatches
select EnglishProductName, EnglishProductSubcategoryName
from DimProduct as P right outer join DimProductSubcategory as S
on P.ProductSubcategoryKey = S.ProductSubcategoryKey
```

Result

	EnglishProductName	EnglishProductSubcategoryName
1	HL Road Frame - Black, 58	Road Frames
2	HL Road Frame - Red, 58	Road Frames
3	Sport-100 Helmet, Red	Helmets
4	Sport-100 Helmet, Red	Helmets
5	Sport-100 Helmet, Red	Helmets
6	Sport-100 Helmet, Black	Helmets
7	Sport-100 Helmet, Black	Helmets
8	Sport-100 Helmet, Black	Helmets
9	Mountain Bike Socks, M	Socks
10	Mountain Bike Socks, L	Socks
11	Sport-100 Helmet, Blue	Helmets
12	Sport-100 Helmet, Blue	Helmets
13	Sport-100 Helmet, Blue	Helmets
14	AWC Logo Cap	Caps
15	AWC Logo Cap	Caps
16	AWC Logo Cap	Caps
17	Long-Sleeve Logo Jersey, S	Jerseys
18	Long-Sleeve Logo Jersey, S	Jerseys

Analysis

A right outer join returns all the records from the right-hand table—that's the table after (to the right of) the join clause. You should have 397 rows. That's the same figure as we had for an inner join. This suggests that every record in the right-hand table (DimProductSubCategory) has a matching record in the left-hand table (DimProduct). In other words, there are no subcategories that have no products belonging to them.

Right Outer Join 2/2

Here there's an Is Null test in the Where clause.

Syntax

```
-- zero records
select EnglishProductName, EnglishProductSubcategoryName
from DimProduct as P right outer join DimProductSubcategory as S
on P.ProductSubcategoryKey = S.ProductSubcategoryKey
where EnglishProductName is null
```

Result

EnglishProductName	EnglishProductSubcategoryName

Analysis

The result of this query confirms our analysis of the previous query. There is no product subcategory that does not contain any products.

Another Inner Join

We changed the tables involved—now there's DimProductCategory with DimProductSubcategory. This is an inner join.

Syntax

```
-- inner join again 37 records
select EnglishProductSubcategoryName, EnglishProductCategoryName
from DimProductSubcategory as S
inner join DimProductCategory as C
on S.ProductCategoryKey = C.ProductCategoryKey
```

Result

	EnglishProductSubcategoryName	EnglishProductCategoryName
1	Mountain Bikes	Bikes
2	Road Bikes	Bikes
3	Touring Bikes	Bikes
4	Handlebars	Components
5	Bottom Brackets	Components
6	Brakes	Components
7	Chains	Components
8	Cranksets	Components
9	Derailleurs	Components
10	Forks	Components
11	Headsets	Components
12	Mountain Frames	Components
13	Pedals	Components
14	Road Frames	Components
15	Saddles	Components
16	Touring Frames	Components
17	Wheels	Components
18	Bib-Shorts	Clothing

Analysis

There are 37 rows.

Another Left Outer Join

Now, let's try a left outer join.

Syntax

```
-- left 37
select EnglishProductSubcategoryName, EnglishProductCategoryName
from DimProductSubcategory as S
left outer join DimProductCategory as C
on S.ProductCategoryKey = C.ProductCategoryKey
```

Result

	EnglishProductSubcategoryName	EnglishProductCategoryName
1	Mountain Bikes	Bikes
2	Road Bikes	Bikes
3	Touring Bikes	Bikes
4	Handlebars	Components
5	Bottom Brackets	Components
6	Brakes	Components
7	Chains	Components
8	Cranksets	Components
9	Derailleurs	Components
10	Forks	Components
11	Headsets	Components
12	Mountain Frames	Components
13	Pedals	Components
14	Road Frames	Components
15	Saddles	Components
16	Touring Frames	Components
17	Wheels	Components
18	Bib-Shorts	Clothing

Analysis

There are still 37 records. This means that every subcategory has a matching category. There are no subcategories without a category.

Another Right Outer Join

This time, it's a right outer join.

Syntax

```
-- right 37
select EnglishProductSubcategoryName, EnglishProductCategoryName
from DimProductSubcategory as S
right outer join DimProductCategory as C
on S.ProductCategoryKey = C.ProductCategoryKey
```

Result

	EnglishProductSubcategoryName	EnglishProductCategoryName
1	Mountain Bikes	Bikes
2	Road Bikes	Bikes
3	Touring Bikes	Bikes
4	Handlebars	Components
5	Bottom Brackets	Components
6	Brakes	Components
7	Chains	Components
8	Cranksets	Components
9	Derailleurs	Components
10	Forks	Components
11	Headsets	Components
12	Mountain Frames	Components
13	Pedals	Components
14	Road Frames	Components
15	Saddles	Components
16	Touring Frames	Components
17	Wheels	Components
18	Bib-Shorts	Clothing

Analysis

This query also results in 37 rows! This suggests that every category has subcategories. The inner, left outer, and right outer joins all give the same result. Our data is pretty good! All categories have subcategories, and all subcategories have categories. There are no orphan records—records in a child table without a matching record in the parent table. And there are no parents without children. Real-world data is not always as straightforward and clean. Our next few queries show how to find less friendly data.

Creating Mismatch 1/2

There are 37 product subcategories—you can verify this by running the Select query first. Then please run the Insert query—this is going to add a new record to the DimProductSubcategory table. If you try the Select again, you should have 38 subcategories.

Syntax

```
-- creating mismatches 1/2
insert into DimProductSubcategory
values (null,'Racing Bikes','','',null)
-- 38 records not 37
select * from DimProductSubcategory
```

Result

```
(1 row(s) affected)
```

Analysis

The result here is from the first query. You should see a new Racing Bikes subcategory as a result of the second query. Don't worry too much about the Insert syntax—it's covered later in the book. The Insert statement has created a new row with an EnglishProductSubcategoryName of Racing Bikes. Please note that the ProductCategoryKey column is null. The Racing Bikes subcategory does not have a category—it's an orphan record. If you're concerned about changing your Adventure Works data in this way, rest assured we remove this new record a little later.

Creating Mismatch 2/2

There are four product categories—you may want to try the Select query first. After running the Insert query, try again with the Select. You should have five categories.

Syntax

```
-- creating mismatches 2/2
insert into DimProductCategory
values (null,'Trikes','','')
-- 5 records not 4
select * from DimProductCategory
```

Result

```
(1 row(s) affected)
```

Analysis

Again, the result is from the first query. We are going to undo this change later, if you are not keen to alter the original Adventure Works data. There is a new row (if you run the second query) with an EnglishProductCategoryName of Trikes. As it stands, this is a parent record with no children. We don't have any subcategories in the DimProductSubcategory table that belong to our new Trikes category. You'll notice that the new record has a ProductCategoryKey value—this is possibly, though not necessarily, 5. The value for that column was not specified in the Insert statement. In fact, that column is set to be autonumbered in the table design—in SQL Server, it's called an *identity column*.

Inner Join

Our query is an inner join on the two amended tables.

Syntax

```
-- inner 37
select EnglishProductSubcategoryName, EnglishProductCategoryName
from DimProductSubcategory as S
inner join DimProductCategory as C
on S.ProductCategoryKey = C.ProductCategoryKey
```

Result

	EnglishProductSubcategoryName	EnglishProductCategoryName
1	Mountain Bikes	Bikes
2	Road Bikes	Bikes
3	Touring Bikes	Bikes
4	Handlebars	Components
5	Bottom Brackets	Components
6	Brakes	Components
7	Chains	Components
8	Cranksets	Components
9	Derailleurs	Components
10	Forks	Components
11	Headsets	Components
12	Mountain Frames	Components
13	Pedals	Components
14	Road Frames	Components
15	Saddles	Components
16	Touring Frames	Components
17	Wheels	Components
18	Bib-Shorts	Clothing

Analysis

There are 37 rows as before. There is no record with a subcategory of Racing Bikes. There is no record with a category of Trikes.

Left Outer Join 1/2

This is a left outer join. The table on the left is DimProductSubcategory.

Syntax

```
-- left outer 38
select EnglishProductSubcategoryName, EnglishProductCategoryName
from DimProductSubcategory as S
left outer join DimProductCategory as C
on S.ProductCategoryKey = C.ProductCategoryKey
```

Result

	EnglishProductSubcategoryName	EnglishProductCategoryName
21	Jerseys	Clothing
22	Shorts	Clothing
23	Socks	Clothing
24	Tights	Clothing
25	Vests	Clothing
26	Bike Racks	Accessories
27	Bike Stands	Accessories
28	Bottles and Cages	Accessories
29	Cleaners	Accessories
30	Fenders	Accessories
31	Helmets	Accessories
32	Hydration Packs	Accessories
33	Lights	Accessories
34	Locks	Accessories
35	Panniers	Accessories
36	Pumps	Accessories
37	Tires and Tubes	Accessories
38	Racing Bikes	NULL

Analysis

You have 38 records now, not 37. You can see the subcategory Racing Bikes with no matching category as the extra record (you may have to scroll down to see it).

Left Outer Join 2/2

This is the same left outer join, but with a null test.

Syntax

```
-- left outer is null 1
select EnglishProductSubcategoryName, EnglishProductCategoryName
from DimProductSubcategory as S
left outer join DimProductCategory as C
on S.ProductCategoryKey = C.ProductCategoryKey
where EnglishProductCategoryName is null
```

Result

	EnglishProductSubcategoryName	EnglishProductCategoryName
1	Racing Bikes	NULL

Analysis

There is only one record to see. This is our new orphan record for Racing Bikes. If you combine outer joins with an Is Null clause, it's a good way to spot orphan records in a table.

Right Outer Join 1/2

This is a right outer join. The table on the right is DimProductCategory.

Syntax

```
-- right outer 38
select EnglishProductSubcategoryName, EnglishProductCategoryName
from DimProductSubcategory as S
right outer join DimProductCategory as C
on S.ProductCategoryKey = C.ProductCategoryKey
```

Result

	EnglishProductSubcategoryName	EnglishProductCategoryName
21	Jerseys	Clothing
22	Shorts	Clothing
23	Socks	Clothing
24	Tights	Clothing
25	Vests	Clothing
26	Bike Racks	Accessories
27	Bike Stands	Accessories
28	Bottles and Cages	Accessories
29	Cleaners	Accessories
30	Fenders	Accessories
31	Helmets	Accessories
32	Hydration Packs	Accessories
33	Lights	Accessories
34	Locks	Accessories
35	Panniers	Accessories
36	Pumps	Accessories
37	Tires and Tubes	Accessories
38	NULL	Trikes

Analysis

We have 38 rows. If you recall, the inner join returned 37 records. The extra record is for the Trikes category—it doesn't have a matching subcategory. But you won't see the subcategory Racing Bikes. This is a right outer join—it's pulling all records from the category table, not from the subcategory table, which is on the left.

Right Outer Join 2/2

This is the same right outer join, but with a null test.

Syntax

```
-- right outer is null 1
select EnglishProductSubcategoryName, EnglishProductCategoryName
from DimProductSubcategory as S
right outer join DimProductCategory as C
on S.ProductCategoryKey = C.ProductCategoryKey
where EnglishProductSubcategoryName is null
```

Result

	EnglishProductSubcategoryName	EnglishProductCategoryName
1	NULL	Trikes

Analysis

There is only the record for the Trikes category. If you combine outer joins with an Is Null clause, it's a good way to spot records in a table that don't have children in another table.

Full Outer Join 1/2

Here's some new join syntax for you. These two queries are full outer join queries (Full Outer Join or Full Join).

Syntax

```
-- full outer 39
select EnglishProductSubcategoryName, EnglishProductCategoryName
from DimProductSubcategory as S
full outer join DimProductCategory as C
on S.ProductCategoryKey = C.ProductCategoryKey
select EnglishProductSubcategoryName, EnglishProductCategoryName
from DimProductSubcategory as S
full join DimProductCategory as C
on S.ProductCategoryKey = C.ProductCategoryKey
```

Result

	EnglishProductSubcategoryName	EnglishProductCategoryName
22	Shorts	Clothing
23	Socks	Clothing
24	Tights	Clothing
25	Vests	Clothing
26	Bike Racks	Accessories
27	Bike Stands	Accessories
28	Bottles and Cages	Accessories
29	Cleaners	Accessories
30	Fenders	Accessories
31	Helmets	Accessories
32	Hydration Packs	Accessories
33	Lights	Accessories
34	Locks	Accessories
35	Panniers	Accessories
36	Pumps	Accessories
37	Tires and Tubes	Accessories
38	Racing Bikes	NULL
39	NULL	Trikes

Analysis

You now have 39 rows. If you scroll down, you'll see the Racing Bikes subcategory with no category, and the Trikes category with no subcategory. Our original inner join gave 37 rows. Our left join returned 38 records: 37 rows plus Racing Bikes from the left table. Our right join gave 38 records: 37 plus Trikes from the right table. The full outer join, in this query, returns 39 records—37 plus Racing Bikes from the left table and Trikes from the right table. A full outer join returns all records from both the left table and the right table, including matched and mismatched records.

Full Outer Join 2/2

This is the full outer join with a double null test.

Syntax

```
-- full outer with two is nulls 2 records
select EnglishProductSubcategoryName, EnglishProductCategoryName
from DimProductSubcategory as S
full outer join DimProductCategory as C
on S.ProductCategoryKey = C.ProductCategoryKey
where EnglishProductSubcategoryName is null
or EnglishProductCategoryName is null
```

Result

	EnglishProductSubcategoryName	EnglishProductCategoryName
1	Racing Bikes	NULL
2	NULL	Trikes

Analysis

Now you have just two rows. These are the two new mismatched records (one from each of the two tables). This is a standard and very useful query to try and discover mismatched records in your tables. Please note that the Is Null clause is used twice on two different columns.

Cleanup 1/2

We've finished our discussion of full outer joins, so it's time to reset your Adventure Works database. The first query removes the new subcategory, Racing Bikes.

Syntax

```
-- clean up back to 37
delete from DimProductSubcategory
where EnglishProductSubcategoryName = 'Racing Bikes'
select * from DimProductSubcategory
```

Result

```
(1 row(s) affected)
```

Analysis

The result here is from the first query. If you run the Select after the Delete, you should be back to 37 records in the DimProductSubcategory table and Racing Bikes should have disappeared. Delete syntax is covered later in this book.

Cleanup 2/2

The first query, here, deletes the new record for Trikes.

Syntax

```
-- clean up back to 4
delete from DimProductCategory
where EnglishProductCategoryName = 'Trikes'
select * from DimProductCategory
```

Result

```
(1 row(s) affected)
```

Analysis

The second Select query (please run the Delete first—which is shown in the result) should confirm that you are back to four records in the DimProductCategory table. Trikes should have gone.

Self Join 1/6

Sometimes, a table may be joined to itself. It has a foreign key that points to the primary key in the same table. A classic example is an employees' table—for example, DimEmployee. Such a table is often referred to as a *self-join table* (other terms include hierarchical table, recursive table, and parent-child table). Please try the following Select on the DimEmployee table.

Syntax

```
-- self join base query (Rob Walters twice)
select EmployeeKey, FirstName, LastName, ParentEmployeeKey, FirstName,
LastName from DimEmployee
```

Result

	EmployeeKey	FirstName	LastName	ParentEmployeeKey	FirstName	LastName
1	1	Guy	Gilbert	18	Guy	Gilbert
2	2	Kevin	Brown	7	Kevin	Brown
3	3	Roberto	Tamburello	14	Roberto	Tamburello
4	4	Rob	Walters	3	Rob	Walters
5	5	Rob	Walters	3	Rob	Walters
6	6	Thierry	D'Hers	267	Thierry	D'Hers
7	7	David	Bradley	112	David	Bradley
8	8	David	Bradley	112	David	Bradley
9	9	JoLynn	Dobney	23	JoLynn	Dobney
10	10	Ruth	Ellerbrock	189	Ruth	Ellerbrock
11	11	Gail	Erickson	3	Gail	Erickson
12	12	Barry	Johnson	189	Barry	Johnson
13	13	Jossef	Goldberg	3	Jossef	Goldberg
14	14	Terri	Duffy	112	Terri	Duffy
15	15	Sidney	Higa	189	Sidney	Higa
16	16	Taylor	Maxwell	23	Taylor	Maxwell
17	17	Jeffrey	Ford	189	Jeffrey	Ford
18	18	Jo	Brown	23	Jo	Brown

Analysis

There are 296 rows. The repetition of the FirstName and LastName columns is deliberate—we're going to use these columns in later queries. The primary key is EmployeeKey and the foreign key is ParentEmployeeKey. The employee called Guy Gilbert has a primary key of 1 and a foreign key of 18. This means he works for the employee with a primary key of 18. That person is Jo Brown, who in turn reports to Peter Krebs. If you understand that, then you understand self joins.

Some employees (for instance, Rob Walters) appear twice. If you are interested, DimEmployee is a slowly changing dimension table. That is not relevant to our self-join queries here, so you can ignore the duplication of employee names.

Self Join 2/6

The first step in constructing a self join is to join the table to itself. DimEmployee is on the left and the right of the inner join.

Syntax

```
-- self join
select EmployeeKey, FirstName, LastName, ParentEmployeeKey, FirstName,
LastName from DimEmployee as E inner join DimEmployee as M
on E.ParentEmployeeKey = M.EmployeeKey
```

Result

```
Msg 209, Level 16, State 1, Line 2
Ambiguous column name 'EmployeeKey'.
Msg 209, Level 16, State 1, Line 2
Ambiguous column name 'FirstName'.
Msg 209, Level 16, State 1, Line 2
Ambiguous column name 'LastName'.
Msg 209, Level 16, State 1, Line 2
Ambiguous column name 'ParentEmployeeKey'.
Msg 209, Level 16, State 1, Line 2
Ambiguous column name 'FirstName'.
Msg 209, Level 16, State 1, Line 2
Ambiguous column name 'LastName'.
```

Analysis

When you join a table to itself, it has to be aliased (here, I've used the aliases E and M). But then you will receive ambiguity error messages on the column names, which is what has happened here.

Self Join 3/6

There are two queries here. Try both if you wish; they are very similar.

Syntax

```
-- correct columns
select E.EmployeeKey, E.FirstName, E.LastName, E.ParentEmployeeKey,
M.FirstName, M.LastName from DimEmployee as E inner join DimEmployee as M
```

```
on E.ParentEmployeeKey = M.EmployeeKey
select E.EmployeeKey, E.FirstName, E.LastName, E.ParentEmployeeKey,
M.EmployeeKey, M.FirstName, M.LastName from DimEmployee as E
inner join DimEmployee as M on E.ParentEmployeeKey = M.EmployeeKey
```

Result

	EmployeeKey	FirstName	LastName	ParentEmployeeKey	EmployeeKey	FirstName	LastName
1	4	Rob	Walters	3	3	Roberto	Tamburello
2	5	Rob	Walters	3	3	Roberto	Tamburello
3	11	Gail	Erickson	3	3	Roberto	Tamburello
4	13	Jossef	Goldberg	3	3	Roberto	Tamburello
5	162	Dylan	Miller	3	3	Roberto	Tamburello
6	267	Ovidiu	Cracium	3	3	Roberto	Tamburello
7	271	Michael	Sullivan	3	3	Roberto	Tamburello
8	274	Sharon	Salavaria	3	3	Roberto	Tamburello
9	275	John	Wood	7	7	David	Bradley
10	276	Mary	Dempsey	7	7	David	Bradley
11	207	Terry	Eminhizer	7	7	David	Bradley
12	2	Kevin	Brown	7	7	David	Bradley
13	48	Sariya	Harnpadoungsataya	7	7	David	Bradley
14	109	Mary	Gibson	7	7	David	Bradley
15	122	Jill	Williams	7	7	David	Bradley
16	273	Wanida	Benshoof	7	7	David	Bradley
17	125	Bryan	Baker	9	9	JoLynn	Dobney
18	78	James	Kramer	9	9	JoLynn	Dobney

Analysis

Notice that the table aliases have been used to qualify the column names (for example, E.LastName). If you can find Guy Gilbert, you can confirm that he does indeed work for Jo Brown. This time we have 295 rows, not 296 as we did earlier—there is a mismatched record somewhere.

It's important to point out that this is not the only way to query a self-join table and join it back to itself. As you progress in your SQL knowledge, you may also want to consider recursive common table expressions (CTEs). CTEs possibly provide a more elegant (but more difficult) approach.

Self Join 4/6

Here, we have some simple column aliases to make the output easier to read.

Syntax

```
-- some tidying up 295 employees
select E.EmployeeKey, E.FirstName, E.LastName,
M.FirstName as ManagerFirstName, M.LastName as ManagerLastName
from DimEmployee as E inner join DimEmployee as M
on E.ParentEmployeeKey = M.EmployeeKey
```

Result

	EmployeeKey	FirstName	LastName	ManagerFirstName	ManagerLastName
1	4	Rob	Walters	Roberto	Tamburello
2	5	Rob	Walters	Roberto	Tamburello
3	11	Gail	Erickson	Roberto	Tamburello
4	13	Jossef	Goldberg	Roberto	Tamburello
5	162	Dylan	Miller	Roberto	Tamburello
6	267	Ovidiu	Cracium	Roberto	Tamburello
7	271	Michael	Sullivan	Roberto	Tamburello
8	274	Sharon	Salavaria	Roberto	Tamburello
9	275	John	Wood	David	Bradley
10	276	Mary	Dempsey	David	Bradley
11	207	Terry	Eminhizer	David	Bradley
12	2	Kevin	Brown	David	Bradley
13	48	Sariya	Harnpadoungsataya	David	Bradley
14	109	Mary	Gibson	David	Bradley
15	122	Jill	Williams	David	Bradley
16	273	Wanida	Benshoof	David	Bradley
17	125	Bryan	Baker	JoLynn	Dobney
18	78	James	Kramer	JoLynn	Dobney

Analysis

There are still only 295 rows.

Self Join 5/6

What if you want the record at the top of a self-join table's hierarchy? You might be tempted to only return the record with a null entry for its manager (that should return the CEO!).

Syntax

```
-- who is CEO?
select E.EmployeeKey, E.FirstName, E.LastName,
M.FirstName as ManagerFirstName, M.LastName as ManagerLastName
from DimEmployee as E inner join DimEmployee as M
on E.ParentEmployeeKey = M.EmployeeKey
where M.LastName is null
```

Result

EmployeeKey	FirstName	LastName	ManagerFirstName	ManagerLastName

Analysis

There are no records—maybe there is no CEO.

Self Join 6/6

There are two queries here. Both use a left outer join rather than an inner join.

Syntax

```
-- 296
select E.EmployeeKey, E.FirstName, E.LastName,
M.FirstName as ManagerFirstName, M.LastName as ManagerLastName
from DimEmployee as E left outer join DimEmployee as M
on E.ParentEmployeeKey = M.EmployeeKey
select E.EmployeeKey, E.FirstName, E.LastName,
M.FirstName as ManagerFirstName, M.LastName as ManagerLastName
from DimEmployee as E left outer join DimEmployee as M
on E.ParentEmployeeKey = M.EmployeeKey
where M.LastName is null
```

Result

	EmployeeKey	FirstName	LastName	ManagerFirstName	ManagerLastName
1	112	Ken	Sánchez	NULL	NULL

Analysis

The first query returns an extra record; there are 296 rather than 295 rows. The second query (the result shown) has an Is Null clause. So, it appears that the CEO is Ken Sánchez.

Cross Join 1/3

The two Select queries return a list of categories and a list of subcategories. We're going to use these tables shortly to examine cross joins.

Syntax

```
-- cross join
-- 4 categories
```

```
select * from DimProductCategory
-- 37 subcategories
select * from DimProductSubcategory
```

Result

	ProductCategoryKey	ProductCategoryAlternateKey	EnglishProductCategoryName	SpanishProductCategoryName	FrenchProductCategoryName
1	1	1	Bikes	Bicicleta	Vélo
2	2	2	Components	Componente	Composant
3	3	3	Clothing	Prenda	Vêtements
4	4	4	Accessories	Accesorio	Accessoire

Analysis

There are 4 categories (result shown) and 37 subcategories.

Cross Join 2/3

This is an inner join between subcategories and categories.

Syntax

```
-- 37 in inner join
select EnglishProductSubcategoryName, EnglishProductCategoryName
from DimProductSubcategory as S
inner join DimProductCategory as C
on S.ProductCategoryKey = C.ProductCategoryKey
```

Result

	EnglishProductSubcategoryName	EnglishProductCategoryName
1	Mountain Bikes	Bikes
2	Road Bikes	Bikes
3	Touring Bikes	Bikes
4	Handlebars	Components
5	Bottom Brackets	Components
6	Brakes	Components
7	Chains	Components
8	Cranksets	Components
9	Derailleurs	Components
10	Forks	Components
11	Headsets	Components
12	Mountain Frames	Components
13	Pedals	Components
14	Road Frames	Components
15	Saddles	Components
16	Touring Frames	Components
17	Wheels	Components
18	Bib-Shorts	Clothing

Analysis

The result has 37 rows. In general, with an inner join, the number of records is equal to the number of records in the table with the most records.

Cross Join 3/3

This is a cross join. There is no join syntax as such in the example, and the table names are comma-separated in the From clause. You might see this if you inherit code, although you can also use the keywords Cross Join.

Syntax

```
-- 148 in cross join
select EnglishProductSubcategoryName, EnglishProductCategoryName
from DimProductSubcategory, DimProductCategory
order by EnglishProductSubcategoryName
```

Result

	EnglishProductSubcategoryName	EnglishProductCategoryName
1	Bib-Shorts	Bikes
2	Bib-Shorts	Components
3	Bib-Shorts	Clothing
4	Bib-Shorts	Accessories
5	Bike Racks	Clothing
6	Bike Racks	Accessories
7	Bike Racks	Components
8	Bike Racks	Bikes
9	Bike Stands	Bikes
10	Bike Stands	Components
11	Bike Stands	Accessories
12	Bike Stands	Clothing
13	Bottles and Cages	Clothing
14	Bottles and Cages	Accessories
15	Bottles and Cages	Components
16	Bottles and Cages	Bikes
17	Bottom Brackets	Components
18	Bottom Brackets	Bikes

Analysis

The number of rows returned by a cross join is the multiplication of the numbers of records in the tables. Here, you should get 148 rows (that is, 4 multiplied by 37).

Chapter 5

Aggregates

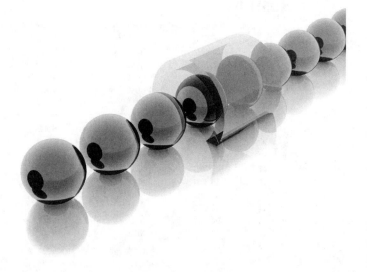

I n this chapter, we look at how to aggregate data. Aggregating data includes counting, totaling, and averaging data. You may also be interested in how to calculate maximum and minimum values. All of these topics are covered in this chapter. We'll be doing the aggregations on all of the records in a table—so, a summation, for example, will result in a grand total. A later chapter, Chapter 8 on Group By, extends this chapter and shows how to perform aggregations against subsets of tables—in other words, how to calculate subtotals as well as grand totals. Being able to produce aggregates makes your reports for end users more informative—they can see the overall picture rather than lots of individual bits of data. Aggregation is also an important concept to understand as you begin to develop your data warehouses.

▶   **Key concepts**   Aggregating data, totaling data, counts, minimums, maximums, sums, averages, standard deviations

▶   **Keywords**   Count(), Count_Big(), Count(distinct), Min(), Max(), Sum(), Avg(), StDev()

Base Query

This is your base query and table (DimProduct) for some subsequent aggregation exercises.

Syntax

```
-- 606 records
select * from DimProduct
```

Result

	ProductKey	ProductAlternateKey	ProductSubcategoryKey	WeightUnitMeasureCode	SizeUnitMeasureCode	EnglishProductName
1	1	AR-5381	NULL	NULL	NULL	Adjustable Race
2	2	BA-8327	NULL	NULL	NULL	Bearing Ball
3	3	BE-2349	NULL	NULL	NULL	BB Ball Bearing
4	4	BE-2908	NULL	NULL	NULL	Headset Ball Bearings
5	5	BL-2036	NULL	NULL	NULL	Blade
6	6	CA-5965	NULL	NULL	NULL	LL Crankarm
7	7	CA-6738	NULL	NULL	NULL	ML Crankarm
8	8	CA-7457	NULL	NULL	NULL	HL Crankarm
9	9	CB-2903	NULL	NULL	NULL	Chainring Bolts
10	10	CN-6137	NULL	NULL	NULL	Chainring Nut
11	11	CR-7833	NULL	NULL	NULL	Chainring
12	12	CR-9981	NULL	NULL	NULL	Crown Race
13	13	CS-2812	NULL	NULL	NULL	Chain Stays
14	14	DC-8732	NULL	NULL	NULL	Decal 1
15	15	DC-9824	NULL	NULL	NULL	Decal 2
16	16	DT-2377	NULL	NULL	NULL	Down Tube
17	17	EC-M092	NULL	NULL	NULL	Mountain End Caps

Analysis

The query returns 606 rows.

Count(*) 1/2

The two queries here both give the same result.

Syntax

```
-- count(*) 606
select COUNT(*) from DimProduct
select COUNT_BIG(*) from DimProduct
```

Result

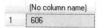

Analysis

Our last query returned 606 rows. These two queries return just 1 row each. That single row contains the count of the number of records in the table (606). Count() returns an int data type while Count_Big() returns a bigint data type. If you are expecting more than about two billion records to be in the table, you must use Count_Big() rather than Count(). Both varieties in the syntax here have an asterisk (*) as a parameter. This has a very specific meaning. It will count a record even if it's a duplicate of another record—a duplicated record counts as two. In addition, it will also count any records that have null values in every single column.

Count(*) 2/2

Aggregate functions, like Count(), do not result in very friendly column names. Our query here employs a simple alias.

Syntax

```
-- aliases good for all aggregates
select COUNT(*) as [Number of Records] from DimProduct
```

Result

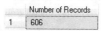

Analysis

Your column header caption should look a little better. As a reminder, the square brackets are obligatory if there are spaces in the column alias name.

Count(column) 1/3

Instead of Count(*), you might like to try Count(EnglishProductName).

Syntax

```
-- count(column) 606
select COUNT(EnglishProductName) from DimProduct
```

Result

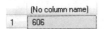

	(No column name)
1	606

Analysis

We get the same answer. The parameter for the Count() function this time is a column name. It too will count a duplicated record as two. However, it will ignore records that have a null value for the specified column—its treatment of nulls is different from Count(*).

Count(column) 2/3

In the syntax there is a simple change to the column name.

Syntax

```
-- and again 397
select COUNT(ProductSubcategoryKey) from DimProduct
```

Result

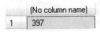

	(No column name)
1	397

Analysis

The aggregation is 397 rather than 606. Just over two hundred records in the DimProduct Table have a null value in the ProductSubcategoryKey column—these records are ignored by the Count() function as it has a column name for a parameter. If you go to the Messages tab, you will see that nulls are eliminated.

Count(column) 3/3

The keyword Distinct precedes the column name in the Count() function.

Syntax

```
-- count distinct 37
select COUNT(distinct ProductSubcategoryKey) from DimProduct
```

Result

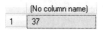

	(No column name)
1	37

Analysis

The answer is 37 rather than 397. Many of the values in the ProductSubcategoryKey column are duplicates. The Distinct keyword causes the Count() function to ignore the duplicates. The syntax here is Count(Distinct ProductSubcategoryKey), and in the previous query it was Count(ProductSubcategoryKey). As an alternative to the latter you can also use Count(All ProductSubcategoryKey).

Min() 1/2

This is the Min() function applied to an alphabetic column.

Syntax

```
-- min alpha
select MIN(EnglishProductName) from DimProduct
```

Result

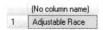

	(No column name)
1	Adjustable Race

Analysis

EnglishProductName has a data type of nvarchar. It's a string, and Min() applied to a string will return the first one in alphabetical order.

Min() 2/2

This is the Min() function applied to a numeric column.

Syntax

```
-- min numeric excludes nulls
select MIN(ListPrice) from DimProduct
```

Result

	(No column name)
1	2.29

Analysis

ListPrice has a data type of money. It's numeric, and Min() applied to a number will return the lowest number. Some of the records have a null value in the ListPrice column—Min() ignores null values.

Max() 1/5

This is the Max() function operating on a string.

Syntax

```
-- max alpha
select MAX(EnglishProductName) from DimProduct
```

Result

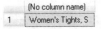

	(No column name)
1	Women's Tights, S

Analysis

It returns the last one in the alphabetical order.

Max() 2/5

Now for the Max() function on a numeric column.

Syntax

```
-- max numeric
select MAX(ListPrice) from DimProduct
```

Result

	(No column name)
1	3578.27

Analysis

This is the price of the most expensive product.

Max() 3/5

Perhaps you want to know the maximum price and the product(s) to which it applies.

Syntax

```
-- problem
select MAX(ListPrice), EnglishProductName from DimProduct
```

Result

```
Msg 8120, Level 16, State 1, Line 2
Column 'DimProduct.EnglishProductName' is invalid in the select list because it is not contained in either an aggregate f
```

Analysis

Unfortunately, this query simply doesn't work. You can't include an aggregate function as part of a normal Select column list. You get to solve this problem shortly.

Max() 4/5

The aggregate function has been removed from the Select query.

Syntax

```
-- one solution
select ListPrice, EnglishProductName from DimProduct
where ListPrice = 3578.27
```

Result

	ListPrice	EnglishProductName
1	3578.27	Road-150 Red, 62
2	3578.27	Road-150 Red, 44
3	3578.27	Road-150 Red, 48
4	3578.27	Road-150 Red, 52
5	3578.27	Road-150 Red, 56

Analysis

Now we know the most expensive products and their price. But in order to write the query you had to use the price in the Where clause. The query assumes that you already know the maximum price, which you might not—unless you write two queries. Even then, the maximum price is hard-coded; it could easily change over time.

Max() 5/5

Here's a solution to the problem. We've not hard-coded the maximum price. We've not written two separate queries—well, not quite. It's a query within a query.

Syntax

```
-- better solution - subquery covered later
select ListPrice, EnglishProductName from DimProduct
where ListPrice = (select MAX(ListPrice) from DimProduct)
```

Result

	ListPrice	EnglishProductName
1	3578.27	Road-150 Red, 62
2	3578.27	Road-150 Red, 44
3	3578.27	Road-150 Red, 48
4	3578.27	Road-150 Red, 52
5	3578.27	Road-150 Red, 56

Analysis

The inner query (called a *subquery*) establishes the maximum price. The outer query uses that maximum price to return the name of the products. Subqueries are covered in a later chapter in this book. I've introduced one here to show a common technique when working with aggregate values—how to display an aggregate in a normal column list. As is often the case, there are many other ways of doing this. Hopefully, this solution is enough to get you started.

Sum() 1/4

We're going to look at a couple of queries using the Sum() function. Here's a Select on a new base table (FactResellerSales) to get us started.

Syntax

```
-- new table
select SalesAmount, CarrierTrackingNumber from FactResellerSales
```

Result

	SalesAmount	CarrierTrackingNumber
1	2024.994	4911-403C-98
2	6074.982	4911-403C-98
3	2024.994	4911-403C-98
4	2039.994	4911-403C-98
5	2039.994	4911-403C-98
6	4079.988	4911-403C-98
7	2039.994	4911-403C-98
8	86.5212	4911-403C-98
9	28.8404	4911-403C-98
10	34.20	4911-403C-98
11	10.373	4911-403C-98
12	80.746	4911-403C-98
13	419.4589	6431-4D57-83
14	874.794	6431-4D57-83
15	809.76	4E0A-4F89-AE
16	714.7043	4E0A-4F89-AE
17	1429.4086	4E0A-4F89-AE
18	20.746	4E0A-4F89-AE

Analysis

The SalesAmount column is numeric with a data type of money. The CarrierTrackingNumber (despite its name) is not numeric—it's a string with a data type of nvarchar.

Sum() 2/4

Let's try the Sum() function on the string column.

Syntax

```
-- sum with alpha
select SUM(CarrierTrackingNumber) from FactResellerSales
```

Result

```
Msg 8117, Level 16, State 1, Line 2
Operand data type nvarchar is invalid for sum operator.
```

Analysis

As you might have expected, it doesn't work. It makes no sense to try to add (as a summation as opposed to a concatenation) strings together.

Sum() 3/4

This is the Sum() function operating on a numeric column.

Syntax

```
-- sum with numeric
select SUM(SalesAmount) from FactResellerSales
```

Result

	(No column name)
1	80450596.9823

Analysis

Now you know what the total sales figure is.

Sum() 4/4

This time, there are four queries. Expect the third one to fail.

Syntax

```
-- formatting
select SUM(SalesAmount) as [Total Sales] from FactResellerSales
select cast(SUM(SalesAmount) as decimal(17,2)) as [Total Sales]
from FactResellerSales
select '$' + cast(SUM(SalesAmount) as decimal(17,2)) as [Total Sales]
from FactResellerSales
select '$' + cast(cast(SUM(SalesAmount) as decimal(17,2)) as varchar)
as [Total Sales] from FactResellerSales
```

Result

	Total Sales
1	$80450596.98

Analysis

Maybe the fourth Select is the best one. It's showing some of the formatting available to you, as you work with aggregates. Please note the double Cast() function in the last query. The third query fails because you can't concatenate a varchar directly to a numeric column—you have to have an additional cast, as shown in the fourth query.

Avg() 1/2

To establish average values, you use the Avg() function.

Syntax

```
-- avg with alpha
select AVG(CarrierTrackingNumber) from FactResellerSales
```

Result

```
Msg 8117, Level 16, State 1, Line 2
Operand data type nvarchar is invalid for avg operator.
```

Analysis

Avg() does not work with strings.

Avg() 2/2

Avg() does work with numeric columns.

Syntax

```
-- avg with numeric
select AVG(SalesAmount) from FactResellerSales
```

Result

	(No column name)
1	1322.0047

Analysis

Avg() gives an average. More specifically, it returns the mean, not the mode or the median.

StDev()

StDev() is used to work out standard deviations. There are three queries here.

Syntax

```
-- stdev
select STDEV(SalesAmount) from FactResellerSales
select STDEV(all SalesAmount) from FactResellerSales
select STDEV(distinct SalesAmount) from FactResellerSales
```

Result

	(No column name)
1	2124.23375848302

Analysis

The first two queries are functionally equivalent (the result shown); the All keyword is optional. The third query returns a different result—the keyword Distinct causes the calculation to ignore duplicate SalesAmount values.

Some Statistics

This is our last query in this chapter devoted to aggregates. It displays more than one aggregation.

Syntax

```
-- more than one aggregate function
select SUM(SalesAmount) as [Total Sales], AVG(SalesAmount)
as [Average Sale], STDEV(all SalesAmount) as [All SD],
STDEV(distinct SalesAmount) as [Distinct SD] from FactResellerSales
```

Result

	Total Sales	Average Sale	All SD	Distinct SD
1	80450596.9823	1322.0047	2124.23375848299	4164.16620976141

Analysis

You can combine different aggregation functions in one Select list. You can even use different columns, provided those columns are all aggregated in some way.

Chapter 6

Select: New Tables

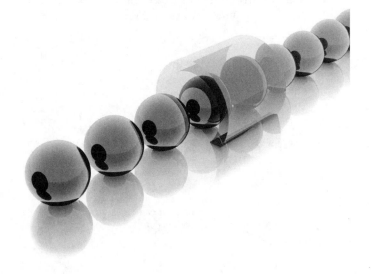

I n this chapter we examine table creation. There are many ways of creating tables—
here we concentrate on creating tables using a Select statement (Select Into).
A later chapter shows how to do so with a Create statement. You'll learn how to
create both permanent and temporary tables. Furthermore, you'll meet three different
types of temporary tables and have a quick look at the tempdb system database. New
permanent and temporary tables have many uses. They can be used to denormalize and
join tables for reporting purposes. In addition, they are invaluable for testing new designs
and testing your SQL when you prefer not to work against live production tables. Also,
when your SQL becomes very complex, you can break it down into simpler steps and
work against a series of temporary staging tables.

► **Key concepts**   Selecting into new tables, permanent tables, local temporary
tables, global temporary tables, semipermanent temporary tables, tempdb database,
deleting data, dropping tables

► **Keywords**   Select Into, #, ##, tempdb, Delete, Drop Table

Base Query

The records returned by this query are going to be used in this chapter to show a variety
of methods for creating new tables with a Select statement.

Syntax

```
-- select
select EnglishProductName, ListPrice - DealerPrice as Discount
from DimProduct
where ListPrice - DealerPrice is not null
order by EnglishProductName
```

Result

	EnglishProductName	Discount
1	All-Purpose Bike Stand	63.60
2	AWC Logo Cap	3.4577
3	AWC Logo Cap	3.4577
4	AWC Logo Cap	3.596
5	Bike Wash - Dissolver	3.18
6	Cable Lock	10.00
7	Chain	8.096
8	Classic Vest, L	25.40
9	Classic Vest, M	25.40
10	Classic Vest, S	25.40
11	Fender Set - Mountain	8.792
12	Front Brakes	42.60
13	Front Derailleur	36.596
14	Full-Finger Gloves, L	15.196
15	Full-Finger Gloves, M	15.196
16	Full-Finger Gloves, S	15.196
17	Half-Finger Gloves, L	9.4192
18	Half-Finger Gloves, L	9.796

Analysis

There are many different ways of creating tables. You can, of course, create tables graphically in SSMS. As this is a book about queries, graphical methods are outside its scope. To create queries directly from the SQL language, you often will use Create Table syntax—this is covered in a later chapter on data definition language (DDL). Create Table results in an empty table, which later has to be populated with records. The next few queries in this chapter show some alternative methods for creating tables (both permanent and temporary tables). The tables are going to be created using a Select statement—this gives the option of populating the table with records as it's created.

Select Into

This query is going to create a new table called NewDimProduct. There is an Into clause before the From clause.

Syntax

```
-- select into
select EnglishProductName, ListPrice - DealerPrice as Discount
into NewDimProduct
from DimProduct
where ListPrice - DealerPrice is not null
```

Result

```
(395 row(s) affected)
```

Analysis

Here, you have a Select statement that doesn't return any records. The result simply informs you how many records have been inserted into the new table. Select Into will fail if the table already exists. When the table already exists, you can use Insert Into Select From. This topic is covered later in the book.

Testing New Table

This is a simple Select (without the Into clause) query to test the new table.

Syntax

```
-- test
select * from NewDimProduct
```

Result

	EnglishProductName	Discount
1	All-Purpose Bike Stand	63.60
2	AWC Logo Cap	3.4577
3	AWC Logo Cap	3.4577
4	AWC Logo Cap	3.596
5	Bike Wash - Dissolver	3.18
6	Cable Lock	10.00
7	Chain	8.096
8	Classic Vest, L	25.40
9	Classic Vest, M	25.40
10	Classic Vest, S	25.40
11	Fender Set - Mountain	8.792
12	Front Brakes	42.60
13	Front Derailleur	36.596
14	Full-Finger Gloves, L	15.196
15	Full-Finger Gloves, M	15.196
16	Full-Finger Gloves, S	15.196
17	Half-Finger Gloves, L	9.4192
18	Half-Finger Gloves, L	9.796

Analysis

The records returned are the same as those in our first base query at the start of the chapter. Select Into not only creates the structure of a new table, but it also copies the data from the source table into the new table. The new table is permanent—you can see it listed in Object Explorer (you may have to right-click and choose Refresh first). The new table has some but not all of the features of the source table. For example, it has the same columns (those specified in the Select column list) with the same data types. It has the same number of records and the same data. If one of the columns has an identity property, this is copied too. However, it will not have any of the keys (for instance, a primary or foreign key) nor any of the indexes from the original table.

If the Select Into is based on two joined tables, you are creating a single table from two source tables. Some people use this method to denormalize data and to create tables for reporting. You can also accomplish this by creating views. Views are discussed in a later chapter. The difference is that a view does not usually create a new permanent object (for simplicity, I am ignoring materialized indexed views, which are a special case). Here, you have a permanent object that persists until it's explicitly dropped.

Deleting from New Table

Please try the Delete query first and then run the Select query.

Syntax

```
-- delete
delete NewDimProduct
select * from NewDimProduct
```

Result

EnglishProductName	Discount

Analysis

The Delete statement does *not* delete the table! You can still see the column names when you execute the Select query. A Delete statement *does* delete data from a table—there are no rows to be seen.

Dropping New Table

Execute the Drop Table query and then try the Select query. Please be careful that you use Drop Table on the correct table, NewDimProduct, *not* DimProduct.

Syntax

```
-- drop
drop table NewDimProduct
select * from NewDimProduct
```

Result

```
Msg 208, Level 16, State 1, Line 1
Invalid object name 'NewDimProduct'.
```

Analysis

Drop Table is different from Delete. Delete removes data but leaves the table intact. Drop Table removes the table completely—if the table contains data, then the data is removed when the table is removed. The Select statement error message confirms that the table no longer exists. If you right-click and choose Refresh in Object Explorer, you can verify that our new table is gone. Maybe a word of caution is in order, if you are using Object Explorer. When you right-click on a table, there is a Delete option in the context menu. This is not the equivalent of the SQL Delete statement; it's actually the equivalent of the SQL Drop Table statement. Please don't experiment on any production database tables!

Creating an Empty Table

You have just created a new table containing data using Select Into. You can also create a new table that does not contain data with Select Into. There is a Where clause at the end of this query.

Syntax

```
-- empty table
select EnglishProductName, ListPrice - DealerPrice as Discount
into NewDimProduct
from DimProduct
where 1 = 0
```

Result

```
(0 row(s) affected)
```

Analysis

The result shows that no records were copied into the new table. The Where clause is never true, so no rows are retrieved by the Select. However, the Select Into does create an empty table structure. This might be handy when you need a few tables that are similar. It's also useful when you want to experiment with a table design—and are rightly wary of doing so on a live production table.

Testing New Table

A simple Select.

Syntax

```
-- test
select * from NewDimProduct
```

Result

EnglishProductName	Discount

Analysis

The table exists but has no records. You know it's there as there's no error message and the column names are returned as column header captions.

Dropping New Table

Please run these two queries separately.

Syntax

```
-- drop
drop table NewDimProduct
select * from NewDimProduct
```

Result

```
Msg 208, Level 16, State 1, Line 1
Invalid object name 'NewDimProduct'.
```

Analysis

The new empty table is gone.

Local Temporary Table

There are a total of four queries here. First, there's a Select Into to create a new table. The new table name has a # prefix. Second, there's a normal Select to test the table. Third, there's a Drop Table to remove the table. Fourth, there's a normal Select to verify that the new table has been removed. Before you run the third query, Drop Table, please read the Analysis for this query.

Syntax

```
-- local temporary
select EnglishProductName, ListPrice - DealerPrice as Discount
into #NewDimProduct
from DimProduct
where ListPrice - DealerPrice is not null
order by EnglishProductName
-- test
select * from #NewDimProduct
-- drop
drop table #NewDimProduct
select * from #NewDimProduct
```

Result

	EnglishProductName	Discount
1	All-Purpose Bike Stand	63.60
2	AWC Logo Cap	3.4577
3	AWC Logo Cap	3.4577
4	AWC Logo Cap	3.596
5	Bike Wash - Dissolver	3.18
6	Cable Lock	10.00
7	Chain	8.096
8	Classic Vest, L	25.40
9	Classic Vest, M	25.40
10	Classic Vest, S	25.40
11	Fender Set - Mountain	8.792
12	Front Brakes	42.60
13	Front Derailleur	36.596
14	Full-Finger Gloves, L	15.196
15	Full-Finger Gloves, M	15.196
16	Full-Finger Gloves, S	15.196
17	Half-Finger Gloves, L	9.4192
18	Half-Finger Gloves, L	9.796

Analysis

The # prefix to the new table name results in the creation of a new temporary table (the ones you created in earlier queries were permanent tables). A single # prefix means a local temporary table. Before you run the Drop Table statement, it's worth considering a few things. As the table is temporary, it will automatically disappear if you close your query editor window—so a Drop Table is not required. I've used Drop Table only to save you closing your editor window. Also, as it's a temporary table, it lives in your tempdb database. You can view it in Object Explorer—open the System Databases folder, then tempdb, and expand Temporary Tables (you may need to right-click and choose Refresh). It's a local temporary table; it can only be seen from the current query editor window. If you were to open a new window, a normal Select on the table would fail.

Try the second Select to verify that the table exists and contains data. Then drop the table and try selecting again to confirm it has disappeared.

Temporary tables are often used as work tables or staging tables or test tables. Maybe you want to experiment with some SQL, but prefer not to do so on a production table.

Global Temporary Table

The new table name in the Select Into query has a ## prefix.

Syntax

```
-- global temporary
select EnglishProductName, ListPrice - DealerPrice as Discount
into ##NewDimProduct
from DimProduct
where ListPrice - DealerPrice is not null
order by EnglishProductName
-- test
select * from ##NewDimProduct
-- drop
drop table ##NewDimProduct
select * from ##NewDimProduct
```

Result

	EnglishProductName	Discount
1	All-Purpose Bike Stand	63.60
2	AWC Logo Cap	3.4577
3	AWC Logo Cap	3.4577
4	AWC Logo Cap	3.596
5	Bike Wash - Dissolver	3.18
6	Cable Lock	10.00
7	Chain	8.096
8	Classic Vest, L	25.40
9	Classic Vest, M	25.40
10	Classic Vest, S	25.40
11	Fender Set - Mountain	8.792
12	Front Brakes	42.60
13	Front Derailleur	36.596
14	Full-Finger Gloves, L	15.196
15	Full-Finger Gloves, M	15.196
16	Full-Finger Gloves, S	15.196
17	Half-Finger Gloves, L	9.4192
18	Half-Finger Gloves, L	9.796

Analysis

The result shown is from the second query. A double ## prefix means a global temporary table. It will reside in your tempdb database until you close the query editor window or issue a Drop Table. In those respects, it's the same as a local temporary table. The difference lies in its scope. A local temporary table is only accessible from the current query editor window (called a *session*). On the other hand, a global temporary table is visible (during its lifetime) from other query editor windows or sessions. Global temporary tables can also be used for testing or as staging tables when you want to start a new SQL query in a new window.

Semipermanent Temporary Table

Take a careful look at the first query here. It's another Select Into but the table name is qualified with a schema name and a database name. The database in question is the system database, tempdb.

Syntax

```
-- semi-permanent temporary
select EnglishProductName, ListPrice - DealerPrice as Discount
into tempdb.dbo.NewDimProduct
from DimProduct
where ListPrice - DealerPrice is not null
```

```
order by EnglishProductName
-- test
select * from tempdb.dbo.NewDimProduct
-- drop
drop table tempdb.dbo.NewDimProduct
select * from tempdb.dbo.NewDimProduct
```

Result

	EnglishProductName	Discount
1	All-Purpose Bike Stand	63.60
2	AWC Logo Cap	3.4577
3	AWC Logo Cap	3.4577
4	AWC Logo Cap	3.596
5	Bike Wash - Dissolver	3.18
6	Cable Lock	10.00
7	Chain	8.096
8	Classic Vest, L	25.40
9	Classic Vest, M	25.40
10	Classic Vest, S	25.40
11	Fender Set - Mountain	8.792
12	Front Brakes	42.60
13	Front Derailleur	36.596
14	Full-Finger Gloves, L	15.196
15	Full-Finger Gloves, M	15.196
16	Full-Finger Gloves, S	15.196
17	Half-Finger Gloves, L	9.4192
18	Half-Finger Gloves, L	9.796

Analysis

The result is from the second query. You are explicitly creating the new table in tempdb. But you won't see it in Object Explorer underneath the tempdb Temporary Tables folder. Rather, it's under the tempdb Tables folder. It's a permanent table in tempdb (your temporary database). I have never discovered the official name for this type of table—so I call them semipermanent temporary tables! They are not truly temporary— if you close the query editor window, the tables are still there for other query editor windows and users. They act just like permanent tables in normal production databases. But then, they are not truly permanent—if you stop and restart SQL Server, they are erased from tempdb. The tempdb database is always re-created and cleared as a result when SQL Server starts up. Again, these tables can be used as test or staging tables.

Chapter 7

Except/Intersect/Union

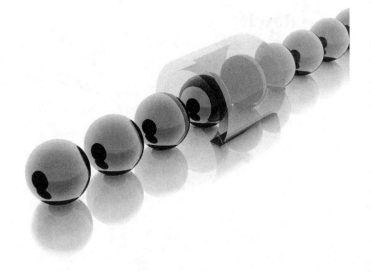

I n this chapter, we examine set operations. The three main keywords introduced are Union, Intersect, and Except. These are set operators that treat each table involved in the operation as a set. If you are familiar with set theory and Venn diagrams from high school math, you already have a good idea how they work. Union puts two or more tables together. Intersect looks at what the tables have in common. Except returns the differences between tables.

▶ **Key concepts**   Set operations, appending tables, common records in tables, different records in tables, except, intersect, union

▶ **Keywords**   Union, Union All, Intersect, Except, Select Into, Insert Into

New Table 1/2

We are going to need two new tables for the exercises in this chapter. Here's a Select Into to create the first of the two new tables. It's followed by a normal Select to verify the new table and its data.

Syntax

```
-- preparing data 1/2
select EnglishProductName, ReorderPoint
into Table1
from DimProduct
where EnglishProductName like 'flat%'
order by EnglishProductName-- 9 records
select * from Table1
```

Result

	EnglishProductName	ReorderPoint
1	Flat Washer 1	750
2	Flat Washer 2	750
3	Flat Washer 3	750
4	Flat Washer 4	750
5	Flat Washer 5	750
6	Flat Washer 6	750
7	Flat Washer 7	750
8	Flat Washer 8	750
9	Flat Washer 9	750

Analysis

Now you have a new table, with a very exciting name! It contains nine products, also with highly stimulating names. I reinstated the Order By clause—the user may want the records sorted.

New Table 2/2

The Select Into here creates the second of the two new tables we need for this chapter.

Syntax

```
-- preparing data 2/2
select EnglishProductName, ReorderPoint
into Table2
from DimProduct
where EnglishProductName = 'flat washer 9'
-- 1 record
select * from Table2
```

Result

	EnglishProductName	ReorderPoint
1	Flat Washer 9	750

Analysis

This new table (Table2) contains just the one record. This record is the same as one of the records in Table1.

Inserting Data

Also, we're going to need another record in the second of the two new tables (Table2). The first query is an Insert Into statement—inserts are covered more fully later in the book.

Syntax

```
-- add a record
insert into Table2
values('Flat Washer 33',999)
-- 2 records
select * from Table2
```

Result

	EnglishProductName	ReorderPoint
1	Flat Washer 33	999
2	Flat Washer 9	750

Analysis

There are now two records in Table2. One of them is the same as one of the records in Table1. The other record is completely different from any of the records in Table1.

Union 1/3

There are actually only two queries here. Each one is composed of two Selects with a Union operator in between. Please try both queries.

Syntax

```
-- union 10 records
select * from Table1
union
select * from Table2
--
select EnglishProductName from Table1
union
select EnglishProductName from Table2
```

Result

	EnglishProductName
1	Flat Washer 1
2	Flat Washer 2
3	Flat Washer 3
4	Flat Washer 33
5	Flat Washer 4
6	Flat Washer 5
7	Flat Washer 6
8	Flat Washer 7
9	Flat Washer 8
10	Flat Washer 9

Analysis

Both queries return 10 rows—the only difference being in the number of columns. Table1 has 9 records and Table2 has 2 records. When you append them with Union, you end up with 10 records, not 11—the common record (Flat Washer 9) appears only once, not twice.

You can union more than two tables—simply add more Union operators and Select statements. A union is not the same as a join. A join puts the tables together horizontally, usually based on a primary-to-foreign-key relationship—it's for creating a single result from often dissimilar tables (denormalization). A union appends tables; it puts them together vertically—it's for creating a single result from similar tables (conforming).

Union 2/3

This query is designed to give an error.

Syntax

```
-- error 1/2
select * from Table1
union
select EnglishProductName from Table2
```

Result

```
Msg 205, Level 16, State 1, Line 2
All queries combined using a UNION, INTERSECT or EXCEPT operator must have an equal number of expressions in their target
```

Analysis

The error occurs as the first Select returns two columns and the second Select returns only one column. When you append tables with the Union operator, there must be an equal number of columns from each table.

Union 3/3

This query, too, is meant to fail!

Syntax

```
-- error 2/2
select ReOrderPoint from Table1
union
select EnglishProductName from Table2
```

Result

```
Msg 245, Level 16, State 1, Line 2
Conversion failed when converting the nvarchar value 'Flat Washer 33' to data type smallint.
```

Analysis

The error is a different one. This time we have the same number of columns, so that's not the problem. However, the data types of the two columns are incompatible. ReOrderPoint is a `smallint` while EnglishProductName is an `nvarchar`.

Union All

But our queries here are meant to work. Please note that Union has been changed to Union All.

Syntax

```
-- union all 11 records
select * from Table1
union all
select * from Table2
```

Result

	EnglishProductName	ReorderPoint
1	Flat Washer 1	750
2	Flat Washer 2	750
3	Flat Washer 3	750
4	Flat Washer 4	750
5	Flat Washer 5	750
6	Flat Washer 6	750
7	Flat Washer 7	750
8	Flat Washer 8	750
9	Flat Washer 9	750
10	Flat Washer 33	999
11	Flat Washer 9	750

Analysis

Here you should get 11 rows (not the 10 we had a couple of queries ago). The record that is common to both tables, Flat Washer 9, is returned twice. The Union operator suppresses duplicates, while Union All does not.

Intersect

The operator between the two Selects is Intersect rather than Union.

Syntax

```
-- intersect 1 record
select * from Table1
intersect
select * from Table2
```

Result

	EnglishProductName	ReorderPoint
1	Flat Washer 9	750

Analysis

Intersect returns the common record (Flat Washer 9) from the two tables. It shows just one copy of the record, not both of them. This is a simple, yet powerful, set operation to see if you have the same data in more than one table.

Except 1/2

The operator is now Except.

Syntax

```
-- except 8 records
select * from Table1
except
select * from Table2
```

Result

	EnglishProductName	ReorderPoint
1	Flat Washer 1	750
2	Flat Washer 2	750
3	Flat Washer 3	750
4	Flat Washer 4	750
5	Flat Washer 5	750
6	Flat Washer 6	750
7	Flat Washer 7	750
8	Flat Washer 8	750

Analysis

You should have eight rows. Except is showing all of the records from Table1 that do not also appear in Table2. Flat Washer 9 is therefore eliminated. Flat Washer 33 from Table2 does not qualify as it's not in Table1. Please note that Table1 is the first table in the query.

Except 2/2

The two tables are in a different order.

Syntax

```
-- except 1 record
select * from Table2
except
select * from Table1
```

Result

	EnglishProductName	ReorderPoint
1	Flat Washer 33	999

Analysis

Just one row—Flat Washer 33. This is the only record in the first table (Table2) that does not appear in Table1. Flat Washer 9 has been eliminated as it's also in the second table (Table1).

You may want to issue two Drop Table statements (against Table1 and Table2) to clean up your Adventure Works database.

Chapter 8

Group By

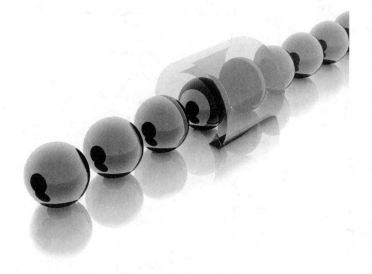

Busines users often ask for reports that show totals and subtotals. These totals are often based on particular categories or groups of data. This chapter introduces the SQL required to group your data and produce meaningful totals. The main emphasis is on the Group By clause used with various aggregation functions, for example Sum(). We also take a quick look at the more specialized Compute and Compute By clauses. Hopefully, you'll learn enough SQL in just this single chapter to begin producing sophisticated reports for your business users.

▶ **Key concepts**   Grouping records, aggregations across groups, totals and subtotals, filtering groups, comparing aggregate values, totals and detail records

▶ **Keywords**   Group By, Having, Compute, Compute By, Count(), Sum(), Min(), Max(), Avg()

Base Query

To get us started on this chapter devoted to grouping records, here's a base query that we'll use a few times.

Syntax

```
select EnglishProductCategoryName, EnglishProductSubcategoryName from
DimProductCategory as C
inner join DimProductSubcategory as S
on C.ProductCategoryKey = S.ProductCategoryKey
```

Result

	EnglishProductCategoryName	EnglishProductSubcategoryName
1	Bikes	Mountain Bikes
2	Bikes	Road Bikes
3	Bikes	Touring Bikes
4	Components	Handlebars
5	Components	Bottom Brackets
6	Components	Brakes
7	Components	Chains
8	Components	Cranksets
9	Components	Derailleurs
10	Components	Forks
11	Components	Headsets
12	Components	Mountain Frames
13	Components	Pedals
14	Components	Road Frames
15	Components	Saddles
16	Components	Touring Frames
17	Components	Wheels
18	Clothing	Bib-Shorts

Analysis

The result of the inner join is a list of categories and corresponding subcategories. There are 37 rows. If you look at the Bikes category, it's composed of three subcategories (Mountain Bikes, Road Bikes, and Touring Bikes).

Count()

The Bikes category has three subcategories. It might be useful to see how many subcategories make up each category for reporting purposes. Here's the Count() aggregate function.

Syntax

```
-- count with error
select EnglishProductCategoryName, COUNT(EnglishProductSubcategoryName)
from DimProductCategory as C
inner join DimProductSubcategory as S
on C.ProductCategoryKey = S.ProductCategoryKey
```

Result

```
Msg 8120, Level 16, State 1, Line 2
Column 'DimProductCategory.EnglishProductCategoryName' is invalid in the select list because it is not contained in eithe
```

Analysis

This is a really common error in SQL queries. There is something wrong with the EnglishProductCategoryName column. It's a non-aggregated column appearing alongside an aggregated column, EnglishProductSubcategoryName. You can't have a non-aggregated column and an aggregated column in a column list, unless you include a Group By clause. You could have aggregated the EnglishProductCategoryName column too—but we don't want that; we simply want to see the category name.

Group By 1/2

The query introduces the Group By clause.

Syntax

```
-- count with group
select EnglishProductCategoryName, COUNT(EnglishProductSubcategoryName)
as [Count Subcategories] from DimProductCategory as C
```

```
inner join DimProductSubcategory as S
on C.ProductCategoryKey = S.ProductCategoryKey
group by EnglishProductCategoryName
```

Result

	EnglishProductCategoryName	Count Subcategories
1	Accessories	12
2	Bikes	3
3	Clothing	8
4	Components	14

Analysis

There are 4 records now, not the 37 we had earlier. The Bikes category has three subcategories. We still have a non-aggregated and an aggregated column in the column list, but the non-aggregated column (EnglishProductCategoryName) this time also appears in the Group By clause. You are asking SQL Server to group on category and return the count of the subcategories in each group.

Group By 2/2

Here we've added a Where clause as well.

Syntax

```
-- count with group with where
select EnglishProductCategoryName, COUNT(EnglishProductSubcategoryName)
as [Count Subcategories] from DimProductCategory as C
inner join DimProductSubcategory as S
on C.ProductCategoryKey = S.ProductCategoryKey
where EnglishProductCategoryName <> 'Bikes'
group by EnglishProductCategoryName
```

Result

	EnglishProductCategoryName	Count Subcategories
1	Accessories	12
2	Clothing	8
3	Components	14

Analysis

Now you can't see the Bikes category. As always, you can extend your SQL by combining clauses and keywords and operators and functions. In this case, the Where clause must appear before the Group By clause.

Having 1/2

You can filter records using a Where clause. You can also filter groups of records by using a Having clause. The difference between Where and Having is examined shortly. Let's try eliminating bikes, by asking only for those categories that contain more than three subcategories.

Syntax

```
-- count with group with having 1/2
select EnglishProductCategoryName, COUNT(EnglishProductSubcategoryName)
as [Count Subcategories] from DimProductCategory as C
inner join DimProductSubcategory as S
on C.ProductCategoryKey = S.ProductCategoryKey
group by EnglishProductCategoryName
having [Count Subcategories] > 3
```

Result

```
Msg 207, Level 16, State 1, Line 6
Invalid column name 'Count Subcategories'.
```

Analysis

Unfortunately, this doesn't quite work. The count of the subcategories is aliased as [Count Subcategories] and that's what we've used in the Having clause.

Having 2/2

Instead of the alias, here we have the aggregation and column in the Having clause.

Syntax

```
-- count with group with having 2/2
select EnglishProductCategoryName, COUNT(EnglishProductSubcategoryName)
as [Count Subcategories] from DimProductCategory as C
inner join DimProductSubcategory as S
on C.ProductCategoryKey = S.ProductCategoryKey
group by EnglishProductCategoryName
having COUNT(EnglishProductSubcategoryName) > 3
```

Result

	EnglishProductCategoryName	Count Subcategories
1	Accessories	12
2	Clothing	8
3	Components	14

Analysis

This time it works fine. You can't use aliases in Having clauses—you have to repeat the original expression, Count(EnglishProductSubcategoryName). A Where clause must precede a Group By clause, while a Having clause has to come after the Group By. You have now managed to eliminate the Bikes category in two queries. Earlier, you did this in a Where clause. Here, you've done it in a Having clause. The two clauses operate differently. A Where clause does not return unwanted rows—they are filtered out at source. A Having clause has to return the records so the grouping and aggregating can be done before they are filtered out. Generally, a Where clause is more efficient than a Having clause. However, if you wish to filter on grouped and aggregated results, you must use a Having clause. You will notice that Bikes is not referred to in the query.

No Aggregation

There are two queries here. The first one has no Group By. Both queries produce the same result, although you might find that the order of the records is different.

Syntax

```
-- when not to use group by
select EnglishProductCategoryName, EnglishProductSubcategoryName from
DimProductCategory as C
inner join DimProductSubcategory as S
on C.ProductCategoryKey = S.ProductCategoryKey
--
select EnglishProductCategoryName, EnglishProductSubcategoryName from
DimProductCategory as C
inner join DimProductSubcategory as S
on C.ProductCategoryKey = S.ProductCategoryKey
group by EnglishProductCategoryName, EnglishProductSubcategoryName
```

Result

	EnglishProductCategoryName	EnglishProductSubcategoryName
1	Accessories	Bike Racks
2	Accessories	Bike Stands
3	Accessories	Bottles and Cages
4	Accessories	Cleaners
5	Accessories	Fenders
6	Accessories	Helmets
7	Accessories	Hydration Packs
8	Accessories	Lights
9	Accessories	Locks
10	Accessories	Panniers
11	Accessories	Pumps
12	Accessories	Tires and Tubes
13	Bikes	Mountain Bikes
14	Bikes	Road Bikes
15	Bikes	Touring Bikes
16	Clothing	Bib-Shorts
17	Clothing	Caps
18	Clothing	Gloves

Analysis

The Group By in the second query is overkill. If your Group By columns match the non-aggregated columns in the column list and there is no aggregated column, then Group By is generally not required.

Grouping on Two Columns

In this query you will see there are two columns in the Group By clause.

Syntax

```
-- when to use group by
select EnglishProductCategoryName, EnglishProductSubcategoryName,
COUNT(EnglishProductName) as [CountOfProducts] from DimProductCategory as C
inner join DimProductSubcategory as S
on C.ProductCategoryKey = S.ProductCategoryKey
inner join DimProduct as P
on S.ProductSubcategoryKey = P.ProductSubcategoryKey
group by EnglishProductCategoryName, EnglishProductSubcategoryName
```

Result

	EnglishProductCategoryName	EnglishProductSubcategoryName	CountOfProducts
1	Clothing	Bib-Shorts	3
2	Accessories	Bike Racks	1
3	Accessories	Bike Stands	1
4	Accessories	Bottles and Cages	3
5	Components	Bottom Brackets	3
6	Components	Brakes	2
7	Clothing	Caps	3
8	Components	Chains	1
9	Accessories	Cleaners	1
10	Components	Cranksets	3
11	Components	Derailleurs	2
12	Accessories	Fenders	1
13	Components	Forks	3
14	Clothing	Gloves	9
15	Components	Handlebars	14
16	Components	Headsets	3
17	Accessories	Helmets	9
18	Accessories	Hydration Packs	1

Analysis

Here Group By makes perfect sense—there is an aggregated column (EnglishProductName) in the column list. We are grouping on two levels and counting the number of products in each subcategory. For each subcategory we are showing the category group to which it belongs.

Jumping a Level

Here there is no reference at all to the subcategory in either the column list or the Group By clause.

Syntax

```
-- grouping at higher level
select EnglishProductCategoryName, COUNT(EnglishProductName)
as [CountOfProducts] from DimProductCategory as C
inner join DimProductSubcategory as S
on C.ProductCategoryKey = S.ProductCategoryKey
inner join DimProduct as P
on S.ProductSubcategoryKey = P.ProductSubcategoryKey
group by EnglishProductCategoryName
```

Result

	EnglishProductCategoryName	CountOfProducts
1	Accessories	35
2	Bikes	125
3	Clothing	48
4	Components	189

Analysis

This query counts the number of products in each category—the result does not show the subcategory. The subcategory table (DimProductSubcategory) is only used so we can join each individual product to its relevant category.

Sum() 1/2

The Count() aggregate function has been replaced by Sum(). Expect this one to return an error.

Syntax

```
-- sum rather than count
select EnglishProductCategoryName, EnglishProductSubcategoryName,
SUM(EnglishProductName) as [SumOfProducts] from DimProductCategory as C
inner join DimProductSubcategory as S
on C.ProductCategoryKey = S.ProductCategoryKey
inner join DimProduct as P
on S.ProductSubcategoryKey = P.ProductSubcategoryKey
group by EnglishProductCategoryName, EnglishProductSubcategoryName
```

Result

```
Msg 8117, Level 16, State 1, Line 2
Operand data type nvarchar is invalid for sum operator.
```

Analysis

EnglishProductName is a string with a data type of nvarchar. Earlier, we used Count() on the same column. You can count product names but you can't sum them.

Sum() 2/2

The aggregated column is now numeric.

Syntax

```
-- sum on numeric, not much good on price
select EnglishProductCategoryName, EnglishProductSubcategoryName,
SUM(ListPrice) as [SumOfProducts] from DimProductCategory as C
inner join DimProductSubcategory as S
on C.ProductCategoryKey = S.ProductCategoryKey
inner join DimProduct as P
on S.ProductSubcategoryKey = P.ProductSubcategoryKey
group by EnglishProductCategoryName, EnglishProductSubcategoryName
```

Result

	EnglishProductCategoryName	EnglishProductSubcategoryName	SumOfProducts
1	Clothing	Bib-Shorts	269.97
2	Accessories	Bike Racks	120.00
3	Accessories	Bike Stands	159.00
4	Accessories	Bottles and Cages	23.97
5	Components	Bottom Brackets	276.72
6	Components	Brakes	213.00
7	Clothing	Caps	26.2784
8	Components	Chains	20.24
9	Accessories	Cleaners	7.95
10	Components	Cranksets	836.97
11	Components	Derailleurs	212.95
12	Accessories	Fenders	21.98
13	Components	Forks	553.20
14	Clothing	Gloves	258.0843
15	Components	Handlebars	1003.3564
16	Components	Headsets	261.22
17	Accessories	Helmets	306.8352
18	Accessories	Hydration Packs	54.99

Analysis

ListPrice has a data type of money—this can be summed (as well as counted, of course). This is just an example, so maybe adding prices is a little meaningless. But Group By with Sum() would work well with something like quantity sold.

Min()

The aggregate function is Min().

Syntax

```
-- min
select EnglishProductCategoryName, EnglishProductSubcategoryName,
MIN(ListPrice) as [MinOfProducts] from DimProductCategory as C
inner join DimProductSubcategory as S
on C.ProductCategoryKey = S.ProductCategoryKey
inner join DimProduct as P
on S.ProductSubcategoryKey = P.ProductSubcategoryKey
group by EnglishProductCategoryName, EnglishProductSubcategoryName
```

Result

	EnglishProductCategoryName	EnglishProductSubcategoryName	MinOfProducts
1	Clothing	Bib-Shorts	89.99
2	Accessories	Bike Racks	120.00
3	Accessories	Bike Stands	159.00
4	Accessories	Bottles and Cages	4.99
5	Components	Bottom Brackets	53.99
6	Components	Brakes	106.50
7	Clothing	Caps	8.6442
8	Components	Chains	20.24
9	Accessories	Cleaners	7.95
10	Components	Cranksets	175.49
11	Components	Derailleurs	91.49
12	Accessories	Fenders	21.98
13	Components	Forks	148.22
14	Clothing	Gloves	23.5481
15	Components	Handlebars	40.4909
16	Components	Headsets	34.20
17	Accessories	Helmets	33.6442
18	Accessories	Hydration Packs	54.99

Analysis

Min() works quite well on a price. The third column shows the price of the cheapest product in each subcategory.

Max()

Max() quite simply returns a maximum value.

Syntax

```
-- max
select EnglishProductCategoryName, EnglishProductSubcategoryName,
MAX(ListPrice) as [MaxOfProducts] from DimProductCategory as C
inner join DimProductSubcategory as S
on C.ProductCategoryKey = S.ProductCategoryKey
inner join DimProduct as P
on S.ProductSubcategoryKey = P.ProductSubcategoryKey
group by EnglishProductCategoryName, EnglishProductSubcategoryName
```

Result

	EnglishProductCategoryName	EnglishProductSubcategoryName	MaxOfProducts
1	Clothing	Bib-Shorts	89.99
2	Accessories	Bike Racks	120.00
3	Accessories	Bike Stands	159.00
4	Accessories	Bottles and Cages	9.99
5	Components	Bottom Brackets	121.49
6	Components	Brakes	106.50
7	Clothing	Caps	8.99
8	Components	Chains	20.24
9	Accessories	Cleaners	7.95
10	Components	Cranksets	404.99
11	Components	Derailleurs	121.46
12	Accessories	Fenders	21.98
13	Components	Forks	229.49
14	Clothing	Gloves	37.99
15	Components	Handlebars	120.27
16	Components	Headsets	124.73
17	Accessories	Helmets	34.99
18	Accessories	Hydration Packs	54.99

Analysis

The third column displays the price of the most expensive product in each subcategory. If Min() and Max() produce the same result, it indicates that each product in a particular subcategory has the same price—or there is only one product in the subcategory.

Avg()

In this query, the aggregate function is Avg().

Syntax

```
-- avg some records avg is same as max
select EnglishProductCategoryName, EnglishProductSubcategoryName,
AVG(ListPrice) as [AvgOfProducts] from DimProductCategory as C
inner join DimProductSubcategory as S
on C.ProductCategoryKey = S.ProductCategoryKey
inner join DimProduct as P
on S.ProductSubcategoryKey = P.ProductSubcategoryKey
group by EnglishProductCategoryName, EnglishProductSubcategoryName
```

Result

	EnglishProductCategoryName	EnglishProductSubcategoryName	AvgOfProducts
1	Clothing	Bib-Shorts	89.99
2	Accessories	Bike Racks	120.00
3	Accessories	Bike Stands	159.00
4	Accessories	Bottles and Cages	7.99
5	Components	Bottom Brackets	92.24
6	Components	Brakes	106.50
7	Clothing	Caps	8.7594
8	Components	Chains	20.24
9	Accessories	Cleaners	7.95
10	Components	Cranksets	278.99
11	Components	Derailleurs	106.475
12	Accessories	Fenders	21.98
13	Components	Forks	184.40
14	Clothing	Gloves	28.676
15	Components	Handlebars	71.6683
16	Components	Headsets	87.0733
17	Accessories	Helmets	34.0928
18	Accessories	Hydration Packs	54.99

Analysis

If Min() and Max() return the same answer for a subcategory, then Avg() will be the same as well.

Two Aggregate Functions

There is nothing to stop you from using two aggregate functions with Group By.

Syntax

```
-- avg and max together
select EnglishProductCategoryName, EnglishProductSubcategoryName,
MAX(ListPrice) as [MaxOfProducts], AVG(ListPrice) as [AvgOfProducts]
from DimProductCategory as C
```

```
inner join DimProductSubcategory as S
on C.ProductCategoryKey = S.ProductCategoryKey
inner join DimProduct as P
on S.ProductSubcategoryKey = P.ProductSubcategoryKey
group by EnglishProductCategoryName, EnglishProductSubcategoryName
```

Result

	EnglishProductCategoryName	EnglishProductSubcategoryName	MaxOfProducts	AvgOfProducts
1	Clothing	Bib-Shorts	89.99	89.99
2	Accessories	Bike Racks	120.00	120.00
3	Accessories	Bike Stands	159.00	159.00
4	Accessories	Bottles and Cages	9.99	7.99
5	Components	Bottom Brackets	121.49	92.24
6	Components	Brakes	106.50	106.50
7	Clothing	Caps	8.99	8.7594
8	Components	Chains	20.24	20.24
9	Accessories	Cleaners	7.95	7.95
10	Components	Cranksets	404.99	278.99
11	Components	Derailleurs	121.46	106.475
12	Accessories	Fenders	21.98	21.98
13	Components	Forks	229.49	184.40
14	Clothing	Gloves	37.99	28.676
15	Components	Handlebars	120.27	71.6683
16	Components	Headsets	124.73	87.0733
17	Accessories	Helmets	34.99	34.0928
18	Accessories	Hydration Packs	54.99	54.99

Analysis

If you can find the Cranksets subcategory in the Components category, the maximum and average prices of products are different. For this subcategory, there must be at least two products with differing ListPrice.

Comparing Two Aggregate Functions

There is a Having clause here. It is using two aggregate functions.

Syntax

```
-- only those where avg and max are different
select EnglishProductCategoryName, EnglishProductSubcategoryName,
MAX(ListPrice) as [MaxOfProducts], AVG(ListPrice) as [AvgOfProducts]
from DimProductCategory as C
inner join DimProductSubcategory as S
on C.ProductCategoryKey = S.ProductCategoryKey
```

```
inner join DimProduct as P
on S.ProductSubcategoryKey = P.ProductSubcategoryKey
group by EnglishProductCategoryName, EnglishProductSubcategoryName
having MAX(ListPrice) <> AVG(ListPrice)
```

Result

	EnglishProductCategoryName	EnglishProductSubcategoryName	MaxOfProducts	AvgOfProducts
1	Accessories	Bottles and Cages	9.99	7.99
2	Components	Bottom Brackets	121.49	92.24
3	Clothing	Caps	8.99	8.7594
4	Components	Cranksets	404.99	278.99
5	Components	Derailleurs	121.46	106.475
6	Components	Forks	229.49	184.40
7	Clothing	Gloves	37.99	28.676
8	Components	Handlebars	120.27	71.6683
9	Components	Headsets	124.73	87.0733
10	Accessories	Helmets	34.99	34.0928
11	Clothing	Jerseys	53.99	50.0286
12	Accessories	Lights	44.99	31.3233
13	Bikes	Mountain Bikes	3399.99	1742.8745
14	Components	Mountain Frames	1364.50	839.4921
15	Components	Pedals	80.99	64.0185
16	Accessories	Pumps	24.99	22.49
17	Bikes	Road Bikes	3578.27	1430.6081
18	Components	Road Frames	1431.50	721.711

Analysis

You should see Cranksets in Components among other rows. A few rows have been eliminated too. The Having clause is comparing the maximum price with the average price. This type of query is very, very difficult to do with a Where clause!

Compute

This is your introduction to the Compute clause. We are still calculating aggregate values, but this time, there's no Group By clause. This query is going to give its result in a completely different way. The structure of the result means you can't use Compute everywhere you might use a Group By—for example, in views and subqueries.

Syntax

```
-- but how to see products as well as aggregrate?
-- compute
select EnglishProductCategoryName, EnglishProductSubcategoryName,
EnglishProductName, ListPrice from DimProductCategory as C
```

```
inner join DimProductSubcategory as S
on C.ProductCategoryKey = S.ProductCategoryKey
inner join DimProduct as P
on S.ProductSubcategoryKey = P.ProductSubcategoryKey
compute MAX(ListPrice), AVG(ListPrice)
```

Result

	EnglishProductCategoryName	EnglishProductSubcategoryName	EnglishProductName	ListPrice
1	Components	Road Frames	HL Road Frame - Black, 58	NULL
2	Components	Road Frames	HL Road Frame - Red, 58	NULL
3	Accessories	Helmets	Sport-100 Helmet, Red	33.6442
4	Accessories	Helmets	Sport-100 Helmet, Red	33.6442
5	Accessories	Helmets	Sport-100 Helmet, Red	34.99
6	Accessories	Helmets	Sport-100 Helmet, Black	33.6442
7	Accessories	Helmets	Sport-100 Helmet, Black	33.6442
8	Accessories	Helmets	Sport-100 Helmet, Black	34.99
9	Clothing	Socks	Mountain Bike Socks, M	9.50
10	Clothing	Socks	Mountain Bike Socks, L	9.50
11	Accessories	Helmets	Sport-100 Helmet, Blue	33.6442
12	Accessories	Helmets	Sport-100 Helmet, Blue	33.6442

	max	avg
1	3578.27	747.6617

Analysis

Group By is incredibly powerful syntax—hopefully, you've seen a couple of examples you might be able to apply to your own data. It shows the groups and the aggregate calculations such as totals. However, it does not show the detail records. For example, if you return the maximum price of products in a subcategory, you don't get to see a list of the individual products in each subcategory as well. The Compute clause is able to show totals and details. There are two result sets here. You can see the individual products and their prices in the first result set. The second result set shows the maximum and average prices. But these are not the maximum and average prices by category or subcategory—they are the maximum and average prices of *all* the products. What we need is to be able to aggregate on groups as well—we need some syntax that combines Compute with Group By. The SQL to do that is the Compute By clause.

Compute By 1/2

This is the Compute By clause—not a Compute clause. This query is an attempt to see both detail records and aggregations at the group level.

Syntax

```
-- compute by error
select EnglishProductCategoryName, EnglishProductSubcategoryName,
EnglishProductName, ListPrice from DimProductCategory as C
inner join DimProductSubcategory as S
on C.ProductCategoryKey = S.ProductCategoryKey
inner join DimProduct as P
on S.ProductSubcategoryKey = P.ProductSubcategoryKey
compute MAX(ListPrice), AVG(ListPrice) by EnglishProductCategoryName
```

Result

```
Msg 143, Level 15, State 1, Line 7
A COMPUTE BY item was not found in the order by list. All expressions in the compute by list must also be present in the
```

Analysis

The Compute By is operating at the category level (EnglishProductCategoryName). But there's an error, and the error mentions the Order By clause!

Compute By 2/2

This is Compute By again, only this time there's also an Order By clause.

Syntax

```
-- compute by
select EnglishProductCategoryName, EnglishProductSubcategoryName,
EnglishProductName, ListPrice from DimProductCategory as C
inner join DimProductSubcategory as S
on C.ProductCategoryKey = S.ProductCategoryKey
inner join DimProduct as P
on S.ProductSubcategoryKey = P.ProductSubcategoryKey
order by EnglishProductCategoryName
compute MAX(ListPrice), AVG(ListPrice) by EnglishProductCategoryName
```

Result

	EnglishProductCategoryName	EnglishProductSubcategoryName	EnglishProductName	ListPrice
1	Accessories	Helmets	Sport-100 Helmet, Blue	33.6442
2	Accessories	Helmets	Sport-100 Helmet, Blue	33.6442
3	Accessories	Helmets	Sport-100 Helmet, Blue	34.99
4	Accessories	Bike Racks	Hitch Rack - 4-Bike	120.00
5	Accessories	Cleaners	Bike Wash - Dissolver	7.95
6	Accessories	Fenders	Fender Set - Mountain	21.98
7	Accessories	Bike Stands	All-Purpose Bike Stand	159.00
8	Accessories	Hydration Packs	Hydration Pack - 70 oz.	54.99

	max	avg
1	159.00	34.2281

	EnglishProductCategoryName	EnglishProductSubcategoryName	EnglishProductName	ListPrice
1	Bikes	Road Bikes	Road-750 Black, 44	539.99
2	Bikes	Road Bikes	Road-750 Black, 48	539.99
3	Bikes	Road Bikes	Road-750 Black, 52	539.99
4	Bikes	Touring Bikes	Touring-2000 Blue,...	1214.85
5	Bikes	Touring Bikes	Touring-1000 Yello...	2384.07
6	Bikes	Touring Bikes	Touring-1000 Yello...	2384.07
7	Bikes	Touring Bikes	Touring-1000 Yello...	2384.07
8	Bikes	Touring Bikes	Touring-1000 Yello...	2384.07

	max	avg
1	3578.27	1524.5937

Analysis

The column(s) you use in a Compute By clause must also appear in an Order By clause. In addition, the Order By clause must precede the Compute By clause. Wow—eight result sets! You should be able to see the product detail records for each of the four categories and the aggregates for each category, too. You may have to use the outer scroll bar to see all the aggregates. You may have to use the inner scroll bars to see all the details.

The result of a Compute By can be a little difficult to read. To get all of the result sets into a single result set would require some extremely complex and probably inefficient SQL. It also gets quite tricky handing the multiple result sets in client applications. If you find yourself writing lots of Compute and Compute By queries, you are probably ready to start building a multidimensional database. However, that requires SSAS cubes, not SQL Server relational tables. Oh, and it might involve learning the MDX query language as well!

Chapter 9

System Functions

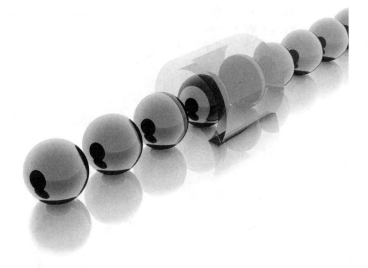

S QL Server has a couple hundred built-in system functions. You can browse them all in Object Explorer where they are arranged by category. You can always write your own functions in SQL, but it makes sense to use the prewritten ones if they serve your purpose. It's going to save you a lot of work and time, if what you want is already there. In this chapter, we investigate some of these system functions. In particular, we concentrate on some of the most popular and useful string functions, mathematical functions, and date functions. A knowledge of these functions will help you to easily manipulate and transform your data, in exactly the way you want to.

▶ **Key concepts**   Using the built-in system functions, string functions, mathematical functions, date functions

▶ **Keywords**   Lower(), Upper(), Left(), Right(), Charindex(), Replace(), Ceiling(), Floor(), Round(), Datepart(), Datename(), Getdate(), Datediff(), Dateadd(), Convert()

Base Query for String Functions

Let's start with a few string functions. This is a base query for these functions.

Syntax

```
-- string functions
-- base query
select distinct EnglishProductName from DimProduct as P
inner join DimProductSubcategory as S
on P.ProductSubcategoryKey = S.ProductSubcategoryKey
inner join DimProductCategory as C
on S.ProductCategoryKey = C.ProductCategoryKey
where EnglishProductCategoryName = 'Bikes'
order by EnglishProductName
```

Result

	EnglishProductName
1	Mountain-100 Black, 38
2	Mountain-100 Black, 42
3	Mountain-100 Black, 44
4	Mountain-100 Black, 48
5	Mountain-100 Silver, 38
6	Mountain-100 Silver, 42
7	Mountain-100 Silver, 44
8	Mountain-100 Silver, 48
9	Mountain-200 Black, 38
10	Mountain-200 Black, 42
11	Mountain-200 Black, 46
12	Mountain-200 Silver, 38
13	Mountain-200 Silver, 42
14	Mountain-200 Silver, 46
15	Mountain-300 Black, 38
16	Mountain-300 Black, 40
17	Mountain-300 Black, 44
18	Mountain-300 Black, 48

Analysis

You should be looking at quite a few bikes.

Lower()

This is your first system function—it's the Lower() string function.

Syntax

```
-- lower
select distinct EnglishProductName, lower(EnglishProductName)
as [Function Result] from DimProduct as P
inner join DimProductSubcategory as S
on P.ProductSubcategoryKey = S.ProductSubcategoryKey
inner join DimProductCategory as C
on S.ProductCategoryKey = C.ProductCategoryKey
where EnglishProductCategoryName = 'Bikes'
order by EnglishProductName
```

Result

	EnglishProductName	Function Result
1	Mountain-100 Black, 38	mountain-100 black, 38
2	Mountain-100 Black, 42	mountain-100 black, 42
3	Mountain-100 Black, 44	mountain-100 black, 44
4	Mountain-100 Black, 48	mountain-100 black, 48
5	Mountain-100 Silver, 38	mountain-100 silver, 38
6	Mountain-100 Silver, 42	mountain-100 silver, 42
7	Mountain-100 Silver, 44	mountain-100 silver, 44
8	Mountain-100 Silver, 48	mountain-100 silver, 48
9	Mountain-200 Black, 38	mountain-200 black, 38
10	Mountain-200 Black, 42	mountain-200 black, 42
11	Mountain-200 Black, 46	mountain-200 black, 46
12	Mountain-200 Silver, 38	mountain-200 silver, 38
13	Mountain-200 Silver, 42	mountain-200 silver, 42
14	Mountain-200 Silver, 46	mountain-200 silver, 46
15	Mountain-300 Black, 38	mountain-300 black, 38
16	Mountain-300 Black, 40	mountain-300 black, 40
17	Mountain-300 Black, 44	mountain-300 black, 44
18	Mountain-300 Black, 48	mountain-300 black, 48

Analysis

This function changes your strings into lowercase, if they are not already in lowercase.

You can browse the system functions in Object Explorer. To do so, expand the Programmability folder under any database, then expand the Functions folder and the System Functions folder. This last folder contains all of the system functions organized into subfolders based on category. As you might expect, string functions are in the String Functions folder, and mathematical functions are in the Mathematical Functions folder. Date functions can be found under the Date and Time Functions folder. Later in the chapter, we're going to use the Convert() function—this appears under the Other Functions folder. If you hover your mouse over a function, you get a tooltip explaining its purpose. If you expand a function, you get a little help with its syntax. As with many other objects in Object Explorer, you can drag and drop the function name into the query editor window to save typing and typos. If you highlight the function in the query editor and press F1, it opens SQL Server Books Online (BOL), giving a full explanation, full syntax, and examples that you can copy and paste. This technique works best if you highlight only the function name without the parentheses.

Upper()

The Upper() function.

Syntax

```
-- upper
select distinct EnglishProductName, upper(EnglishProductName) as
[Function Result] from DimProduct as P
inner join DimProductSubcategory as S
on P.ProductSubcategoryKey = S.ProductSubcategoryKey
inner join DimProductCategory as C
on S.ProductCategoryKey = C.ProductCategoryKey
where EnglishProductCategoryName = 'Bikes'
order by EnglishProductName
```

Result

	EnglishProductName	Function Result
1	Mountain-100 Black, 38	MOUNTAIN-100 BLACK, 38
2	Mountain-100 Black, 42	MOUNTAIN-100 BLACK, 42
3	Mountain-100 Black, 44	MOUNTAIN-100 BLACK, 44
4	Mountain-100 Black, 48	MOUNTAIN-100 BLACK, 48
5	Mountain-100 Silver, 38	MOUNTAIN-100 SILVER, 38
6	Mountain-100 Silver, 42	MOUNTAIN-100 SILVER, 42
7	Mountain-100 Silver, 44	MOUNTAIN-100 SILVER, 44
8	Mountain-100 Silver, 48	MOUNTAIN-100 SILVER, 48
9	Mountain-200 Black, 38	MOUNTAIN-200 BLACK, 38
10	Mountain-200 Black, 42	MOUNTAIN-200 BLACK, 42
11	Mountain-200 Black, 46	MOUNTAIN-200 BLACK, 46
12	Mountain-200 Silver, 38	MOUNTAIN-200 SILVER, 38
13	Mountain-200 Silver, 42	MOUNTAIN-200 SILVER, 42
14	Mountain-200 Silver, 46	MOUNTAIN-200 SILVER, 46
15	Mountain-300 Black, 38	MOUNTAIN-300 BLACK, 38
16	Mountain-300 Black, 40	MOUNTAIN-300 BLACK, 40
17	Mountain-300 Black, 44	MOUNTAIN-300 BLACK, 44
18	Mountain-300 Black, 48	MOUNTAIN-300 BLACK, 48

Analysis

This function changes your strings into uppercase.

Left()

The Left() function.

Syntax

```
-- just road bikes - left (could use like 'Road%')
select distinct EnglishProductName, left(EnglishProductName,4) as
[Function Result] from DimProduct as P
inner join DimProductSubcategory as S
```

```
on P.ProductSubcategoryKey = S.ProductSubcategoryKey
inner join DimProductCategory as C
on S.ProductCategoryKey = C.ProductCategoryKey
where EnglishProductCategoryName = 'Bikes' and
left(EnglishProductName,4) = 'Road'
order by EnglishProductName
```

Result

	EnglishProductName	Function Result
1	Road-150 Red, 44	Road
2	Road-150 Red, 48	Road
3	Road-150 Red, 52	Road
4	Road-150 Red, 56	Road
5	Road-150 Red, 62	Road
6	Road-250 Black, 44	Road
7	Road-250 Black, 48	Road
8	Road-250 Black, 52	Road
9	Road-250 Black, 58	Road
10	Road-250 Red, 44	Road
11	Road-250 Red, 48	Road
12	Road-250 Red, 52	Road
13	Road-250 Red, 58	Road
14	Road-350-W Yellow, 40	Road
15	Road-350-W Yellow, 42	Road
16	Road-350-W Yellow, 44	Road
17	Road-350-W Yellow, 48	Road
18	Road-450 Red, 44	Road

Analysis

Left() is used here in both the column list and the Where clause. The second parameter is the number of characters to return.

Right()

The Right() function.

Syntax

```
-- just size 42 - right
select distinct EnglishProductName, right(EnglishProductName,2) as
[Function Result] from DimProduct as P
inner join DimProductSubcategory as S
on P.ProductSubcategoryKey = S.ProductSubcategoryKey
inner join DimProductCategory as C
```

```
on S.ProductCategoryKey = C.ProductCategoryKey
where EnglishProductCategoryName = 'Bikes' and
right(EnglishProductName,2) = '42'
order by EnglishProductName
```

Result

	EnglishProductName	Function Result
1	Mountain-100 Black, 42	42
2	Mountain-100 Silver, 42	42
3	Mountain-200 Black, 42	42
4	Mountain-200 Silver, 42	42
5	Mountain-400-W Silver, 42	42
6	Mountain-500 Black, 42	42
7	Mountain-500 Silver, 42	42
8	Road-350-W Yellow, 42	42
9	Road-550-W Yellow, 42	42

Analysis

The second parameter of the Right() function is the number of characters to return.

Charindex()

The Charindex() function.

Syntax

```
-- just black - charindex
select distinct EnglishProductName, charindex('Black',EnglishProductName,1)
as [Function Result] from DimProduct as P
inner join DimProductSubcategory as S
on P.ProductSubcategoryKey = S.ProductSubcategoryKey
inner join DimProductCategory as C
on S.ProductCategoryKey = C.ProductCategoryKey
where EnglishProductCategoryName = 'Bikes'
and charindex('Black',EnglishProductName,1) > 0
order by EnglishProductName
```

Result

	EnglishProductName	Function Result
1	Mountain-100 Black, 38	14
2	Mountain-100 Black, 42	14
3	Mountain-100 Black, 44	14
4	Mountain-100 Black, 48	14
5	Mountain-200 Black, 38	14
6	Mountain-200 Black, 42	14
7	Mountain-200 Black, 46	14
8	Mountain-300 Black, 38	14
9	Mountain-300 Black, 40	14
10	Mountain-300 Black, 44	14
11	Mountain-300 Black, 48	14
12	Mountain-500 Black, 40	14
13	Mountain-500 Black, 42	14
14	Mountain-500 Black, 44	14
15	Mountain-500 Black, 48	14
16	Mountain-500 Black, 52	14
17	Road-250 Black, 44	10
18	Road-250 Black, 48	10

Analysis

Charindex() returns the start position of a string within an expression. It's looking for 'Black' within the EnglishProductName column, beginning from the first letter. If there's no match, Charindex() returns 0. The Where clause will only return those products that contain 'Black' and belong to the Bikes category.

Replace()

The Replace() function.

Syntax

```
-- replace black
select distinct EnglishProductName,
replace(EnglishProductName,'Black','Blk') as [Function Result]
from DimProduct as P
inner join DimProductSubcategory as S
on P.ProductSubcategoryKey = S.ProductSubcategoryKey
inner join DimProductCategory as C
on S.ProductCategoryKey = C.ProductCategoryKey
where EnglishProductCategoryName = 'Bikes'
and charindex('Black',EnglishProductName,1) > 0
order by EnglishProductName
```

Result

	EnglishProductName	Function Result
1	Mountain-100 Black, 38	Mountain-100 Blk, 38
2	Mountain-100 Black, 42	Mountain-100 Blk, 42
3	Mountain-100 Black, 44	Mountain-100 Blk, 44
4	Mountain-100 Black, 48	Mountain-100 Blk, 48
5	Mountain-200 Black, 38	Mountain-200 Blk, 38
6	Mountain-200 Black, 42	Mountain-200 Blk, 42
7	Mountain-200 Black, 46	Mountain-200 Blk, 46
8	Mountain-300 Black, 38	Mountain-300 Blk, 38
9	Mountain-300 Black, 40	Mountain-300 Blk, 40
10	Mountain-300 Black, 44	Mountain-300 Blk, 44
11	Mountain-300 Black, 48	Mountain-300 Blk, 48
12	Mountain-500 Black, 40	Mountain-500 Blk, 40
13	Mountain-500 Black, 42	Mountain-500 Blk, 42
14	Mountain-500 Black, 44	Mountain-500 Blk, 44
15	Mountain-500 Black, 48	Mountain-500 Blk, 48
16	Mountain-500 Black, 52	Mountain-500 Blk, 52
17	Road-250 Black, 44	Road-250 Blk, 44
18	Road-250 Black, 48	Road-250 Blk, 48

Analysis

Replace() replaces one string with another string. Here the string 'Black' is replaced with the string 'Blk'.

Base Query for Mathematical Functions

Now maybe we should try some of the mathematical functions. Here's our base query.

Syntax

```
-- numeric
-- base query
select EnglishProductName, ListPrice from DimProduct
where ListPrice is not null
```

Result

	EnglishProductName	ListPrice
1	Sport-100 Helmet, Red	33.6442
2	Sport-100 Helmet, Red	33.6442
3	Sport-100 Helmet, Red	34.99
4	Sport-100 Helmet, Black	33.6442
5	Sport-100 Helmet, Black	33.6442
6	Sport-100 Helmet, Black	34.99
7	Mountain Bike Socks, M	9.50
8	Mountain Bike Socks, L	9.50
9	Sport-100 Helmet, Blue	33.6442
10	Sport-100 Helmet, Blue	33.6442
11	Sport-100 Helmet, Blue	34.99
12	AWC Logo Cap	8.6442
13	AWC Logo Cap	8.6442
14	AWC Logo Cap	8.99
15	Long-Sleeve Logo Jersey, S	48.0673
16	Long-Sleeve Logo Jersey, S	48.0673
17	Long-Sleeve Logo Jersey, S	49.99
18	Long-Sleeve Logo Jersey, M	48.0673

Analysis

The upcoming mathematical functions are going to operate on the ListPrice column.

Ceiling()

The Ceiling() function.

Syntax

```
-- ceiling
select EnglishProductName, ListPrice, ceiling(ListPrice) as
[Function Result] from DimProduct
where ListPrice is not null
```

Result

	EnglishProductName	ListPrice	Function Result
1	Sport-100 Helmet, Red	33.6442	34.00
2	Sport-100 Helmet, Red	33.6442	34.00
3	Sport-100 Helmet, Red	34.99	35.00
4	Sport-100 Helmet, Black	33.6442	34.00
5	Sport-100 Helmet, Black	33.6442	34.00
6	Sport-100 Helmet, Black	34.99	35.00
7	Mountain Bike Socks, M	9.50	10.00
8	Mountain Bike Socks, L	9.50	10.00
9	Sport-100 Helmet, Blue	33.6442	34.00
10	Sport-100 Helmet, Blue	33.6442	34.00
11	Sport-100 Helmet, Blue	34.99	35.00
12	AWC Logo Cap	8.6442	9.00
13	AWC Logo Cap	8.6442	9.00
14	AWC Logo Cap	8.99	9.00
15	Long-Sleeve Logo Jersey, S	48.0673	49.00
16	Long-Sleeve Logo Jersey, S	48.0673	49.00
17	Long-Sleeve Logo Jersey, S	49.99	50.00
18	Long-Sleeve Logo Jersey, M	48.0673	49.00

Analysis

Ceiling() rounds up to the smallest integer greater than or equal to the number.

Floor()

The Floor() function.

Syntax

```
-- floor
select EnglishProductName, ListPrice, floor(ListPrice) as
[Function Result] from DimProduct
where ListPrice is not null
```

Result

	EnglishProductName	ListPrice	Function Result
1	Sport-100 Helmet, Red	33.6442	33.00
2	Sport-100 Helmet, Red	33.6442	33.00
3	Sport-100 Helmet, Red	34.99	34.00
4	Sport-100 Helmet, Black	33.6442	33.00
5	Sport-100 Helmet, Black	33.6442	33.00
6	Sport-100 Helmet, Black	34.99	34.00
7	Mountain Bike Socks, M	9.50	9.00
8	Mountain Bike Socks, L	9.50	9.00
9	Sport-100 Helmet, Blue	33.6442	33.00
10	Sport-100 Helmet, Blue	33.6442	33.00
11	Sport-100 Helmet, Blue	34.99	34.00
12	AWC Logo Cap	8.6442	8.00
13	AWC Logo Cap	8.6442	8.00
14	AWC Logo Cap	8.99	8.00
15	Long-Sleeve Logo Jersey, S	48.0673	48.00
16	Long-Sleeve Logo Jersey, S	48.0673	48.00
17	Long-Sleeve Logo Jersey, S	49.99	49.00
18	Long-Sleeve Logo Jersey, M	48.0673	48.00

Analysis

Floor(), would you believe, is the opposite of Ceiling(). Both functions always return integer values.

Round()

The Round() function.

Syntax

```
-- round
select EnglishProductName, ListPrice, round(ListPrice,2) as
[Function Result] from DimProduct
where ListPrice is not null
```

Result

	EnglishProductName	ListPrice	Function Result
1	Sport-100 Helmet, Red	33.6442	33.64
2	Sport-100 Helmet, Red	33.6442	33.64
3	Sport-100 Helmet, Red	34.99	34.99
4	Sport-100 Helmet, Black	33.6442	33.64
5	Sport-100 Helmet, Black	33.6442	33.64
6	Sport-100 Helmet, Black	34.99	34.99
7	Mountain Bike Socks, M	9.50	9.50
8	Mountain Bike Socks, L	9.50	9.50
9	Sport-100 Helmet, Blue	33.6442	33.64
10	Sport-100 Helmet, Blue	33.6442	33.64
11	Sport-100 Helmet, Blue	34.99	34.99
12	AWC Logo Cap	8.6442	8.64
13	AWC Logo Cap	8.6442	8.64
14	AWC Logo Cap	8.99	8.99
15	Long-Sleeve Logo Jersey, S	48.0673	48.07
16	Long-Sleeve Logo Jersey, S	48.0673	48.07
17	Long-Sleeve Logo Jersey, S	49.99	49.99
18	Long-Sleeve Logo Jersey, M	48.0673	48.07

Analysis

Round(), in this example, is rounding the price to two decimal places. There is an extension to its syntax that you can use for truncation of a number, rather than rounding.

Base Query for Date Functions 1/2

Time for time (or date) functions. We're going to construct the base query in two stages.

Syntax

```
-- dates
-- base query analyze orders by date
select FullDateAlternateKey as [Date], round(SalesAmount,2) as [Sales]
from DimDate as D
inner join FactResellerSales as F
on D.DateKey = F.OrderDateKey
```

Result

	Date	Sales
1	2001-07-01	2024.99
2	2001-07-01	6074.98
3	2001-07-01	2024.99
4	2001-07-01	2039.99
5	2001-07-01	2039.99
6	2001-07-01	4079.99
7	2001-07-01	2039.99
8	2001-07-01	86.52
9	2001-07-01	28.84
10	2001-07-01	34.20
11	2001-07-01	10.37
12	2001-07-01	80.75
13	2001-07-01	419.46
14	2001-07-01	874.79
15	2001-07-01	809.76
16	2001-07-01	714.70
17	2001-07-01	1429.41
18	2001-07-01	20.75

Analysis

The query returns 60,855 rows of dates and sales figures.

Base Query for Date Functions 2/2

Now we're grouping the records by date.

Syntax

```
-- group on date
select FullDateAlternateKey as [Date], round(sum(SalesAmount),2) as
[Sales] from DimDate as D
inner join FactResellerSales as F
on D.DateKey = F.OrderDateKey
group by FullDateAlternateKey
```

Result

	Date	Sales
1	2001-07-01	489328.58
2	2001-08-01	1538408.31
3	2001-09-01	1165897.08
4	2001-10-01	844721.00
5	2001-11-01	2324135.80
6	2001-12-01	1702944.54
7	2002-01-01	713116.69
8	2002-02-01	1900788.93
9	2002-03-01	1455280.41
10	2002-04-01	882899.94
11	2002-05-01	2269116.71
12	2002-06-01	1001803.77
13	2002-07-01	2393689.53
14	2002-08-01	3601190.71
15	2002-09-01	2885359.20
16	2002-10-01	1802154.21
17	2002-11-01	3053816.33
18	2002-12-01	2185213.21

Analysis

This reduces the number of rows to 40 and aggregates sales for each date.

Datepart() 1/5

The Datepart(yy) function.

Syntax

```
-- year
select datepart(yy,FullDateAlternateKey) as [Year],
round(sum(SalesAmount),2) as [Sales] from DimDate as D
inner join FactResellerSales as F
on D.DateKey = F.OrderDateKey
group by FullDateAlternateKey
```

Result

	Year	Sales
1	2001	489328.58
2	2001	1538408.31
3	2001	1165897.08
4	2001	844721.00
5	2001	2324135.80
6	2001	1702944.54
7	2002	713116.69
8	2002	1900788.93
9	2002	1455280.41
10	2002	882899.94
11	2002	2269116.71
12	2002	1001803.77
13	2002	2393689.53
14	2002	3601190.71
15	2002	2885359.20
16	2002	1802154.21
17	2002	3053816.33
18	2002	2185213.21

Analysis

Datepart(yy) extracts the year from a date.

Datepart() 2/5

This query uses the Datepart(yy) function again, but we're also grouping using the function.

Syntax

```
-- group on year
select datepart(yy,FullDateAlternateKey) as [Year],
round(sum(SalesAmount),2) as [Sales] from DimDate as D
inner join FactResellerSales as F
on D.DateKey = F.OrderDateKey
group by datepart(yy,FullDateAlternateKey)
```

Result

	Year	Sales
1	2001	8065435.31
2	2002	24144429.65
3	2003	32202669.43
4	2004	16038062.60

Analysis

You should see only four rows this time.

Datepart() 3/5

The Datepart(qq) function.

Syntax

```
-- by quarter wrong
select datepart(qq,FullDateAlternateKey) as [Quarter],
round(sum(SalesAmount),2) as [Sales] from DimDate as D
inner join FactResellerSales as F
on D.DateKey = F.OrderDateKey
group by datepart(qq,FullDateAlternateKey)
```

Result

	Quarter	Sales
1	1	16438214.65
2	2	19823101.73
3	3	23000069.49
4	4	21189211.10

Analysis

Datepart(qq) returns the quarter of a date. This query gives a result, but it's wrong if you want to see the quarters for each year. The previous query gave four years—surely, there should be more than four quarters?

Datepart() 4/5

The Datepart(qq) function again.

Syntax

```
-- by quarter correct
select datepart(yy,FullDateAlternateKey) as [Year],
datepart(qq,FullDateAlternateKey) as [Quarter],
round(sum(SalesAmount),2) as [Sales] from DimDate as D
inner join FactResellerSales as F
on D.DateKey = F.OrderDateKey
```

```
group by datepart(yy,FullDateAlternateKey),
datepart(qq,FullDateAlternateKey)
order by datepart(yy,FullDateAlternateKey),
datepart(qq,FullDateAlternateKey)
```

Result

	Year	Quarter	Sales
1	2001	3	3193633.97
2	2001	4	4871801.34
3	2002	1	4069186.04
4	2002	2	4153820.42
5	2002	3	8880239.44
6	2002	4	7041183.75
7	2003	1	5266343.51
8	2003	2	6733903.82
9	2003	3	10926196.09
10	2003	4	9276226.01
11	2004	1	7102685.11
12	2004	2	8935377.49

Analysis

This is better. The previous query did not differentiate quarters by year—this one does. The important change is in the Group By clause.

Datepart() 5/5

The Datepart(mm) function. Only a single table (DimDate) is being used in this query.

Syntax

```
-- also months
select FullDateAlternateKey as [Date],
datepart(mm,FullDateAlternateKey) as [Month Number] from DimDate
```

Result

	Date	Month Number
1	2001-07-01	7
2	2001-07-02	7
3	2001-07-03	7
4	2001-07-04	7
5	2001-07-05	7
6	2001-07-06	7
7	2001-07-07	7
8	2001-07-08	7
9	2001-07-09	7
10	2001-07-10	7
11	2001-07-11	7
12	2001-07-12	7
13	2001-07-13	7
14	2001-07-14	7
15	2001-07-15	7
16	2001-07-16	7
17	2001-07-17	7
18	2001-07-18	7

Analysis

Datepart(mm) extracts the month as a number from a date.

Datename() 1/2

The Datename(mm) function.

Syntax

```
-- also as names
select FullDateAlternateKey as [Date],
datename(mm,FullDateAlternateKey) as [Month Name] from DimDate
```

Result

	Date	Month Name
1	2001-07-01	July
2	2001-07-02	July
3	2001-07-03	July
4	2001-07-04	July
5	2001-07-05	July
6	2001-07-06	July
7	2001-07-07	July
8	2001-07-08	July
9	2001-07-09	July
10	2001-07-10	July
11	2001-07-11	July
12	2001-07-12	July
13	2001-07-13	July
14	2001-07-14	July
15	2001-07-15	July
16	2001-07-16	July
17	2001-07-17	July
18	2001-07-18	July

Analysis

Datename(mm) returns the month as a name from a date. Please note that it's Datename(), not Datepart().

Datename() 2/2

The Datename(mm) function again.

Syntax

```
-- handy for star schema
select distinct FullDateAlternateKey as [Date],
'CY ' + cast(datepart(yy, FullDateAlternateKey) as char(4)) + ' '
+ datename(mm,FullDateAlternateKey) as [Calendar Month]
from DimDate
```

Result

	Date	Calendar Month
1	2001-07-01	CY 2001 July
2	2001-07-02	CY 2001 July
3	2001-07-03	CY 2001 July
4	2001-07-04	CY 2001 July
5	2001-07-05	CY 2001 July
6	2001-07-06	CY 2001 July
7	2001-07-07	CY 2001 July
8	2001-07-08	CY 2001 July
9	2001-07-09	CY 2001 July
10	2001-07-10	CY 2001 July
11	2001-07-11	CY 2001 July
12	2001-07-12	CY 2001 July
13	2001-07-13	CY 2001 July
14	2001-07-14	CY 2001 July
15	2001-07-15	CY 2001 July
16	2001-07-16	CY 2001 July
17	2001-07-17	CY 2001 July
18	2001-07-18	CY 2001 July

Analysis

This type of query is going to help you build time dimension attributes for star schemas and cubes. Building relational and multidimensional dimension attributes is beyond the scope of this book—I've included this query for readers who already have some knowledge of those topics.

New Base Query for Date Functions

A change of table and columns, so you can try a few more date functions. The query includes the Getdate() function.

Syntax

```
-- new base query
select FirstName, LastName, BirthDate, getdate() as [Today] from DimEmployee
```

Result

	FirstName	LastName	BirthDate	Today
1	Guy	Gilbert	1972-05-15	2009-08-30 01:18:17.533
2	Kevin	Brown	1977-06-03	2009-08-30 01:18:17.533
3	Roberto	Tamburello	1964-12-13	2009-08-30 01:18:17.533
4	Rob	Walters	1965-01-23	2009-08-30 01:18:17.533
5	Rob	Walters	1965-01-23	2009-08-30 01:18:17.533
6	Thierry	D'Hers	1949-08-29	2009-08-30 01:18:17.533
7	David	Bradley	1965-04-19	2009-08-30 01:18:17.533
8	David	Bradley	1965-04-19	2009-08-30 01:18:17.533
9	JoLynn	Dobney	1946-02-16	2009-08-30 01:18:17.533
10	Ruth	Ellerbrock	1946-07-06	2009-08-30 01:18:17.533
11	Gail	Erickson	1942-10-29	2009-08-30 01:18:17.533
12	Barry	Johnson	1946-04-27	2009-08-30 01:18:17.533
13	Jossef	Goldberg	1949-04-11	2009-08-30 01:18:17.533
14	Terri	Duffy	1961-09-01	2009-08-30 01:18:17.533
15	Sidney	Higa	1946-10-01	2009-08-30 01:18:17.533
16	Taylor	Maxwell	1946-05-03	2009-08-30 01:18:17.533
17	Jeffrey	Ford	1946-08-12	2009-08-30 01:18:17.533
18	Jo	Brown	1946-11-09	2009-08-30 01:18:17.533

Analysis

I guess your Today column is going to show a different result from mine. Getdate() returns a `datetime` data type. If you are using SQL Server 2008 AdventureWorksDW2008 database, BirthDate is a `date` data type (there is no time). If you are using SQL Server 2005 AdventureWorksDW, BirthDate is `datetime`.

Convert()

The Convert() function is applied to the Getdate() function.

Syntax

```
-- in UK try 103
select FirstName, LastName, convert(varchar,BirthDate,101) as
[Birth Date], convert(varchar,getdate(),101) as [Today]
from DimEmployee
```

Result

	FirstName	LastName	Birth Date	Today
1	Guy	Gilbert	05/15/1972	08/30/2009
2	Kevin	Brown	06/03/1977	08/30/2009
3	Roberto	Tamburello	12/13/1964	08/30/2009
4	Rob	Walters	01/23/1965	08/30/2009
5	Rob	Walters	01/23/1965	08/30/2009
6	Thierry	D'Hers	08/29/1949	08/30/2009
7	David	Bradley	04/19/1965	08/30/2009
8	David	Bradley	04/19/1965	08/30/2009
9	JoLynn	Dobney	02/16/1946	08/30/2009
10	Ruth	Ellerbrock	07/06/1946	08/30/2009
11	Gail	Erickson	10/29/1942	08/30/2009
12	Barry	Johnson	04/27/1946	08/30/2009
13	Jossef	Goldberg	04/11/1949	08/30/2009
14	Terri	Duffy	09/01/1961	08/30/2009
15	Sidney	Higa	10/01/1946	08/30/2009
16	Taylor	Maxwell	05/03/1946	08/30/2009
17	Jeffrey	Ford	08/12/1946	08/30/2009
18	Jo	Brown	11/09/1946	08/30/2009

Analysis

The third parameter for the Convert() function is 101—this gives dates in U.S. format. U.K. and other European readers may want to try 103 instead of 101.

Datediff()

The Datediff(yy) function.

Syntax

```
-- datediff to find age
select FirstName, LastName, convert(varchar,BirthDate,101) as
[Birth Date], convert(varchar,getdate(),101) as [Today],
datediff(YY,BirthDate,getdate()) as [Age] from DimEmployee
```

Result

	FirstName	LastName	Birth Date	Today	Age
1	Guy	Gilbert	05/15/1972	08/30/2009	37
2	Kevin	Brown	06/03/1977	08/30/2009	32
3	Roberto	Tamburello	12/13/1964	08/30/2009	45
4	Rob	Walters	01/23/1965	08/30/2009	44
5	Rob	Walters	01/23/1965	08/30/2009	44
6	Thierry	D'Hers	08/29/1949	08/30/2009	60
7	David	Bradley	04/19/1965	08/30/2009	44
8	David	Bradley	04/19/1965	08/30/2009	44
9	JoLynn	Dobney	02/16/1946	08/30/2009	63
10	Ruth	Ellerbrock	07/06/1946	08/30/2009	63
11	Gail	Erickson	10/29/1942	08/30/2009	67
12	Barry	Johnson	04/27/1946	08/30/2009	63
13	Jossef	Goldberg	04/11/1949	08/30/2009	60
14	Terri	Duffy	09/01/1961	08/30/2009	48
15	Sidney	Higa	10/01/1946	08/30/2009	63
16	Taylor	Maxwell	05/03/1946	08/30/2009	63
17	Jeffrey	Ford	08/12/1946	08/30/2009	63
18	Jo	Brown	11/09/1946	08/30/2009	63

Analysis

Your Today and Age columns are likely to be different from mine. Datediff(yy) works out the number of years between two dates.

Dateadd 1/2

The Dateadd(yy) function.

Syntax

```
-- dateadd to find retirement date
select FirstName, LastName, convert(varchar,BirthDate,101) as [Birth
Date], datediff(YY,BirthDate,getdate()) as [Age], convert(varchar,dateadd
(yy,65,BirthDate),101) as [Retirement Day?] from DimEmployee
```

Result

	FirstName	LastName	Birth Date	Age	Retirement Day?
1	Guy	Gilbert	05/15/1972	37	05/15/2037
2	Kevin	Brown	06/03/1977	32	06/03/2042
3	Roberto	Tamburello	12/13/1964	45	12/13/2029
4	Rob	Walters	01/23/1965	44	01/23/2030
5	Rob	Walters	01/23/1965	44	01/23/2030
6	Thierry	D'Hers	08/29/1949	60	08/29/2014
7	David	Bradley	04/19/1965	44	04/19/2030
8	David	Bradley	04/19/1965	44	04/19/2030
9	JoLynn	Dobney	02/16/1946	63	02/16/2011
10	Ruth	Ellerbrock	07/06/1946	63	07/06/2011
11	Gail	Erickson	10/29/1942	67	10/29/2007
12	Barry	Johnson	04/27/1946	63	04/27/2011
13	Jossef	Goldberg	04/11/1949	60	04/11/2014
14	Terri	Duffy	09/01/1961	48	09/01/2026
15	Sidney	Higa	10/01/1946	63	10/01/2011
16	Taylor	Maxwell	05/03/1946	63	05/03/2011
17	Jeffrey	Ford	08/12/1946	63	08/12/2011
18	Jo	Brown	11/09/1946	63	11/09/2011

Analysis

Dateadd(yy) adds a number of years (65) to a date—the assumption here is that 65 is the retirement age.

Dateadd 2/2

The Datediff(yy) and Dateadd(yy) functions again.

Syntax

```
-- who is near or past retirement age?
select FirstName, LastName, convert(varchar,BirthDate,101) as
[Birth Date], datediff(YY,BirthDate,getdate()) as [Age], convert(varchar,
dateadd(yy,65,BirthDate),101) as [Retirement Day?] from DimEmployee
where datediff(YY,BirthDate,getdate()) >= 60
order by datediff(YY,BirthDate,getdate()) desc
```

Result

	FirstName	LastName	Birth Date	Age	Retirement Day?
1	José	Saraiva	01/11/1930	79	01/11/1995
2	Gordon	Hee	12/30/1932	77	12/30/1997
3	Kim	Abercrombie	01/14/1933	76	01/14/1998
4	Betsy	Stadick	01/17/1933	76	01/17/1998
5	Eric	Brown	01/08/1933	76	01/08/1998
6	Sootha	Charncherngkha	01/05/1933	76	01/05/1998
7	Shu	Ito	04/10/1934	75	04/10/1999
8	Stephen	Jiang	11/17/1941	68	11/17/2006
9	Frank	Pellow	06/13/1942	67	06/13/2007
10	Frank	Martinez	04/03/1942	67	04/03/2007
11	Gail	Erickson	10/29/1942	67	10/29/2007
12	Prasanna	Samarawickrama	06/01/1943	66	06/01/2008
13	Jo	Berry	05/25/1944	65	05/25/2009
14	Maciej	Dusza	03/02/1945	64	03/02/2010
15	Barry	Johnson	04/27/1946	63	04/27/2011
16	JoLynn	Dobney	02/16/1946	63	02/16/2011
17	Ruth	Ellerbrock	07/06/1946	63	07/06/2011
18	Sidney	Higa	10/01/1946	63	10/01/2011

Analysis

The result is a list of employees who are 60 or over (in descending order of age) on the day you run the query. It also shows age and possible retirement dates.

Chapter 10

Subqueries

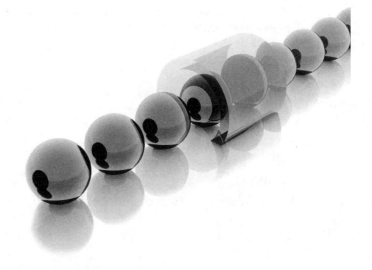

T his chapter looks at queries within queries—that's Select statements with Select statements. These are often called *subqueries* or *nested queries*. Subqueries have lots of uses, some of them quite advanced, like derived tables. As this is an introductory book, we'll concentrate on one of the more popular and simpler uses for subqueries. We examine how to use a subquery in a Where clause. As is often the case, there are many ways of doing the same thing in SQL. You can arrive at the same results as you do with subqueries by possibly using joins or temporary tables or some procedural programming with variables. Those other topics are covered in other chapters in this book.

- ▶ **Key concepts** Subqueries or nested queries
- ▶ **Keywords** Select, In, Exists, Not, Any, All

Where Revision

This chapter is going to have subqueries (or nested queries) in Where clauses. Here are four queries to give you some revision of simple Where clauses—if you need it.

Syntax

```
-- simple where revision
select FirstName, LastName from DimEmployee
where LastName = 'Munson'
select FirstName, LastName from DimEmployee
where LastName <> 'Munson'
select FirstName, LastName from DimEmployee
where LastName in ('Munson','Brown')
select FirstName, LastName from DimEmployee
where LastName not in ('Munson','Brown')
```

Result

	FirstName	LastName
1	Kevin	Brown
2	Jo	Brown
3	Stuart	Munson
4	Eric	Brown

Analysis

The result shown is from the third of the four Select statements.

Subquery In

There are two Selects and two tables in one query. The second Select, in parentheses, is
the subquery.

Syntax

```
-- employee and customer table no direct join
-- same surname
select FirstName, LastName from DimEmployee
where LastName in (select LastName from DimCustomer)
```

Result

	FirstName	LastName
1	Frank	Lee
2	Kimberly	Zimmerman
3	Samantha	Smith
4	Denise	Smith
5	Shane	Kim
6	John	Campbell
7	David	Campbell
8	Dan	Wilson
9	Ashvini	Sharma
10	Lane	Sacksteder
11	Barry	Johnson
12	David	Johnson
13	Willis	Johnson
14	Patrick	Wedge
15	Michael	Ray
16	Michael	Rothkugel
17	Janet	Sheperdigian
18	Ken	Sánchez

Analysis

The result is a list of your employees who share surnames with your customers. The
subquery must be enclosed within parentheses. A good way to test queries containing
subqueries is to make sure the subquery itself works. This is true for the subqueries in this
book—there is a type of subquery called a *correlated subquery* where it no longer holds.
You test by highlighting the subquery and executing it individually as a stand-alone query.
If it fails, the whole query (the outer and inner queries together) is also going to fail. This
subquery could be rewritten as a join between the tables. You can do this, even if there
is no primary-to-foreign-key relationship between the tables. In this example, the join
column would be LastName.

Subquery Not In

This variation on the previous query includes the logical operator Not.

Syntax

```
-- different surnames
select FirstName, LastName from DimEmployee
where LastName not in (select LastName from DimCustomer)
```

Result

	FirstName	LastName
1	Guy	Gilbert
2	Roberto	Tamburello
3	Rob	Walters
4	Rob	Walters
5	Thierry	D'Hers
6	JoLynn	Dobney
7	Ruth	Ellerbrock
8	Gail	Erickson
9	Terri	Duffy
10	Sidney	Higa
11	Taylor	Maxwell
12	Jeffrey	Ford
13	Doris	Hartwig
14	Diane	Glimp
15	Peter	Krebs
16	Stuart	Munson
17	Greg	Alderson
18	Zheng	Mu

Analysis

You should be looking at a list of employees who do not share surnames with your customers.

Subquery Exists

This time our two queries contain the Exists keyword and the subqueries have their own Where clauses.

Syntax

```
-- exists
select FirstName, LastName from DimEmployee
where exists (select LastName from DimCustomer where LastName =
'Zimmerman')
--
select FirstName, LastName from DimEmployee
where exists (select LastName from DimCustomer where LastName = 'Munson')
```

Result

FirstName	LastName

Analysis

The result shown is from the second of the two queries. The keyword Exists tests to see if there are any records in the subquery. The first query returns all of your employees only if there are one or more customers with a LastName of Zimmerman. The second query does so if one or more customers have a surname of Munson. As that query returns no employees, it means no customer has a LastName of Munson. On large tables, you may find that using an asterisk (*) rather than a specific column name in the subquery Select is more efficient.

Subquery Not Exists

This time, we're using Not Exists.

Syntax

```
-- not exists
select FirstName, LastName from DimEmployee
where not exists (select LastName from DimCustomer
where LastName = 'Zimmerman')
--
select FirstName, LastName from DimEmployee
where not exists (select LastName from DimCustomer
where LastName = 'Munson')
```

Result

	FirstName	LastName
1	Guy	Gilbert
2	Kevin	Brown
3	Roberto	Tamburello
4	Rob	Walters
5	Rob	Walters
6	Thierry	D'Hers
7	David	Bradley
8	David	Bradley
9	JoLynn	Dobney
10	Ruth	Ellerbrock
11	Gail	Erickson
12	Barry	Johnson
13	Jossef	Goldberg
14	Terri	Duffy
15	Sidney	Higa
16	Taylor	Maxwell
17	Jeffrey	Ford
18	Jo	Brown

Analysis

The results of these two queries are the opposite of those from the previous two queries. The result shown here is from the second query. You can see your employees because no customer has a LastName of Munson.

Base Query

In order to explore subqueries a little more, we need a new base query.

Syntax

```
-- new base query
-- inner query first 1742 is largest average
select avg(ListPrice) from DimProduct
group by ProductSubcategoryKey
order by avg(ListPrice) asc
```

Result

	(No column name)
1	NULL
2	7.95
3	7.99
4	8.7594
5	9.245
6	19.4827
7	20.24
8	21.98
9	22.49
10	25.00
11	28.676
12	31.3233
13	34.0928
14	39.6333
15	50.0286
16	54.99
17	63.50
18	64.0185

Analysis

The lowest, non-null, average price of the products within each subcategory is 7.95.
There is also a null value for one of the subcategories. The highest average price is
about 1742—you may need to scroll to the end to see it.

Subquery Any

There are a couple of points to make. First, the outer query has the Any keyword in its
Where clause. Second, the Order By clause is part of the outer query—Order By does
not work inside a subquery.

Syntax

```
-- any
-- remove inner order by
select EnglishProductName, ListPrice from DimProduct
where ListPrice > any(select avg(ListPrice) from DimProduct
group by ProductSubcategoryKey)
order by ListPrice asc
```

Result

	EnglishProductName	ListPrice
1	AWC Logo Cap	8.6442
2	AWC Logo Cap	8.6442
3	AWC Logo Cap	8.99
4	Road Bottle Cage	8.99
5	Racing Socks, M	8.99
6	Racing Socks, L	8.99
7	Mountain Bike Socks, M	9.50
8	Mountain Bike Socks, L	9.50
9	Mountain Bottle Cage	9.99
10	Taillights - Battery-Powered	13.99
11	Minipump	19.99
12	Chain	20.24
13	LL Road Tire	21.49
14	Fender Set - Mountain	21.98
15	Half-Finger Gloves, S	23.5481
16	Half-Finger Gloves, M	23.5481
17	Half-Finger Gloves, L	23.5481
18	Half-Finger Gloves, L	24.49

Analysis

This is quite a tricky query to decipher. It's asking for a list of products whose price is greater than *any* of the average list prices from the subquery. The lowest average is 7.95. Therefore it's showing all of those products with a ListPrice of more than 7.95.

Subquery All 1/2

The keyword Any has been replaced by the keyword All.

Syntax

```
-- all with nulls
select EnglishProductName, ListPrice from DimProduct
where ListPrice > all(select avg(ListPrice) from DimProduct
group by ProductSubcategoryKey)
order by ListPrice asc
```

Result

EnglishProductName	ListPrice

Analysis

The query returns no records. It's looking for all products with a price greater than all of the average prices from the subquery. In other words, it's looking for all those products whose price is greater than the highest of the subcategory average prices. That figure is about 1742—from two queries ago. But there was an average price (two queries ago) with a null value. A null value, if you like, is indeterminate—so the figure of 1742 cannot be guaranteed to *really* be the maximum. The maximum is unknown, so the outer query fails to show any records.

Subquery All 2/2

I've added a Having clause to the subquery—this is going to eliminate all average prices with null values.

Syntax

```
-- all without nulls
select EnglishProductName, ListPrice from DimProduct
where ListPrice > all(select avg(ListPrice) from DimProduct group by
ProductSubcategoryKey having avg(ListPrice) is not null)
order by ListPrice asc
```

Result

	EnglishProductName	ListPrice
1	Mountain-200 Black, 38	2049.0982
2	Mountain-200 Black, 46	2049.0982
3	Mountain-200 Black, 42	2049.0982
4	Mountain-200 Silver, 46	2071.4196
5	Mountain-200 Silver, 38	2071.4196
6	Mountain-200 Silver, 42	2071.4196
7	Road-250 Red, 58	2181.5625
8	Road-250 Black, 44	2181.5625
9	Road-250 Black, 48	2181.5625
10	Road-250 Black, 52	2181.5625
11	Road-250 Black, 58	2181.5625
12	Mountain-200 Black, 42	2294.99
13	Mountain-200 Black, 38	2294.99
14	Mountain-200 Black, 46	2294.99
15	Mountain-200 Silver, 46	2319.99
16	Mountain-200 Silver, 42	2319.99
17	Mountain-200 Silver, 38	2319.99
18	Touring-1000 Yellow, 46	2384.07

Analysis

With the null average prices removed from the subquery, the maximum average price for any subcategory is *definitely* about 1742. The outer query can therefore now return all those products with a price greater than that maximum average price. The ListPrice of such products starts at around 2049 and rises to about 3578.

Chapter 11

Delete/Insert/Update

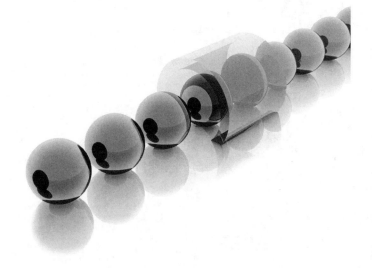

Many of the other chapters deal with getting data out of your tables and databases—lots and lots of Select statements. This assumes, of course, that the data is already there and is in the form you require it. By contrast, this chapter is dedicated to entering and maintaining the data in the first place. Without data, your Select statements will return nothing. Without good data, your Select statements will return erroneous or obsolete data. Here, we look at data entry using the Insert statement and maintaining data accuracy with the Update statement. In addition, you learn how to remove obsolete or unwanted data with the Delete statement. There are also example queries showing how to work with identity (auto-numbering) columns.

▶ **Key concepts** Inserting records, updating records, deleting records, truncating tables, dropping tables, working with identity columns

▶ **Keywords** Insert Into ... Select, Insert Into ... Values, Select Into, Update ... Set, Delete, Truncate Table, DBCC Checkident(), Set Identity_Insert, Drop Table

Select Into

Our first query in this chapter creates a new table, Scenario, based on an existing table called DimScenario. There's a second Select to test this new table. The new table is used for exercises shortly. The first query also demonstrates Select Into, which is one way (out of a few) to put data into a table.

Syntax

```
-- base table select into
select *
into Scenario
from DimScenario
--
select * from Scenario
```

Result

	ScenarioKey	ScenarioName
1	1	Actual
2	2	Budget
3	3	Forecast

Analysis

Select Into creates a new table and populates it with data from the source table. If the destination table already exists, the query will fail. To put data into an existing table from a source table, you use Insert Select, not Select Into. If you don't have a source table, you can manually enter data with Insert Values. Both Insert Select and Insert Values are also covered in this chapter.

Truncate Table

Here's a Truncate Table query followed by a Select.

Syntax

```
-- truncate
truncate table Scenario
--
select * from Scenario
```

Result

ScenarioKey	ScenarioName

Analysis

Truncate Table removes all the data from the table. It does not remove the table. You can also use Delete to remove data from a table—Delete is discussed shortly. Truncate Table is faster than Delete on large tables. However, Truncate Table is never logged (Delete is logged if you have logging turned on—through the Recovery Model property of a database), which means it's more difficult to recover after an accidental removal of records. In addition, Truncate Table will fail if the table is involved in a referential integrity relationship with another table. Here it works fine, and you should be left with an empty Scenario table.

Drop Table (the next query) is completely different from Truncate Table and Delete. The latter two leave the table structure intact. Drop Table not only removes the data from the table but it also removes the table itself.

Drop Table

This is a Drop Table query followed by a Select to test the results.

Syntax

```
-- drop
drop table Scenario
--
select * from Scenario
```

Result

```
Msg 208, Level 16, State 1, Line 4
Invalid object name 'Scenario'.
```

Analysis

Our new Scenario table has disappeared completely.

Delete

There are a total of four queries here. The initial Select Into re-creates the new Scenario table and populates it with data from the DimScenario table. That's followed by a normal Select to verify the results. Then there's a Delete statement and a final Select statement to see what the Delete has done.

Syntax

```
-- delete
select *
into Scenario
from DimScenario
--
select * from Scenario
-- delete from works too
delete Scenario
--
select * from Scenario
```

Result

ScenarioKey	ScenarioName

Analysis

The result is from the last Select showing the effect of the Delete statement. Instead of Delete, you can use Delete From. The effect of a Delete is similar to that of a Truncate

Table—there is a small difference that we examine later. Please remember that Delete is safer than Truncate Table as it is logged. In addition, a Delete can have a Where clause so you don't have to Delete all the records. Truncate Table always deletes every single record.

Select Into

Our Scenario table is now empty after the last Delete. Here's a Select Into to try and repopulate it with records.

Syntax

```
-- error
select *
into Scenario
from DimScenario
```

Result

```
Msg 2714, Level 16, State 6, Line 2
There is already an object named 'Scenario' in the database.
```

Analysis

Select Into does not work if the table already exists. In such a case, you have to use Insert Into … Select or Insert Into … Values. There is another possibility, Insert Into … Exec—this one is not covered in this book.

Insert Into … Select 1/3

The previous Select Into failed as the table already existed. Instead, let's try an Insert Into … Select, which is one way to enter data into existing tables.

Syntax

```
-- also an error
insert into Scenario
select * from DimScenario
```

Result

```
Msg 8101, Level 16, State 1, Line 2
An explicit value for the identity column in table 'Scenario' can only be specified when a column list is used and IDENTI
```

Analysis

We seem to have a problem with something called an identity column. An identity column is auto-numbering. SQL Server automatically enters data in the column for you. By default, it won't let you enter your own values. When you use Select Into to create a new table, it will also make a column into an identity if such a column exists in the source table. In the original DimScenario table, the ScenarioKey is an identity column. Also, the ScenarioKey column in our new Scenario table is an identity. Our Insert Into ... Select is trying to copy data into this identity column, which is why it fails.

Insert Into ... Select 2/3

This time we are only going to insert data into one column.

Syntax

```
-- better?
insert into Scenario
select ScenarioName from DimScenario
```

Result

```
(3 row(s) affected)
```

Analysis

You should see that three rows are affected. Our Insert Into ... Select has worked.

Insert Into ... Select 3/3

This is even better. You have explicitly listed the destination column as well as the source column.

Syntax

```
-- even better
insert into Scenario (ScenarioName)
select ScenarioName from DimScenario
--
select * from Scenario
```

Result

	ScenarioKey	ScenarioName
1	4	Actual
2	5	Budget
3	6	Forecast
4	7	Actual
5	8	Budget
6	9	Forecast

Analysis

If you followed the steps exactly so far, you should have six rows. Three records were inserted by the last query and three by this query. But if you look carefully, the identity column ScenarioKey now starts at number 4!

Truncate Table with Identity

Let's clear out the table with a Truncate Table before our next Insert Into ... Select.

Syntax

```
-- identities!
truncate table Scenario
--
insert into Scenario (ScenarioName)
select ScenarioName from DimScenario
--
select * from Scenario
```

Result

	ScenarioKey	ScenarioName
1	1	Actual
2	2	Budget
3	3	Forecast

Analysis

The ScenarioKey column now starts at 1. Truncate Table resets an identity column so it can start auto-numbering from the beginning again.

Delete with Identity 1/2

This time, we'll use Delete rather than Truncate Table before repopulating the Scenario table.

Syntax

```
-- delete again
delete Scenario
-- delete from Scenario also works
--
insert into Scenario (ScenarioName)
select ScenarioName from DimScenario
--
select * from Scenario
```

Result

	ScenarioKey	ScenarioName
1	4	Actual
2	5	Budget
3	6	Forecast

Analysis

Now ScenarioKey starts at 4. It picks up where it left off counting last time. Delete (unlike Truncate Table) does not reset the identity column.

Delete with Identity 2/2

So, how do you reset an identity column after a Delete? The second query here uses DBCC Checkident().

Syntax

```
-- delete with identities
delete Scenario
-- reseed
dbcc checkident(Scenario, reseed, 0)
--
insert into Scenario (ScenarioName)
select ScenarioName from DimScenario
--
select * from Scenario
```

Result

	ScenarioKey	ScenarioName
1	1	Actual
2	2	Budget
3	3	Forecast

Analysis

Your ScenarioKey column should start at 1 again. DBCC Checkident() accepts a table name, the Reseed keyword, and a reseed value. This is all a bit convoluted, so why bother?

Truncate Table removes all the records from a table. Delete (without a Where clause) does the same. Truncate Table resets the identity column but Delete does not. However, Truncate Table can be dangerous as it's not logged. Anyway, it will not work if the table is involved in a referential integrity relationship. So you may prefer to or be forced to use Delete to clear out a table. But why bother worrying about reseeding the identity column with DBCC Checkident after a Delete? Okay, it looks nicer if it restarts at 1 again. More importantly, though, you might simply run out of numbers, and further inserts will not work. The point at which you are going to run out of numbers depends on the data type of the identity column. Tinyint limits you to a couple of hundred, smallint has a limit of just over 32,000, and the int limit is somewhere around two billion. In terms of performance and storage space, tinyint is better than smallint, which, in turn, is better than int. You are going to hit a trade-off between performance and number limits. DBCC Checkident(), which resets the identity column, can help you avoid this trade-off.

Delete with Where

If all is well, you should have three records in the new Scenario table, starting with an identity column value of 1. So far, our Truncate Table and Delete statements have managed to remove *all* the records from the table each time. Truncate Table and Delete can be very, very dangerous! Delete is a little safer if you have logging turned on (through the Recovery Model property of a database)—it's easy to undo it. Delete is a lot safer if you remember to add a Where clause (Truncate Table does not support the Where clause).

Syntax

```
-- delete with where
delete Scenario
where ScenarioName = 'Budget'
--
select * from Scenario
```

Result

	ScenarioKey	ScenarioName
1	1	Actual
2	3	Forecast

Analysis

You should have two records intact. The Delete has a Where clause, which means that only one record (for Budget) gets removed.

Re-creating Base Table

Before we move onto another topic, Update, let's re-create the Scenario table again.

Syntax

```
-- reset
truncate table Scenario
--
insert into Scenario (ScenarioName)
select ScenarioName from DimScenario
--
select * from Scenario
```

Result

	ScenarioKey	ScenarioName
1	1	Actual
2	2	Budget
3	3	Forecast

Analysis

You are back to three rows.

Update

This is the Update … Set syntax. As you might expect, Update changes existing data.

Syntax

```
-- update
-- one column
update Scenario
set ScenarioName = 'Revised forecast'
--
select * from Scenario
```

Result

	ScenarioKey	ScenarioName
1	1	Revised forecast
2	2	Revised forecast
3	3	Revised forecast

Analysis

Whoops, I forgot to use a Where clause! All the ScenarioName columns now have the same data.

Update with Where 1/2

In this query, we have a Where clause with the Update statement.

Syntax

```
-- where clause doesn't have to be same column
update Scenario
set ScenarioName = 'New revised forecast'
where ScenarioKey = 3
--
select * from Scenario
```

Result

	ScenarioKey	ScenarioName
1	1	Revised forecast
2	2	Revised forecast
3	3	New revised forecast

Analysis

Hopefully, we all just learned a very important lesson. An Update without a Where will update every single record in the table. Similarly, a Delete without a Where will remove all of the records from a table. Unless you have a very good reason not to, Updates and Deletes should always be written with a Where clause.

Update with Where 2/2

You can update more than one column by having a comma-separated list of column names and their new values.

Syntax

```
-- two columns, fails because of identity
update Scenario
set ScenarioKey = 99,
ScenarioName = 'Budget'
where ScenarioKey = 3
```

Result

```
Msg 8102, Level 16, State 1, Line 2
Cannot update identity column 'ScenarioKey'.
```

Analysis

ScenarioKey is an identity column. You can't update the number that SQL Server has already automatically assigned to the column. If you must change an identity value, you have to delete the record and re-insert it.

Re-creating Base Table

We're going to try to override an identity column. First, we need to get our Scenario table back to how it was.

Syntax

```
-- insert - reset table first
drop table Scenario
--
select *
into Scenario
from DimScenario
--
select * from Scenario
```

Result

	ScenarioKey	ScenarioName
1	1	Actual
2	2	Budget
3	3	Forecast

Analysis

Instead of Drop Table followed by Select Into, we could have used Delete (or Truncate Table) followed by Insert … Select. Both Drop Table and Truncate Table will reseed the identity without the need for DBCC Checkident().

Insert … Values 1/3

Let's attempt to force a value into the first column, which is the identity column ScenarioKey.

Syntax

```
-- insert values table
insert into Scenario
values(99,'Forecast 2011')
```

Result

```
Msg 8101, Level 16, State 1, Line 2
An explicit value for the identity column in table 'Scenario' can only be specified when a column list is used and IDENTI
```

Analysis

Not only can you not update an identity, but by default, you can't insert one either. The next query shows a way around this.

Insert … Values 2/3

The first query here introduces Set Identity_Insert. The second query (the first Insert) will fail. The third query (the second Insert) should work.

Syntax

```
-- identity column
set identity_insert Scenario on
--
```

```
insert into Scenario
values(99,'Forecast 2011')
--
insert into Scenario (ScenarioKey, ScenarioName)
values(99,'Forecast 2011')
--
set identity_insert Scenario off
--
select * from Scenario
```

Result

	ScenarioKey	ScenarioName
1	99	Forecast 2011
2	1	Actual
3	2	Budget
4	3	Forecast

Analysis

The second Insert worked as it has a column list—this is obligatory for inserting identities. This is how you override an identity column. But why might you want to do so? There are a number of reasons for doing this. When you delete records, the identity number is not reused. You can use the method here to fill the "gaps" with new records—this will prevent SQL Server from hitting the number limit, especially if it's a tinyint or smallint column. Or maybe you must have a specific number for a specific ScenarioName, especially if the identity column is the primary key. If you've already got a ScenarioName with a number you don't want, simply delete it and re-insert it as here.

Insert ... Values 3/3

Here are a couple of variations on Insert syntax. Both Inserts should succeed.

Syntax

```
-- insert values table again
insert into Scenario (ScenarioName)
values ('Forecast 2012')
-- shorthand
insert into Scenario
values ('Forecast 2013')
--
select * from Scenario
```

Result

	ScenarioKey	ScenarioName
1	99	Forecast 2011
2	100	Forecast 2012
3	101	Forecast 2013
4	1	Actual
5	2	Budget
6	3	Forecast

Analysis

The first Insert explicitly nominates the destination column—the second Insert does not. Yet, the second Insert works too. SQL Server will automatically populate the identity column in a table, so it knows that, and values in the Value list should go into your nonidentity column(s). If you have more than one column, then you need a comma-separated list of values.

Insert Select

This query is for practice.

Syntax

```
-- insert select
insert into Scenario
select ScenarioName from DimScenario
--
select * from Scenario
```

Result

	ScenarioKey	ScenarioName
1	99	Forecast 2011
2	100	Forecast 2012
3	101	Forecast 2013
4	102	Actual
5	103	Budget
6	104	Forecast
7	1	Actual
8	2	Budget
9	3	Forecast

Analysis

Please note the ScenarioKey values for the three new records.

Drop Table

Let's get rid of our practice table.

Syntax

```
-- drop table to clean up
drop table Scenario
```

Result

```
Command(s) completed successfully.
```

Analysis

Hopefully, you should be back to an unblemished Adventure Works.

Chapter 12

Views/User-Defined Functions

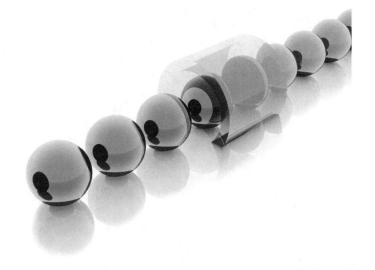

A s business user demands for more and more sophisticated reports increase, your SQL is going to become more and more complex. Rather than having to code the same syntax over and over again, you can save your SQL. There are three main ways of doing this. You can create views for complex Select statements—a *view* is really a stored query. You (and others) can reuse it at any time, without having to be aware of all the complex SQL you originally put into it. This is called *encapsulation*. A second way of saving SQL is to create your own user-defined functions. These are normally used for storing calculations (we are not going to cover table functions that can store Selects). A third way is to create stored procedures. Stored procedures can be used to store both calculations and Selects. Views and functions are covered in this chapter. The next chapter discusses stored procedures. Functions and stored procedures allow you to do sophisticated procedural programming, which views do not.

▶   **Key concepts**   Creating views, encapsulating and hiding complex SQL, creating your own functions

▶   **Keywords**   Create View, Alter View, Drop View, Create Function, Drop Function

Select from Tables

Here's some moderately complex SQL—it's a Select joining three tables.

Syntax

```
-- a select
select EnglishProductName, EnglishProductSubcategoryName,
EnglishProductCategoryName from DimProduct as P
inner join DimProductSubcategory as S
on P.ProductSubcategoryKey = S.ProductSubcategoryKey
inner join DimProductCategory as C
on S.ProductCategoryKey = C.ProductCategoryKey
where EnglishProductCategoryName = 'Bikes' or
EnglishProductCategoryName = 'Accessories'
```

Result

	EnglishProductName	EnglishProductSubcategoryName	EnglishProductCategoryName
1	Sport-100 Helmet, Red	Helmets	Accessories
2	Sport-100 Helmet, Red	Helmets	Accessories
3	Sport-100 Helmet, Red	Helmets	Accessories
4	Sport-100 Helmet, Black	Helmets	Accessories
5	Sport-100 Helmet, Black	Helmets	Accessories
6	Sport-100 Helmet, Black	Helmets	Accessories
7	Sport-100 Helmet, Blue	Helmets	Accessories
8	Sport-100 Helmet, Blue	Helmets	Accessories
9	Sport-100 Helmet, Blue	Helmets	Accessories
10	Road-150 Red, 62	Road Bikes	Bikes
11	Road-150 Red, 44	Road Bikes	Bikes
12	Road-150 Red, 48	Road Bikes	Bikes
13	Road-150 Red, 52	Road Bikes	Bikes
14	Road-150 Red, 56	Road Bikes	Bikes
15	Road-450 Red, 58	Road Bikes	Bikes
16	Road-450 Red, 60	Road Bikes	Bikes
17	Road-450 Red, 44	Road Bikes	Bikes
18	Road-450 Red, 48	Road Bikes	Bikes

Analysis

It would be nice not to have to type this every time you needed it. It might also be useful if you could make it easily available to other SQL developers in your company.

Create View

This is the same Select as in the last query, but it has Create View syntax before the Select.

Syntax

```
-- a view
create view MyView as
select EnglishProductName, EnglishProductSubcategoryName,
EnglishProductCategoryName from DimProduct as P
inner join DimProductSubcategory as S
on P.ProductSubcategoryKey = S.ProductSubcategoryKey
inner join DimProductCategory as C
on S.ProductCategoryKey = C.ProductCategoryKey
where EnglishProductCategoryName = 'Bikes'
or EnglishProductCategoryName = 'Accessories'
```

Result

```
Command(s) completed successfully.
```

Analysis

You'll notice that the Select itself doesn't run—there are no rows returned. It's good practice to give the view a name that describes its purpose—I guess MyView is not a particularly good name! Your SQL is now stored in the view. You can see the view in Object Explorer under the Views folder for the database—you may need to right-click and choose Refresh first on the folder. It's gone into the dbo schema.

Select from View

Using a view you've created is straightforward.

Syntax

```
-- encapsulation
select * from MyView
```

Result

	EnglishProductName	EnglishProductSubcategoryName	EnglishProductCategoryName
1	Sport-100 Helmet, Red	Helmets	Accessories
2	Sport-100 Helmet, Red	Helmets	Accessories
3	Sport-100 Helmet, Red	Helmets	Accessories
4	Sport-100 Helmet, Black	Helmets	Accessories
5	Sport-100 Helmet, Black	Helmets	Accessories
6	Sport-100 Helmet, Black	Helmets	Accessories
7	Sport-100 Helmet, Blue	Helmets	Accessories
8	Sport-100 Helmet, Blue	Helmets	Accessories
9	Sport-100 Helmet, Blue	Helmets	Accessories
10	Road-150 Red, 62	Road Bikes	Bikes
11	Road-150 Red, 44	Road Bikes	Bikes
12	Road-150 Red, 48	Road Bikes	Bikes
13	Road-150 Red, 52	Road Bikes	Bikes
14	Road-150 Red, 56	Road Bikes	Bikes
15	Road-450 Red, 58	Road Bikes	Bikes
16	Road-450 Red, 60	Road Bikes	Bikes
17	Road-450 Red, 44	Road Bikes	Bikes
18	Road-450 Red, 48	Road Bikes	Bikes

Analysis

This is encapsulation (the original complex SQL is hidden) and reusability. Subject to permissions, it's also available to other SQL developers and report designers—they don't have to know anything more than how to write a simple Select like the one here.

Alter View 1/2

You can retrospectively change a view, too. Here, we're trying to change the product categories in the Where clause.

Syntax

```
-- altering a view error
create view MyView as
select EnglishProductName, EnglishProductSubcategoryName,
EnglishProductCategoryName from DimProduct as P
inner join DimProductSubcategory as S
on P.ProductSubcategoryKey = S.ProductSubcategoryKey
inner join DimProductCategory as C
on S.ProductCategoryKey = C.ProductCategoryKey
where EnglishProductCategoryName = 'Clothing' or
EnglishProductCategoryName = 'Components'
```

Result

```
Msg 2714, Level 16, State 3, Procedure MyView, Line 3
There is already an object named 'MyView' in the database.
```

Analysis

You can't run Create View more than once on the same view.

Alter View 2/2

Instead, you might want to try this Alter View. It's followed by a simple Select to verify the change to the categories in the Where clause of the view. You'll have to run the two queries separately to avoid a syntax error.

Syntax

```
-- altering a view no error
alter view MyView as
select EnglishProductName, EnglishProductSubcategoryName,
EnglishProductCategoryName from DimProduct as P
inner join DimProductSubcategory as S
on P.ProductSubcategoryKey = S.ProductSubcategoryKey
inner join DimProductCategory as C
on S.ProductCategoryKey = C.ProductCategoryKey
where EnglishProductCategoryName = 'Clothing' or
EnglishProductCategoryName = 'Components'
--
select * from MyView
```

Result

	EnglishProductName	EnglishProductSubcategoryName	EnglishProductCategoryName
1	HL Road Frame - Black, 58	Road Frames	Components
2	HL Road Frame - Red, 58	Road Frames	Components
3	Mountain Bike Socks, M	Socks	Clothing
4	Mountain Bike Socks, L	Socks	Clothing
5	AWC Logo Cap	Caps	Clothing
6	AWC Logo Cap	Caps	Clothing
7	AWC Logo Cap	Caps	Clothing
8	Long-Sleeve Logo Jersey, S	Jerseys	Clothing
9	Long-Sleeve Logo Jersey, S	Jerseys	Clothing
10	Long-Sleeve Logo Jersey, S	Jerseys	Clothing
11	Long-Sleeve Logo Jersey, M	Jerseys	Clothing
12	Long-Sleeve Logo Jersey, M	Jerseys	Clothing
13	Long-Sleeve Logo Jersey, M	Jerseys	Clothing
14	Long-Sleeve Logo Jersey, L	Jerseys	Clothing
15	Long-Sleeve Logo Jersey, L	Jerseys	Clothing
16	Long-Sleeve Logo Jersey, L	Jerseys	Clothing
17	Long-Sleeve Logo Jersey, XL	Jerseys	Clothing
18	Long-Sleeve Logo Jersey, XL	Jerseys	Clothing

Analysis

Your view has been successfully changed.

Select from View

As well as being stored queries, views are also virtual tables. You can manipulate a view from a Select just as you would a table.

Syntax

```
-- like a table
select EnglishProductName from MyView
--
select * from MyView
where EnglishProductCategoryName = 'Components'
--
select * from MyView
order by EnglishProductName desc
```

Result

	EnglishProductName	EnglishProductSubcategoryName	EnglishProductCategoryName
1	Women's Tights, S	Tights	Clothing
2	Women's Tights, M	Tights	Clothing
3	Women's Tights, L	Tights	Clothing
4	Women's Mountain Shorts, S	Shorts	Clothing
5	Women's Mountain Shorts, M	Shorts	Clothing
6	Women's Mountain Shorts, L	Shorts	Clothing
7	Touring Rear Wheel	Wheels	Components
8	Touring Pedal	Pedals	Components
9	Touring Front Wheel	Wheels	Components
10	Short-Sleeve Classic Jersey, XL	Jerseys	Clothing
11	Short-Sleeve Classic Jersey, S	Jerseys	Clothing
12	Short-Sleeve Classic Jersey, M	Jerseys	Clothing
13	Short-Sleeve Classic Jersey, L	Jerseys	Clothing
14	Rear Derailleur	Derailleurs	Components
15	Rear Brakes	Brakes	Components
16	Racing Socks, M	Socks	Clothing
17	Racing Socks, L	Socks	Clothing
18	Mountain Bike Socks, M	Socks	Clothing

Analysis

We are manipulating the content from the original three tables just as if it were a single table.

Insert/Update/Delete View

Although a view is like a single virtual table for Selects, it gets a little more complicated if you try an Insert, Update, or Delete. This query is a Delete on the view.

Syntax

```
-- views can sometimes be updated and inserted and deleted
delete MyView where EnglishProductName = 'AWC Logo Cap'
```

Result

```
Msg 4405, Level 16, State 1, Line 2
View or function 'MyView' is not updatable because the modification affects multiple base tables.
```

Analysis

This Delete doesn't work. The rules governing whether you can update, insert into, or delete from a view are reasonably arcane. However, the main reason for having a view is simply to write Selects against it.

Drop View

The syntax to remove a view is quite simple.

Syntax

```
-- removing a view
drop view MyView
--
select * from MyView
```

Result

```
Msg 208, Level 16, State 1, Line 4
Invalid object name 'MyView'.
```

Analysis

The Select can't find the view.

Select Calculation

The Select here is using some predefined, built-in system functions. One of the columns is a calculation to work out the tax on the price of a product.

Syntax

```
-- programming
-- functions user-defined scalar
-- calculation in a select
select EnglishProductName as [Product], round(ListPrice,2) as [Price],
ceiling(ListPrice * 0.15) as [Tax] from DimProduct
where ListPrice is not null
```

Result

	Product	Price	Tax
1	Sport-100 Helmet, Red	33.64	6
2	Sport-100 Helmet, Red	33.64	6
3	Sport-100 Helmet, Red	34.99	6
4	Sport-100 Helmet, Black	33.64	6
5	Sport-100 Helmet, Black	33.64	6
6	Sport-100 Helmet, Black	34.99	6
7	Mountain Bike Socks, M	9.50	2
8	Mountain Bike Socks, L	9.50	2
9	Sport-100 Helmet, Blue	33.64	6
10	Sport-100 Helmet, Blue	33.64	6
11	Sport-100 Helmet, Blue	34.99	6
12	AWC Logo Cap	8.64	2
13	AWC Logo Cap	8.64	2
14	AWC Logo Cap	8.99	2
15	Long-Sleeve Logo Jersey, S	48.07	8
16	Long-Sleeve Logo Jersey, S	48.07	8
17	Long-Sleeve Logo Jersey, S	49.99	8
18	Long-Sleeve Logo Jersey, M	48.07	8

Analysis

The Tax column is a calculated column. If you repeatedly use the same calculation, it might be a good idea to save it somewhere for reuse whenever you need it.

Create Function

So, here's a function that saves the calculation.

Syntax

```
-- encapsulation re-usable library
create function Tax (@price money)
returns int
as
begin
return ceiling(@price * 0.15)
end
```

Result

```
Command(s) completed successfully.
```

Analysis

The function is going to accept an input parameter with a data type of money and return a value with a data type of int (in reality, this might be money too, but I just wanted to show different data types in the syntax). The actual return value is the calculation. The Begin and End keywords that define a Begin ... End block are obligatory.

You can see the function in Object Explorer. Under the database, expand the Programmability, Functions, and Scalar-valued Functions folders. You'll probably have to right-click on the latter folder and choose Refresh. If the built-in system functions do not meet your requirements, you might consider creating your own functions as here.

Select Function 1/2

To use a function, you issue a Select against it—but the syntax has got to be exactly right. There are five queries here—the first three generate errors! If you are using SQL Server 2005 (rather than SQL Server 2008), you'll have to adapt the database name in the final query.

Syntax

```
-- calling a function
select Tax
--
select dbo.Tax
--
select Tax(20)
--
select dbo.Tax(20)
--
select AdventureWorksDW2008.dbo.Tax(20)
```

Result

	(No column name)
1	3

Analysis

A call to a function must preface the function name with the schema name. In addition, the function name must be followed by parentheses. If any input parameters are expected by the function, they go inside the parentheses. If there's more than one input parameter, create a comma-separated list.

Select Function 2/2

You can add the function call to any Select list.

Syntax

```
-- as part of a select from table
select EnglishProductName as [Product], round(ListPrice,2) as [Price],
dbo.Tax(ListPrice) as Tax from DimProduct
where ListPrice is not null
```

Result

	Product	Price	Tax
1	Sport-100 Helmet, Red	33.64	6
2	Sport-100 Helmet, Red	33.64	6
3	Sport-100 Helmet, Red	34.99	6
4	Sport-100 Helmet, Black	33.64	6
5	Sport-100 Helmet, Black	33.64	6
6	Sport-100 Helmet, Black	34.99	6
7	Mountain Bike Socks, M	9.50	2
8	Mountain Bike Socks, L	9.50	2
9	Sport-100 Helmet, Blue	33.64	6
10	Sport-100 Helmet, Blue	33.64	6
11	Sport-100 Helmet, Blue	34.99	6
12	AWC Logo Cap	8.64	2
13	AWC Logo Cap	8.64	2
14	AWC Logo Cap	8.99	2
15	Long-Sleeve Logo Jersey, S	48.07	8
16	Long-Sleeve Logo Jersey, S	48.07	8
17	Long-Sleeve Logo Jersey, S	49.99	8
18	Long-Sleeve Logo Jersey, M	48.07	8

Analysis

Now you don't have to redo the calculation every time you need it. The input parameter to the Tax function is the ListPrice column.

Drop Function

Removing a function is easy.

Syntax

```
-- clean up
drop function Tax
```

Result

```
Command(s) completed successfully.
```

Analysis

Any subsequent calls to this function will not work.

Create Function

Here's some practice on a final function. There are four queries—please run them separately.

Syntax

```
-- another example
create function [Calculate Volume] (@x int, @y int, @z int)
returns int
as
begin
return @x * @y * @z
end
--
select dbo.[Calculate Volume](12,5,3) as [Volume]
--
select dbo.[Calculate Volume](12.9,5,3) as [Volume]
--
drop function [Calculate Volume]
```

Result

	Volume
1	180

Analysis

This function accepts three input parameters. In the second call to the function, notice the truncation of 12.9 to 12—that's because the input parameter data type is int. You might want to experiment with decimal(5,2) for the input parameters and the Returns data types.

Chapter 13

Stored Procedures/ Programming

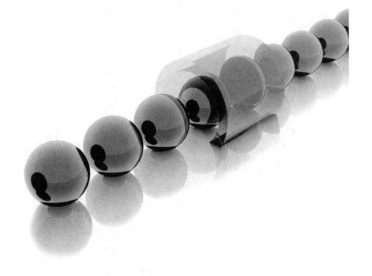

Τ his is the chapter for procedural programmers. It introduces lots of syntax that you may not think of as SQL. Indeed, strictly speaking, some of it is not SQL. We should rather call it T-SQL (Transact-SQL), which is the SQL Server version of SQL that contains lots of keywords and concepts that extend standard SQL. These extensions are very powerful and help you make your SQL queries truly dynamic and versatile. For example, you can dynamically change a Where clause at run time. The main emphasis of the chapter (after exploring some basic programming constructs) is on stored procedures. These allow you to change your SQL dynamically based on conditional factors—and a whole lot more. In addition, stored procedures provide encapsulation of your code. If you get it right, a Select in a stored procedure can also run much faster than it normally would as a stand-alone query. This is SQL on steroids!

▶ **Key concepts**   Debugging with Select and Print, user-defined variables, while loops, conditional branching, system variables, creating stored procedures, calling stored procedures, input parameters, output parameters, return values, default parameters, error handling

▶ **Keywords**   Select, Print, Declare, @, Set, @@Version, @@Rowcount, While, Begin ... End, Return, If ... Else, Case ... When ... End, Create Proc, Alter Proc, Out, Default, Try ... Catch, ERROR_MESSAGE()

Select

You can use Select to display literals and variables onscreen.

Syntax

```
-- select
select 'Got here'
```

Result

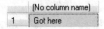

	(No column name)
1	Got here

Analysis

The result appears on the Results tab. Dumping variable values to screen is very handy when you are debugging complex procedural code.

Print

You can also use Print.

Syntax

```
-- print
print 'Got here'
```

Result

```
Got here
```

Analysis

Print displays its result on the Messages tab. If you are dumping out lots of values, Print possibly gives a cleaner display than Select.

String Variable

This query shows how to declare a variable, assign it a value, and check the value onscreen. This example is for a string variable.

Syntax

```
-- variable alpha
declare @X varchar(25)
set @X = 'hello world'
print @X
```

Result

```
hello world
```

Analysis

Please note the use of the Declare statement to create the variable. Variables you define must begin with an at sign (@). The Set statement is used to assign a value to the variable. Finally, the Print statement displays the value of the variable.

Numeric Variable

Here, it's a numeric variable of data type int.

Syntax

```
-- variable numeric
declare @Y int
set @Y = 123
print @Y
```

Result

```
123
```

Analysis

The value of the variable is 123.

System Variable 1/2

This is a system variable.

Syntax

```
-- system variable @@version
select @@VERSION
```

Result

(No column name)
1	Microsoft SQL Server 2008 (RTM) - 10.0.1600.22 (Intel X86) Jul 9 2008 14:43:34 Copyright (c) 1988-2008 Microsoft Corporation Developer Edition ...

Analysis

System variables begin with a double at sign (@@). With system variables, you don't create them, nor do you assign them a value—SQL Server does that for you.

System Variable 2/2

Some system variables are only given values by SQL Server after you've done something.

Syntax

```
-- system variable @@rowcount
select * from DimCustomer
select @@ROWCOUNT
```

Result

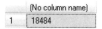

	[No column name]
1	18484

Analysis

@@Rowcount tells you how many records have been affected by a previous statement. Here, it returns the number of records from the first Select.

While 1/3

This is the first of a few queries (I guess they're not really queries—but they're in the query editor, so I'll keep on calling them queries) on the While loop. There is no End While. After you run it, click on the Messages tab. Wait a few seconds and then click the Stop (Cancel Executing Query) button on the toolbar.

Syntax

```
-- while - click the stop button
declare @counter int
set @counter = 1
while @counter < 3
print @counter
```

Result

```
1
1
1
1
1
1
1
1
1
1
1
1
1
1
1
1
1
1
1
1
1
1
1
1
1
1
```

Analysis

If you don't click the Stop button, then this query is going to run forever—or, at least until you run out of stack space. There is nothing in the code to terminate the While.

While 2/3

Hopefully, this version of the While loop stops by itself.

Syntax

```
-- better only prints 3?
declare @counter int
set @counter = 1
while @counter < 3
set @counter = @counter + 1
print @counter
```

Result

```
3
```

Analysis

It only prints 3! The Print statement is *not* part of the While loop. It comes after the While loop terminates and the value of @counter is 3.

While 3/3

There is a Begin ... End block in the While loop.

Syntax

```
-- much better
declare @counter int
set @counter = 1
print @counter
while @counter < 3
begin
set @counter = @counter + 1
print @counter
end
```

Result

```
1
2
3
```

Analysis

As there's no End While, the While loop is simply the next line—unless you have a Begin ... End block as in this query. The Print statement is now inside the loop.

Return

Our queries here introduce the Return statement. Please run the two queries separately to appreciate the effect.

Syntax

```
-- return
print 'starting'
print 'finished'
--
print 'starting'
return
print 'finished'
```

Result

```
starting
```

Analysis

Return stops program execution unconditionally.

If ... Else 1/6

This is an introduction to If and Else. There is no Then and no End If. Please run each of the four queries separately.

Syntax

```
-- if
if 1 = 0
print 'true'
--
if 1 <> 0
print 'true'
--
if 1 = 0
print 'true'
else
print 'false'
--
if 1 <> 0
print 'true'
else
print 'false'
```

Result

```
true
```

Analysis

If you have a background in Visual Basic, it might seem strange without Then and without End If.

If ... Else 2/6

This query is deliberately written to fail.

Syntax

```
-- more on if
if 1 <> 0
print 'true'
print 'got here'
else
print 'false'
```

Result

```
Msg 156, Level 15, State 1, Line 5
Incorrect syntax near the keyword 'else'.
```

Analysis

The error may be a little perplexing at first. An Else must come after an If. But the If is actually only the first Print ('true'). The second Print ('got here') is not part of the If—therefore the Else does not follow the If; it follows a stand-alone Print ('got here').

If ... Else 3/6

Now, there's a Begin ... End block after the If.

Syntax

```
-- better
if 1 <> 0
begin
print 'true'
print 'got here'
end
else
print 'false'
```

Result

```
true
got here
```

Analysis

The Begin ... End block means that both the first two Print statements ('true' and 'got here') are part of the If. Now, the Else does follow the If, and we have eliminated the error.

If ... Else 4/6

Perhaps this query is quite strange too.

Syntax

```
-- more on else
if 1 <> 0
begin
print 'true'
print 'got here'
end
else
print 'false'
print 'got here too'
```

Result

```
true
got here
got here too
```

Analysis

It reached the final Print ('got here too'). That's because it's not part of the Else; it's a stand-alone Print statement.

If ... Else 5/6

Here we introduce another Begin ... End block after the Else.

Syntax

```
-- getting there!
if 1 <> 0
begin
print 'true'
print 'got here'
```

```
end
else
begin
print 'false'
print 'got here too'
end
```

Result

```
true
got here
```

Analysis

This is more like it. Hopefully, you are beginning to appreciate just how important Begin ... End blocks are to your code.

If ... Else 6/6

The If test at the top has changed.

Syntax

```
-- one more on if else
if 1 = 0
begin
print 'true'
print 'got here'
end
else
begin
print 'false'
print 'got here too'
end
```

Result

```
false
got here too
```

Analysis

I hope, by now, this is making perfect sense. Isn't this much easier than Visual Basic?

Case ... When ... End

Instead of If ... Else, you might like to take a look at Case ... When ... End. Yes, this one does have a Then and an End—maybe it's a little more structured.

Syntax

```
-- case
declare @minute tinyint
set @minute = datepart(mi,getdate())
declare @OddEven bit
set @OddEven = @minute %2
select
case @OddEven
when 0 then 'Even'
when 1 then 'Odd'
else 'Unknown'
end as [Minute]
```

Result

Analysis

If you run this a few times, the result should change. Hopefully, you never see 'Unknown'. Getdate() returns the current date and time. Datepart(mi) extracts the minute from the time. %2 means modulo 2—so divide by 2 and return the remainder, which is always going to be 0 or 1.

Variable in Select

You can use variables to replace literals in your "standard" SQL queries. You can use If and Case to determine the value of the variable. You can use While to repeat operations. Here's a variable in a Where clause.

Syntax

```
-- variable in where clause
declare @maritalstatus nchar(1)
set @maritalstatus = 'M'
select * from DimCustomer
where MaritalStatus = @maritalstatus
```

Result

	CustomerKey	GeographyKey	CustomerAlternateKey	Title	FirstName	MiddleName	LastName	NameStyle	BirthDate	MaritalStatus	Suffix	Genc
1	11000	26	AW00011000	NULL	Jon	V	Yang	0	1966-04-08	M	NULL	M
2	11002	31	AW00011002	NULL	Ruben	NULL	Torres	0	1965-08-12	M	NULL	M
3	11007	40	AW00011007	NULL	Marco	NULL	Mehta	0	1964-05-09	M	NULL	M
4	11011	22	AW00011011	NULL	Curtis	NULL	Lu	0	1963-11-04	M	NULL	M
5	11012	611	AW00011012	NULL	Lauren	M	Walker	0	1968-01-18	M	NULL	F
6	11013	543	AW00011013	NULL	Ian	M	Jenkins	0	1968-08-06	M	NULL	M
7	11016	329	AW00011016	NULL	Wyatt	L	Hill	0	1979-04-28	M	NULL	M
8	11022	609	AW00011022	NULL	Ethan	G	Zhang	0	1978-10-12	M	NULL	M
9	11023	298	AW00011023	NULL	Seth	M	Edwards	0	1978-10-11	M	NULL	M
10	11024	311	AW00011024	NULL	Russell	NULL	Xie	0	1978-09-17	M	NULL	M
11	11025	24	AW00011025	NULL	Alejandro	NULL	Beck	0	1945-12-23	M	NULL	M
12	11027	40	AW00011027	NULL	Jessie	R	Zhao	0	1946-12-07	M	NULL	M
13	11028	17	AW00011028	NULL	Jill	NULL	Jimenez	0	1946-04-11	M	NULL	F
14	11029	32	AW00011029	NULL	Jimmy	L	Moreno	0	1946-12-21	M	NULL	M
15	11030	28	AW00011030	NULL	Bethany	G	Yuan	0	1947-02-22	M	NULL	F
16	11031	8	AW00011031	NULL	Theresa	G	Ramos	0	1947-08-22	M	NULL	F
17	11032	35	AW00011032	NULL	Denise	NULL	Stone	0	1947-06-11	M	NULL	F

Analysis

Only the married customers are returned.

Base Query

It's about time we moved on to stored procedures, now that you have the programming background. Here's a base query to get us started.

Syntax

```
-- base select
select FirstName + ' ' + LastName as [Full Name], MaritalStatus, Gender
from DimCustomer
```

Result

	Full Name	MaritalStatus	Gender
1	Jon Yang	M	M
2	Eugene Huang	S	M
3	Ruben Torres	M	M
4	Christy Zhu	S	F
5	Elizabeth Johnson	S	F
6	Julio Ruiz	S	M
7	Janet Alvarez	S	F
8	Marco Mehta	M	M
9	Rob Verhoff	S	F
10	Shannon Carlson	S	M
11	Jacquelyn Suarez	S	F
12	Curtis Lu	M	M
13	Lauren Walker	M	F
14	Ian Jenkins	M	M
15	Sydney Bennett	S	F
16	Chloe Young	S	F
17	Wyatt Hill	M	M
18	Shannon Wang	S	F

Analysis

I guess, by now, you might find this kind of SQL far too easy.

Create Proc

This is your first stored procedure. There are two varieties—please run one or the other; if you attempt to run both, you'll get an error on the second one.

Syntax

```
-- first stored procedure
create proc GetCustomers as
select FirstName + ' ' + LastName as [Full Name], MaritalStatus, Gender
from DimCustomer
-- better
create proc GetCustomers as
begin
select FirstName + ' ' + LastName as [Full Name], MaritalStatus, Gender
from DimCustomer
end
```

Result

Command(s) completed successfully.

Analysis

The second version has a Begin ... End block. This is obligatory in a function—it's optional in a stored procedure, but maybe it looks better. When you run one of these Create Proc queries, you won't see any data returned by the Select statement.

You can see your stored procedure in Object Explorer. Under the database, expand Programmability and the Stored Procedures folder. As usual, you'll have to right-click on the last folder and choose Refresh.

Alter Proc

Here there is a very minor cosmetic change to the stored procedure. The column alias is now FullName, not Full Name.

Syntax

```
alter proc GetCustomers as
begin
select FirstName + ' ' + LastName as [FullName], MaritalStatus, Gender
from DimCustomer
end
```

Result

Command(s) completed successfully.

Analysis

When you change a stored procedure, you have to use Alter Proc. You can't run Create Proc more than once on the same stored procedure.

Running a Stored Procedure 1/3

One way to run a stored procedure is to highlight its name in your Create Proc or Alter Proc syntax and execute. This is handy while you're still developing. But, mostly, you'll not have that code showing any more and you'll want to run it as a separate stand-alone query.

Syntax

```
-- calling a stored procedure
GetCustomers
```

Result

	FullName	MaritalStatus	Gender
1	Jon Yang	M	M
2	Eugene Huang	S	M
3	Ruben Torres	M	M
4	Christy Zhu	S	F
5	Elizabeth Johnson	S	F
6	Julio Ruiz	S	M
7	Janet Alvarez	S	F
8	Marco Mehta	M	M
9	Rob Verhoff	S	F
10	Shannon Carlson	S	M
11	Jacquelyn Suarez	S	F
12	Curtis Lu	M	M
13	Lauren Walker	M	F
14	Ian Jenkins	M	M
15	Sydney Bennett	S	F
16	Chloe Young	S	F
17	Wyatt Hill	M	M
18	Shannon Wang	S	F

Analysis

All you have to do is type the name (or drag and drop from Object Explorer—it will put the schema name in front) and run. Now, you will see the result of the Select inside the stored procedure.

Running a Stored Procedure 2/3

To be doubly sure, you might want to run it twice. This is going to fail if you don't do them separately.

Syntax

```
-- calling it twice
GetCustomers
GetCustomers
```

Result

```
Msg 8146, Level 16, State 1, Procedure GetCustomers, Line 0
Procedure GetCustomers has no parameters and arguments were supplied.
```

Analysis

Simply entering the name of the stored procedure doesn't work on second and subsequent lines. The fix is in the next query.

Running a Stored Procedure 3/3

Notice the Exec on the second line.

Syntax

```
-- better
GetCustomers
exec GetCustomers
```

Result

	FullName	MaritalStatus	Gender
1	Jon Yang	M	M
2	Eugene Huang	S	M
3	Ruben Torres	M	M
4	Christy Zhu	S	F
5	Elizabeth Johnson	S	F
6	Julio Ruiz	S	M
7	Janet Alvarez	S	F
8	Marco Mehta	M	M

	FullName	MaritalStatus	Gender
1	Jon Yang	M	M
2	Eugene Huang	S	M
3	Ruben Torres	M	M
4	Christy Zhu	S	F
5	Elizabeth Johnson	S	F
6	Julio Ruiz	S	M
7	Janet Alvarez	S	F
8	Marco Mehta	M	M

Analysis

It's good practice to always use Exec anyway, even if it's just a one-line query. It makes it explicit that it's a stored procedure that's being run.

Alter Proc

Don't run this query yet! This is quite a nasty one. If you do run it, the Exec GetCustomers line becomes part of the GetCustomers stored procedure. When you subsequently try the stored procedure, it will run itself, repeatedly. So, please run the top query first and the Exec GetCustomers separately.

Syntax

```
-- more hard-coded where clause
alter proc GetCustomers as
begin
select FirstName + ' ' + LastName as [Full Name], MaritalStatus, Gender
from DimCustomer
where MaritalStatus = 'S' and Gender = 'F'
end
--
exec GetCustomers
```

Result

	Full Name	MaritalStatus	Gender
1	Christy Zhu	S	F
2	Elizabeth Johnson	S	F
3	Janet Alvarez	S	F
4	Rob Verhoff	S	F
5	Jacquelyn Suarez	S	F
6	Sydney Bennett	S	F
7	Chloe Young	S	F
8	Shannon Wang	S	F
9	Destiny Wilson	S	F
10	Chloe Garcia	S	F
11	Carol Rai	S	F
12	Heidi Lopez	S	F
13	Ashlee Andersen	S	F
14	Angela Murphy	S	F
15	Tiffany Liang	S	F
16	Carolyn Navarro	S	F
17	Linda Serrano	S	F
18	Casey Luo	S	F

Analysis

The Alter Proc has added a Where clause.

Variables

There are two queries here. Please run the top one first. If you accidentally run all of this syntax, the stored procedure is going to run itself. If that happens, highlight everything apart from Exec GetCustomers and run again. Then try Exec GetCustomers by itself.

Syntax

```
-- variables in where clause
alter proc GetCustomers as
begin
declare @maritalstatus nchar(1)
declare @gender nvarchar(1)
set @maritalstatus = 'S'
set @gender = 'F'
select FirstName + ' ' + LastName as [Full Name], MaritalStatus, Gender
from DimCustomer
where MaritalStatus = @maritalstatus and Gender = @gender
end
--
exec GetCustomers
```

Result

	Full Name	MaritalStatus	Gender
1	Christy Zhu	S	F
2	Elizabeth Johnson	S	F
3	Janet Alvarez	S	F
4	Rob Verhoff	S	F
5	Jacquelyn Suarez	S	F
6	Sydney Bennett	S	F
7	Chloe Young	S	F
8	Shannon Wang	S	F
9	Destiny Wilson	S	F
10	Chloe Garcia	S	F
11	Carol Rai	S	F
12	Heidi Lopez	S	F
13	Ashlee Andersen	S	F
14	Angela Murphy	S	F
15	Tiffany Liang	S	F
16	Carolyn Navarro	S	F
17	Linda Serrano	S	F
18	Casey Luo	S	F

Analysis

The literal values in the Where clause have been replaced by variables. Please note the two Declare statements and the two Set statements.

Parameters

This version shows an important and fundamental change. There are *two* queries again. The two Declares have gone. The two Sets have gone. And the former variable names (@maritalstatus and @gender) have been placed before the As keyword and separated by a comma. These are stored procedure input parameters.

Syntax

```
-- parameters in where clause
-- no declare and before as and no set
alter proc GetCustomers
@maritalstatus nchar(1),
@gender nvarchar(1)
as
begin
select FirstName + ' ' + LastName as [Full Name], MaritalStatus, Gender
from DimCustomer
where MaritalStatus = @maritalstatus and Gender = @gender
end
--
exec GetCustomers
```

Result

```
Msg 201, Level 16, State 4, Procedure GetCustomers, Line 0
Procedure or function 'GetCustomers' expects parameter '@maritalstatus', which was not supplied.
```

Analysis

The Alter Proc should succeed. The Exec GetCustomers should fail, complaining about a parameter.

Passing Parameters

If a stored procedure expects input parameters, you must supply the values for those parameters.

Syntax

```
-- calling with parameters
exec GetCustomers 'S', 'F'
--
exec GetCustomers 'S', 'M'
```

Result

	Full Name	MaritalStatus	Gender
1	Eugene Huang	S	M
2	Julio Ruiz	S	M
3	Shannon Carlson	S	M
4	Clarence Rai	S	M
5	Luke Lal	S	M
6	Jordan King	S	M
7	Harold Sai	S	M
8	Leonard Nara	S	M
9	Daniel Johnson	S	M
10	Caleb Carter	S	M
11	Levi Arun	S	M
12	Blake Anderson	S	M
13	Donald Gonzalez	S	M
14	Lucas Phillips	S	M
15	Trevor Bryant	S	M
16	Cedric Ma	S	M
17	Chad Kumar	S	M
18	Jessie Liu	S	M

Analysis

You will get two different result sets from the two queries. We had to provide the values for the parameters. In the next query we'll look at default values for the parameters, so you don't always have to provide the values when you call the stored procedure.

Default Parameter Values

There are three queries this time. The Alter Proc is setting default values for the two input parameters (single for marital status and female for gender).

Syntax

```
-- default value
alter proc GetCustomers
@maritalstatus nchar(1) = 'S',
@gender nvarchar(1) = 'F'
```

```
as
begin
select FirstName + ' ' + LastName as [Full Name], MaritalStatus, Gender
from DimCustomer
where MaritalStatus = @maritalstatus and Gender = @gender
end
--
exec GetCustomers
--
exec GetCustomers 'M', 'M'
```

Result

	Full Name	MaritalStatus	Gender
1	Christy Zhu	S	F
2	Elizabeth Johnson	S	F
3	Janet Alvarez	S	F
4	Rob Verhoff	S	F
5	Jacquelyn Suarez	S	F
6	Sydney Bennett	S	F
7	Chloe Young	S	F
8	Shannon Wang	S	F
9	Destiny Wilson	S	F
10	Chloe Garcia	S	F
11	Carol Rai	S	F
12	Heidi Lopez	S	F
13	Ashlee Andersen	S	F
14	Angela Murphy	S	F
15	Tiffany Liang	S	F
16	Carolyn Navarro	S	F
17	Linda Serrano	S	F
18	Casey Luo	S	F

Analysis

The first Exec GetCustomers returns single females, even without the values being passed in (the result shown). The second Exec GetCustomers 'M', 'M' returns married males—the provided values are overriding the default values for the parameters.

Output Parameter 1/4

As well as input parameters, stored procedures also support output parameters—that is, you can get values being returned from the procedure. This query rebuilds the procedure with an output parameter called @count.

Syntax

```
-- output parameter
alter proc GetCustomers
@maritalstatus nchar(1) = 'S',
@gender nvarchar(1) = 'F',
@count int out
as
begin
select FirstName + ' ' + LastName as [Full Name], MaritalStatus, Gender
from DimCustomer
where MaritalStatus = @maritalstatus and Gender = @gender
set @count = @@ROWCOUNT
end
```

Result

```
Command(s) completed successfully.
```

Analysis

Output parameters require the keyword Out (or Output) and appear before the As keyword. If there are two or more input and/or output parameters, they must be comma-separated. The output parameter here, @count, is of data type int. In the main body of the procedure, this parameter is being set to @@Rowcount. @@Rowcount is a system variable that returns the number of records affected by the previous statement. Consequently, @count holds the number of records returned by the Select statement.

Output Parameter 2/4

Let's attempt to run our stored procedure. All three queries here are going to fail.

Syntax

```
-- calling to get output parameter
exec GetCustomers
--
exec GetCustomers 'M', 'F'
--
exec GetCustomers @count out
```

Result

```
Msg 137, Level 15, State 2, Line 1
Must declare the scalar variable "@count".
```

Analysis

The result shows the error from the third query. When you do call a stored procedure with an output parameter, you can't provide the value. Instead you use a variable followed by the keyword Out. In the third query, the error is telling you that the variable (@count, in this case) has not been declared.

Output Parameter 3/4

This time, the variable is declared first. The variable here (@count) will hold the value of the output parameter (@count).

Syntax

```
-- better
declare @count int
exec GetCustomers 'M', 'M', @count out
select @count as [Records]
```

Result

	Records
1	5266

Analysis

The final Select is dumping the value of the variable (@count) to screen. The result shows the result of this Select—please note that you can't run this Select separately from the preceding syntax. Your variable does not have to have the same name as the output parameter—but it's probably good practice to do so.

Output Parameter 4/4

If you recall, our stored procedure has default values for the two input parameters. The question is, how do you call the stored procedure with those default values? There are two attempts here.

Syntax

```
-- with defaults
declare @count int
exec GetCustomers , , @count out
select @count as [Records]
--
declare @count int
exec GetCustomers default, default, @count out
select @count as [Records]
```

Result

	Records
1	4388

Analysis

The first try won't work. The second attempt will return all single female customers. It also returns the number of records (result shown). Please note the use of the Default keyword. You could have used this just for one input parameter and provided a literal value for the other one.

Return 1/4

Without any work on your part, stored procedures also provide a return value—this is simply a value with a data type of int.

Syntax

```
-- return value
declare @count int
declare @return int
exec @return = GetCustomers default, default, @count out
select @count as [Records]
select @return as [Return]
```

Result

	Return
1	0

Analysis

If a stored procedure runs successfully, the return value is 0. Here, we've created a variable (@return) to capture, hold, and display the return value. Please note the new syntax for the Exec line. You must run all of the syntax in one go—the result shown is from Select @return. Altogether, there are three results.

Return 2/4

In our last query, the return value was set implicitly by the stored procedure. You can, if you wish, also set it explicitly. There are two queries here; please run them separately.

Syntax

```
alter proc GetCustomers
@maritalstatus nchar(1) = 'S',
@gender nvarchar(1) = 'F',
@count int out
as
begin
select FirstName + ' ' + LastName as [Full Name], MaritalStatus, Gender
from DimCustomer
where MaritalStatus = @maritalstatus and Gender = @gender
set @count = @@ROWCOUNT
return 0
end
--
declare @count int
declare @return int
exec @return = GetCustomers default, default, @count out
select @count as [Records]
select @return as [Return]
```

Result

	Return
1	0

Analysis

To set the return value from a stored procedure explicitly, you use the Return statement. A Return statement also causes the stored procedure to stop and exit. The result shown is the return value.

Return 3/4

In this example, the values for the two input parameters are deliberately wrong.

Syntax

```
declare @count int
declare @return int
exec @return = GetCustomers 'X', 'Y', @count out
select @count as [Records]
select @return as [Return]
```

Result

	Return
1	0

Analysis

There are no records returned. We are going to see how to trap this happening. Once again, the result shown in the preceding illustration is the return value.

Return 4/4

Here there are two queries—they need to be executed separately.

Syntax

```
-- trapped
alter proc GetCustomers
@maritalstatus nchar(1) = 'S',
@gender nvarchar(1) = 'F',
@count int out
as
begin
declare @err int
select FirstName + ' ' + LastName as [Full Name], MaritalStatus, Gender
from DimCustomer
where MaritalStatus = @maritalstatus and Gender = @gender
set @count = @@ROWCOUNT
if @count = 0
return -99
else
```

```
return 0
end
--
declare @count int
declare @return int
exec @return = GetCustomers 'X', 'Y', @count out
select @count as [Records]
select @return as [Return]
```

Result

	Return
1	-99

Analysis

Now, our stored procedure has two possible return values—in this case, it returns -99 (see the result). You can use these values in an If test to determine how to react. This is often done in a stored procedure that calls a stored procedure.

Two Stored Procedures

Once again, there are two queries, to be executed one at a time.

Syntax

```
-- call the sp from a sp
create proc CallGetCustomers as
begin
declare @count int
declare @return int
exec @return = GetCustomers 'S', 'F', @count out
select @count as [Records]
select @return as [Return]
end
--
exec CallGetCustomers
```

Result

	Full Name	MaritalStatus	Gender
1	Christy Zhu	S	F
2	Elizabeth Johnson	S	F
3	Janet Alvarez	S	F
4	Rob Verhoff	S	F
5	Jacquelyn Suarez	S	F
6	Sydney Bennett	S	F
7	Chloe Young	S	F
8	Shannon Wang	S	F
9	Destiny Wilson	S	F
10	Chloe Garcia	S	F
11	Carol Rai	S	F
12	Heidi Lopez	S	F
13	Ashlee Andersen	S	F
14	Angela Murphy	S	F
15	Tiffany Liang	S	F
16	Carolyn Navarro	S	F
17	Linda Serrano	S	F
18	Casey Luo	S	F

Analysis

Our new stored procedure, CallGetCustomers, is running the original stored procedure, GetCustomers.

Try ... Catch 1/2

You can trap errors in called stored procedures by having a Try ... Catch construct in the calling stored procedure. There are two separate queries here.

Syntax

```
-- try catch
alter proc CallGetCustomers as
begin
declare @count int
declare @return int
begin try
exec @return = GetCustomers 'S', 'F', @count out
end try
begin catch
set @count = 0
set @return = -100
```

```
print ERROR_MESSAGE()
end catch
select @count as [Records]
select @return as [Return]
end
--
exec CallGetCustomers
```

Result

	Return
1	0

Analysis

Our calling stored procedure (CallGetCustomers) is going to try to run the inner stored procedure (GetCustomers). If the Try fails, the Catch block will be triggered.

Try ... Catch 2/2

Yet again, we have two queries. The first introduces no changes. If you take a look at the table name, it's DimCustomer. The second query, which executes CallGetCustomers, should print out a return value of 0. If you want to experiment, change the table name to DimX in the Alter Proc and run again. Now, when you run the second query, the return value is -100—and if you go to the Messages tab, you can see what ERROR_MESSAGE does. Please make sure you correct the table name (if you have experimented) and re-run the Alter Proc before you move on.

Syntax

```
-- correct tablename
alter proc GetCustomers
@maritalstatus nchar(1) = 'S',
@gender nvarchar(1) = 'F',
@count int out
as
begin
select FirstName + ' ' + LastName as [Full Name], MaritalStatus, Gender
from DimCustomer
where MaritalStatus = @maritalstatus and Gender = @gender
set @count = @@ROWCOUNT
if @count = 0
```

```
return -99
else
return 0
end
--
exec CallGetCustomers
```

Result

	Records
1	4388

Analysis

The result shows the number of records returned. Hopefully, you are beginning to get the hang of stored procedures. If you did experiment and change the table name, you are seeing the Catch block being triggered. A Catch block is fired when a Try block fails. Make sure the table name is reset to DimCustomer, before you attempt the next query.

Your Last Stored Procedure

Almost done. This has been a long chapter but there is one outstanding problem to fix. The calling procedure (CallGetCustomers) has always been passing hard-coded values to the input parameters of the called procedure (GetCustomers). We are always getting single females (not that I'm complaining)! Here, we parameterize the outer, calling stored procedure as well. There are a total of four queries, to be run one at a time.

Syntax

```
-- parameters on calling proc
alter proc CallGetCustomers
@maritalstatus nchar(1) = 'S',
@gender nvarchar(1) = 'F'
as
begin
declare @count int
declare @return int
begin try
exec @return = GetCustomers @maritalstatus, @gender, @count out
end try
begin catch
set @count = 0
```

```
set @return = -100
print ERROR_MESSAGE()
end catch
select @count as [Records]
select @return as [Return]
end
--
exec CallGetCustomers 'X', 'Y'
--
exec CallGetCustomers default, default
--
exec CallGetCustomers 'S', 'M'
```

Result

	Full Name	MaritalStatus	Gender
1	Eugene Huang	S	M
2	Julio Ruiz	S	M
3	Shannon Carlson	S	M
4	Clarence Rai	S	M
5	Luke Lal	S	M
6	Jordan King	S	M
7	Harold Sai	S	M
8	Leonard Nara	S	M
9	Daniel Johnson	S	M
10	Caleb Carter	S	M

	Records
1	4085

	Return
1	0

Analysis

If you wish, you can leave out the two Default keywords in the middle Exec CallGetCustomers. If you got this far through the chapter, you have done really well.

Chapter 14

Data Definition Language (DDL) and Data Control Language (DCL)

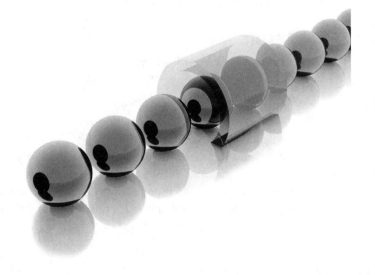

Data definition language (DDL) is that part of SQL concerned with creating and maintaining the database objects you will need. Data control language (DCL) is the part of SQL dedicated to setting up security on the objects you've created. This chapter is dedicated to DDL and DCL. You will see how to create a database, tables, keys, indexes, and other objects. Once those objects have been created, you'll also learn how to create a login and a user, and to control and test access to the objects.

▶ **Key concepts**   Data definition language, data control language, creating databases, creating tables, creating primary keys, creating foreign keys, creating indexes, creating logins, creating users, security, giving and removing permissions

▶ **Keywords**   Create Database, Use, Create Table, Alter Table, Add Constraint, Primary Key, Foreign Key, References, Create Index, Create Login, Create User, Execute As, Revert, Grant, Revoke, Deny, Drop Database, Drop Login

Create Database

Creating a database from a SQL query can be very simple or very complex. This query is about the simplest you can get. I would recommend that you don't try the exercises in this chapter on a production server.

Syntax

```
-- create database
-- you must be sysadmin
-- make sure it doesn't already exist
create database MyDatabase
```

Result

```
Command(s) completed successfully.
```

Analysis

There's not a lot of syntax here! Creating a database this way means it will have all of the default values configured for your SQL Server databases. The full syntax is complex and beyond the scope of an introductory book. By default, you can only create databases if you are a member of the sysadmin server role. You can also create databases if you have been given explicit permissions or have been added to the dbcreator role. If you are logged in as an administrator, it's possible that you are a member of this role already. If you're not sure, you may want to consult with your SQL Server DBA.

Use

You are going to create some tables in this new database. If you are currently connected to AdventureWorksDW2008 (or AdventureWorksDW in SQL Server 2005), then the tables you create shortly will go into that database. To ensure that the tables go into your new MyDatabase, you have three choices. First, as you create other new objects, preface the object name with the database and schema (dbo) names. Second, switch the context to MyDatabase by using the drop-down on the toolbar. Third, issue the Use statement as shown in this query.

Syntax

```
-- either switch database from combo or use MyDatabase
use MyDatabase
```

Result

```
Command(s) completed successfully.
```

Analysis

If you issue the Use statement as shown here, the new database context can be seen in the drop-down on the toolbar. The tab of your query editor window also displays the current context. Database context is vital. Many times I have inadvertently created objects and then lost them—only to discover later that I accidentally created them in the master database!

Create Table

There are two alternative queries here to create a table. Please try just one of them, preferably the first one. If you do try the first one, make sure that the database context is MyDatabase.

Syntax

```
-- check context is right before creating table
-- either
create table Suppliers
(
SupplierID int not null,
SupplierName varchar(25) not null
)
```

```
-- or when not in context
create table MyDatabase.dbo.Suppliers
(
SupplierID int not null,
SupplierName varchar(25) not null
)
```

Result

```
Command(s) completed successfully.
```

Analysis

When you create a table, you'll need a comma-separated list of column names enclosed within parentheses. Each column has to have a data type, and, optionally, you can specify the nullability of the column. In this case, either of our two columns will allow null values. All the objects we are creating during this chapter can be viewed in Object Explorer (you may need to right-click and then choose Refresh for them to display).

Testing the Table

You can now start to use the new Suppliers table. Here's a Select query.

Syntax

```
-- query new table
select * from Suppliers
-- or
select * from MyDatabase.dbo.Suppliers
```

Result

SupplierID	SupplierName

Analysis

There's no data in the table, so all you get is the column names as captions to the column headers in the result.

Insert Into ... Values

Maybe we should add some data to the table. We can use a couple of Inserts followed by a Select.

Syntax

```
-- put some data in
insert into Suppliers
values (1,'Adventure Works')
insert into Suppliers
values (2,'Northwind')
--
select * from Suppliers
```

Result

	SupplierID	SupplierName
1	1	Adventure Works
2	2	Northwind

Analysis

You should have two rows. There are no new concepts or syntax here.

Primary Key

The Alter Table query here makes the first column (SupplierID) into a primary key using Add Constraint syntax. PK_SupplerID is the name you invent for the key. There are also two Inserts and a Select—expect the first Insert to fail.

Syntax

```
-- primary key
alter table Suppliers
add constraint PK_SupplierID primary key (SupplierID)
--
insert into Suppliers
values (1,'Pubs')
--
insert into Suppliers
values (3,'Pubs')
--
select * from Suppliers
```

Result

	SupplierID	SupplierName
1	1	Adventure Works
2	2	Northwind
3	3	Pubs

Analysis

The Select should return three rows. The second Insert was successful. The first Insert failed as there's now a primary key on the table. The primary key is on the SupplierID column. One of the features of a primary key is that it puts a unique index on the column. This means you can't have duplicate values—a supplier (Adventure Works) already has a SupplierID of 1, and the attempt to add a new supplier (Pubs) with the same SupplierID generates a primary key violation error. The second attempt to add Pubs is fine.

Create Table

Here's a second table called Products to add to our new database.

Syntax

```
-- second table
create table Products
(
ProductID int not null primary key,
ProductName varchar(25) not null,
ProductPrice money,
SupplierID int not null
)
```

Result

```
Command(s) completed successfully.
```

Analysis

This syntax is a slight variation on the syntax we used for the first Suppliers table. This time, the primary key definition is part of the Create Table—we don't need to have a subsequent Alter Table.

Foreign Key

We are going to define a foreign key and set up referential integrity between the two tables.

Syntax

```
-- foreign key DRI
alter table Products
add constraint FK_SupplierID foreign key (SupplierID)
references dbo.Suppliers (SupplierID)
```

Result

```
Command(s) completed successfully.
```

Analysis

The foreign key in the Products table is SupplierID. This refers back to the SupplierID column in the parent table (Suppliers). SupplierID is the primary key in the Suppliers table. FK_SupplierID is the name you decide to give the foreign key. You can see the foreign key in Object Explorer under the Keys folder underneath the table.

Foreign Key Violation

This query is an Insert Into … Values. The last entry in the Values list is the foreign key (SupplierID).

Syntax

```
-- inserting data fails DRI
insert into Products
values(1,'Red racing bike',2500,99)
```

Result

```
Msg 547, Level 16, State 0, Line 2
The INSERT statement conflicted with the FOREIGN KEY constraint "FK_SupplierID". The conflict occurred in database "MyDat
The statement has been terminated.
```

Analysis

The Insert should fail. You tried to insert a value of 99 as the SupplierID. The foreign key constraint will only allow values for the foreign key (SupplierID) that already exist in the primary key (SupplierID) column of the parent table (Suppliers).

Insert Into ... Values

You have three Inserts and a Select here. You can run them all at once if you wish.

Syntax

```
-- valid values
insert into Products
values(1,'Red racing bike',2500,1)
insert into Products
values(2,'Green tea',15,2)
insert into Products
values(3,'Black racing bike',2000,1)
--
select * from Products
```

Result

	ProductID	ProductName	ProductPrice	SupplierID
1	1	Red racing bike	2500.00	1
2	2	Green tea	15.00	2
3	3	Black racing bike	2000.00	1

Analysis

You should be looking at three rows—all of the foreign keys are valid; there is no violation of referential integrity.

Create Index

Let's add an index to the ProductName column of the Products table. IX_ProductName is simply a name you make up for the index.

Syntax

```
-- index
create index IX_ProductName
on Products (ProductName)
-- faster
select * from Products
where ProductName = 'Green tea'
```

Result

	ProductID	ProductName	ProductPrice	SupplierID
1	2	Green tea	15.00	2

Analysis

On a large table, a Select like this will run faster if it uses an index. The index is under the Indexes folder under the table in Object Explorer.

Inner Join

Now we can join the two tables together. The join is on the primary-to-foreign-key relationship between the two tables.

Syntax

```
-- inner join
select SupplierName, ProductName from Suppliers as S
inner join Products as P
on S.SupplierID = P.SupplierID
```

Result

	SupplierName	ProductName
1	Adventure Works	Red racing bike
2	Northwind	Green tea
3	Adventure Works	Black racing bike

Analysis

Three rows.

Create View

Let's create a view on the join. You have to run these two queries separately.

Syntax

```
-- view
create view SimpleView as
select SupplierName, ProductName from Suppliers as S
inner join Products as P
```

```
on S.SupplierID = P.SupplierID
--
select * from SimpleView
order by SupplierName, ProductName
```

Result

	SupplierName	ProductName
1	Adventure Works	Black racing bike
2	Adventure Works	Red racing bike
3	Northwind	Green tea

Analysis

You can treat a view like a table.

Create Function

Now for a function to help us perform calculations. Please run the two queries separately.

Syntax

```
-- function
create function Discount (@price money)
returns money
as
begin
return @price * 0.9
end
--
select ProductName as Product, ProductPrice as Price,
dbo.Discount(ProductPrice) as [Price after discount] from Products
```

Result

	Product	Price	Price after discount
1	Red racing bike	2500.00	2250.00
2	Green tea	15.00	13.50
3	Black racing bike	2000.00	1800.00

Analysis

You can reuse this function at any time.

Create Proc

Why not a stored procedure too? Please run separately—otherwise the stored procedure will run itself recursively.

Syntax

```
-- stored procedure
create proc ProductsBySupplier
@supplier varchar(25)
as
select SupplierName, ProductName from Suppliers as S
inner join Products as P
on S.SupplierID = P.SupplierID
where SupplierName = @supplier
--
exec ProductsBySupplier 'Adventure Works'
```

Result

	SupplierName	ProductName
1	Adventure Works	Red racing bike
2	Adventure Works	Black racing bike

Analysis

You may want to vary the parameter value in the call to the stored procedure.

Create Login

We are going to look at security now. This query creates a login. Before you execute it, please be aware of a couple of important points. You have to be sysadmin for this to work. Please don't do this on a production server; try it out on a development server. It might not work anyway!

Syntax

```
-- DCL
-- create login
-- integrated security create login [Domain\User] from windows
create login TestLogin with password = ''
```

Result

```
Command(s) completed successfully.
```

Analysis

This is only going to work if your SQL Server security model is set to SQL Server and Windows Authentication mode. A setting of Windows Authentication mode (the recommended setting) will result in an error. If you are sysadmin and are working on a development server, then you can change the security model (or ask your SQL Server DBA). Please don't try to change the security model on a production server. If you can't switch the security mode, then use [Domain\User] instead of TestLogin as the login name. [Domain\User] is in the form of domain name followed by Windows user name.

Create User

Now that we have a new login at the server level, we need to add this login as a user to our new database. Please make sure that the database context is MyDatabase.

Syntax

```
-- create user
create user TestLogin for login TestLogin
```

Result

```
Command(s) completed successfully.
```

Analysis

You can see the new user in Object Explorer (under the Users folder under the Security folder underneath your database). If you were unable to create a login in the last query, then you won't be able to create the user here—sorry, you'll just have to read and not try the next few security exercises.

Execute As

Run all of these as one complete query. It's demonstrating impersonation.

Syntax

```
-- impersonation
select USER
execute as login = 'TestLogin'
select USER
revert
select USER
```

Result

	(No column name)
1	TestLogin

Analysis

Execute As allows you to impersonate another user in the database. You are briefly the TestLogin user (the result shown). Revert switches you back to yourself (you are, in fact, the dbo user).

Testing Security

Run this as one complete query. You are briefly trying to access the Products table as TestLogin.

Syntax

```
-- test security on select
execute as login = 'TestLogin'
select * from Products
revert
```

Result

```
Msg 229, Level 14, State 5, Line 3
The SELECT permission was denied on the object 'Products', database 'MyDatabase', schema 'dbo'.
```

Analysis

You are locked out of the table.

Grant

This will work as one query. It includes the Grant statement.

Syntax

```
-- give permission
grant select on Products to TestLogin
--
execute as login = 'TestLogin'
select * from Products
revert
```

Result

	ProductID	ProductName	ProductPrice	SupplierID
1	1	Red racing bike	2500.00	1
2	2	Green tea	15.00	2
3	3	Black racing bike	2000.00	1

Analysis

You have given permission for the TestLogin user to perform a Select on the Products table.

Revoke

There is also a Revoke statement. The first Grant statement is a repeat from the last query; it's not strictly necessary again. Please try the top Execute As block first. Then run the Revoke statement line, and finally try the bottom Execute As block.

Syntax

```
-- revoke
grant select on Products to TestLogin
--
execute as login = 'TestLogin'
select * from Products
revert
--
revoke select on Products to TestLogin
--
execute as login = 'TestLogin'
select * from Products
revert
```

Result

```
Msg 229, Level 14, State 5, Line 2
The SELECT permission was denied on the object 'Products', database 'MyDatabase', schema 'dbo'.
```

Analysis

On the first try, you can see the table as TestLogin. Your second try should fail. In addition to Grant and Revoke, there is also a Deny statement. There is a subtle difference between Revoke and Deny—we're not going to cover that in this book. However, if you have to implement security for real, you will need to understand the difference. You are referred to SQL Server Books Online (BOL).

Here, you've been looking at Select permissions. You can also set permissions for Insert, Update, and Delete.

Execute Permission

It's also possible to allow users to run stored procedures. There are three Execute As blocks this time. Run the first one, then the Grant statement. Then, run the second one followed by the Deny statement. Finally, run the third Execute As block.

Syntax

```
-- test security on stored procedure
execute as login = 'TestLogin'
exec  ProductsBySupplier 'Adventure Works'
revert
--
grant execute on ProductsBySupplier to TestLogin
--
execute as login = 'TestLogin'
exec  ProductsBySupplier 'Adventure Works'
revert
--
deny execute on ProductsBySupplier to TestLogin
--
execute as login = 'TestLogin'
exec  ProductsBySupplier 'Adventure Works'
revert
```

Result

```
Msg 229, Level 14, State 5, Procedure ProductsBySupplier, Line 1
The EXECUTE permission was denied on the object 'ProductsBySupplier', database 'MyDatabase', schema 'dbo'.
```

Analysis

You have used Deny this time rather than Revoke. In our very simplified example, both Deny and Revoke have the same effect—in reality, you may find differences between Deny and Revoke.

Drop Database

After our tour of DDL and DCL, it's time to clean up your server. Try the first Drop Database—it will fail, probably. If it does, try the Use with the second Drop Database. Finally, try the Drop Login.

Syntax

```
-- drop database removes user tables view stored proc index
-- primary and foreign keys
-- but not login
-- login (drop or sp_revokelogin 'Domain\User')
--
drop database MyDatabase
--
use master
drop database MyDatabase
--
drop login TestLogin
```

Result

```
Command(s) completed successfully.
```

Analysis

You can't drop a database if it's in context and you have a connection to it. The Use statement flips you into the master database, and then you can drop MyDatabase. Dropping a database removes the database and any objects it contains (tables, views, functions, stored procedures, and users). However, it won't remove the login we created. Users live in databases, but logins are at the server level. That's why you needed the final Drop Login.

Well done, that's our last query. But please be careful! Your database context may now be master. Remember to change back to AdventureWorksDW2008 (AdventureWorksDW in SQL Server 2005) before you start experimenting with any more SQL. To change the database, issue another Use statement or use the drop-down on the toolbar.

Chapter 15

After You Finish

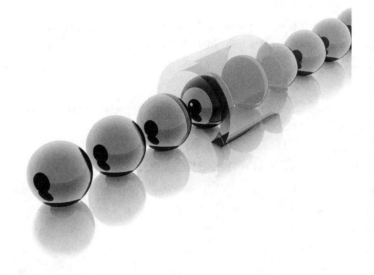

Where to Use SQL

Throughout this book, you've been using SSMS to write your SQL queries and display the results. It's unlikely that your users will have SSMS—indeed, it's not recommended for end users as it's simply too powerful and potentially dangerous. This chapter presents some alternative software and methods for getting SQL query results to the end user.

SSRS

SQL Server Reporting Services (SSRS) can generate quite complex SQL for you, but you may want some of the even more sophisticated queries you've seen in this book. You will need a SQL Server connection to do this. To use your own SQL, paste the code you might have developed in SSMS into the SQL Pane in Query Designer (or click Edit As Text on the toolbar first).

SSIS

With SQL Server Integration Services (SSIS) you can get the SQL results into a data pipeline using a Data Flow task. It's then quite easy to convert it into a text file, an Excel worksheet, or a SQL Server table. You will need an OLE DB or ADO NET source with a SQL Server connection. Then change the Data access mode from Table or View to SQL Command and paste in your SQL from SSMS. Alternatively, on the SSIS Control Flow, you can use an Execute SQL task and configure the ResultSet property appropriately.

DMX

If you need to train an SSAS data mining model or run a DMX prediction query against a relational database, you can use SQL inside the DMX.

XMLA

Your SQL queries can also be nested inside XMLA. To do so, use an <Execute> <Command> <Statement> construct.

Winforms and Webforms

If you are a .NET developer, you can create your own Windows applications (Winforms) or web pages (Webforms) to display the results of your SQL queries. The simplest way to do so is to use a datagrid.

The SQL can return the data as a dataset or datareader or as XML. Here's some sample VB.NET code that creates a dataset (you may have to adapt the Data Source and Initial Catalog properties as well as the table name in the From clause):

```
Dim con As New SqlClient.SqlConnection("Data Source=localhost;
Initial Catalog=AdventureWorksDW2008;Integrated Security=SSPI")
con.Open()
Dim cmd As New SqlClient.SqlCommand("select * from DimCustomer", con)
Dim adt As New SqlClient.SqlDataAdapter(cmd)
Dim dst As New DataSet
adt.Fill(dst)

        'or use a DATAREADER
        'Dim rdr As AdomdDataReader = cmd.ExecuteReader
        'do stuff with reader
        'rdr.Close()

        'or use an XMLREADER
        'Dim xml As System.Xml.XmlReader = cmd.ExecuteXmlReader
        'do stuff with XML

DataGridView1.DataSource = dst.Tables(0)
'for a Webform add .DataBind
con.Close()
```

Third-Party Software

There is an infinite variety of third-party software applications available that allow you to paste in your SQL.

Copy and Paste

Or you can right-click on the Results pane in SSMS and choose Select All. Then right-click again and choose Copy. You can then paste the SQL results (rather than the SQL itself) into an application of your choice.

Index